D0358791

TIME FLIES
HEATHROW AT 60

TIME FLIES
HEATHROW AT 60

ALAN GALLOP

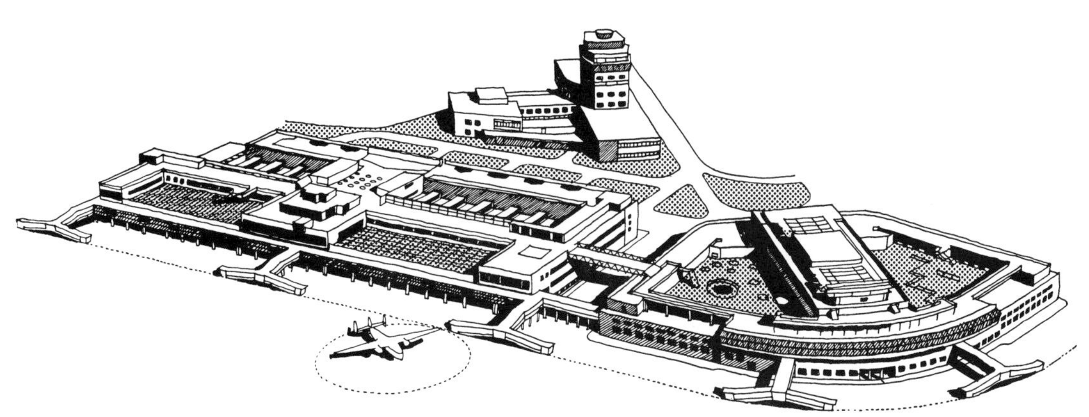

SUTTON PUBLISHING

First published in 2005 by
Sutton Publishing Limited · Phoenix Mill
Thrupp · Stroud · Gloucestershire GL5 2BU

Reprinted 2006

British Library Cataloguing in Publication Data
A catalogue record for this book is available from the British Library.

ISBN 0-7509-3840-4

Endpapers: London Airport 1957 from a painting by C.E. Turner. *(Reproduced by kind permission of the Dunlop Rubber Company)*

The author dedicates this book to the happy memory of his friend, Mike Braund, and his family, with whom there was always much laughter.

Typeset in 10.5/14.5pt GillSans Light
Typesetting and origination by
Sutton Publishing Limited.
Printed and bound in England by
J.H. Haynes & Co. Ltd, Sparkford.

CONTENTS

ACKNOWLEDGEMENTS

THIS BOOK WOULD NOT HAVE BEEN POSSIBLE to write without the help, guidance, comments, contributions and referrals given to me by many people who are part of the story of Heathrow Airport.

In 2003 a number of newspapers and radio stations carried stories about my search for people who had worked at the airport during its early years, generating over 100 letters, e-mails and telephone calls. Most of the responses were interesting, many were fascinating and a small number were real gems of remembrances about the airport's early years.

A postcard from Keith Hayward, who started life as a 16-year old school leaver working for British South American Airways in London and later at Heathrow, triggered off an incredible trail leading to people who were at the airport on its very first day of operations on 1 January 1946. Thanks to Keith (who at the age of 76 years young is still at Heathrow working in the British Airways Archives in a voluntary capacity a couple of days each week), I was put in touch with two people who flew on that first flight – Mary Cunningham, the country's first peacetime air stewardess and Captain Cliff Alabaster, navigator of the BSAA Avro Lancastrian service to South America. All three were kind enough to give me their time and recall their airport memories for the benefit of my tape recorder.

Another set of fascinating memories came from John Boulding, MBE, BOAC's former chief investigator of accidents and air safety who lives just 100 steps away from my own home in Ashford, Middlesex. Special thanks also to Fred Gore, Ray Berry, Ben Lewers and Flo Kingdon who also freely shared their airport memories.

Thanks, too, to Dennis Martin for providing me with information on the rise and fall of British Eagle, Nicky Carter for material on the villages of Heath Row and Perry Oakes and Simon Newbold, BAA Heathrow movement area officer – and his airside operations (safety and security) colleagues – for making it possible for me to view old and newer parts of the airport.

Others who shared material and memories with me included Betty Richardson, Paul Townend, Ted Carpenter, Derek Rylatt, Gordon Pankhurst, Leslie Green, Stan Stern, Gordon Chubb, Phillip Gordon-Marshall, Eric Driver, June Pearce and her brother

Dennis Sparks, June Pike, Tony Hesketh-Gardener, Gwen Humphries, Don Parry, Vincent Vere, Tom Marks, Father Peter Knott and airport pressmen Steve Meller, Russell Clisby and David Dyson.

I would also like to acknowledge the generous assistance given to me by David Smith, marketing director of Taylor Woodrow Construction Ltd; Sonia Sampson and Liz Nicholls at the excellent Heathrow Airport Visitor Centre; Vanessa Finneran, BAA Heathrow's senior media relations manager in the press and public relations office and my friend Barry Dix who, along with others mentioned above, were kind enough to loan me fascinating photographs from their archives and private collections.

I have been asked to point out that Heathrow's owner, BAA plc, has had no involvement in the writing, editing or publishing of *Time Flies*, although it has permitted many of its archive photographs to be used. Accordingly, none of the views expressed in this book are those of BAA plc, which makes no representations or warranties about the accuracy, completeness or suitability for any purpose of the information contained within this story.

INTRODUCTION

TIME FLIES IS *NOT* A BOOK ABOUT HOW Heathrow Airport works in its sixtieth anniversary year. It is the story of how an airport everyone in the world has heard about, millions use every year, and where thousands go to work 365 days of the year, was born and has evolved over the last six decades.

The year 2006 marks Heathrow's sixtieth anniversary. It was opened at a time when flying had already proved itself in two world wars and had linked all parts of the British Empire together in days, instead of weeks and months. The first flight from Heathrow departed just 46 years after Wilbur Wright wrote to a friend: 'I am intending to start out in a few days for a trip to the north coast of North Carolina for the purpose of making some experiments with a flying machine.' In just over four decades, man had learned how to fly from just a few feet across sand dunes to destinations across the globe. In six decades, Heathrow has controversially grown from a single concrete runway to what many claim to be the world's number one civil airport.

For anyone growing up in suburban west London in the 1950s, London Airport – which we now refer to today as Heathrow – played an important part in our lives. Few of us ever actually travelled from the place because we had no need to. If we took holidays, they were within the UK. Foreign travel was for the rich and most people going abroad used trains and boats – not planes – to reach their destination. But it cost very little to actually visit the airport as a sightseer and thrill to the sight of planes arriving and departing to and from the places we one day dreamed of visiting.

Many interviewed for this book describe the airport's early days as 'primitive'. To the visitors who came to the airport by the London Underground and bus or suburban rail services, it was far from primitive. If we had been given an opportunity to move forward in time and experience the airport as it would become in later years, we might have agreed. But in the 1950s, the airport was the single most advanced place any of us were privileged to visit.

I was born in Staines, a busy town to the south-west of the airport. Unlike many other communities closer to the airport or under its flight path, we were never bothered by aircraft noise, although we could see them taking off and landing in the far distance. I remember lying in bed on cold winter nights and hearing a high-pitched 'whirring' sound far away and being told that it was coming from aeroplanes revving their engines to avoid freezing up. For me, that was a very good sound to fall asleep with.

In later years, when the Queen's Building's famous Roof Gardens opened to the public, my friends and I would spend entire school holidays plane spotting and later walking around terminals begging for leaflets, stickers, timetables and postcards – or anything else - from airlines. They rarely turned us away.

A friend once told me that he knew an old house along the Bath Road that had been turned into offices, which filled its dustbins with wasted airline material and photographs. One day during the school holidays we went in search of it and soon came across the shabby old building – and its dustbins overflowing with glossy black and white prints of planes and people coming and going through the airport. Through a grimy window we could see people inside the office typing and talking on the telephone. As we quickly grabbed a handful of dustbin booty, there was a loud rap on the window and an angry cry of 'Gedoutoffit!' We dropped our spoils and beat it up the Bath Road. Three years later – in the summer of 1966 – I went back to that same shabby building for an interview for a school leaver wanting to train as a news agency reporter at the airport. The man who interviewed me was the same man who had rapped on the window. I didn't mention the incident. He gave me the job.

I stayed at the airport as a reporter until 1978 – possibly the airport's most interesting time. But everyone who has worked at Heathrow from the 1940s to the present day makes the same claim. For all of us, every period was the best time to work at the airport.

Heathrow means many things to different people. Anyone who has ever worked at the airport in the last six decades, travelled in or out of it or simply collected a passenger from one of its terminals, identifies with it in some way. Staff employed there generally love the place. Passengers either like it or loathe it. Many are frightened by the size of the place, the confusion it can cause and the security rituals that each passenger must undergo today. Thousands living under its flight path hate Heathrow. Tens of thousands are thankful that Heathrow provides them with a job. Scores of industries depend on British airports – particularly Heathrow – for their survival. Exporters and importers across the country are grateful to airline cargo services from Heathrow, which reach just about every important place in the world, mostly within 24 hours. The airport has always been – and remains – a favourite news hunting ground for reporters, photographers and TV camera crews.

Personally, I love the place. It has been part of my life for as long as I can remember. I love flying from and always look forward to landing back, because I'm home again. But I would feel very differently about Heathrow if its aircraft screamed over my rooftop, if its noise disturbed my sleep, if my home or livelihood was threatened by its expansion. The airport is a wonderful place for many and hell on earth to others. This book takes no sides in telling the story of its development.

However, one airport veteran interviewed for this book, Tom Marks, told me: 'Imagine that for some reason Heathrow was taken away, closed down for good. Think about the thousands of people who would be thrown out of work, most of them folks who earn a decent living from the airport who would find it difficult to secure other jobs paying similar salaries, many with attractive travel "perks" thrown in for good measure. Many of these people live in communities close to the airport and their economies depend in part on Heathrow's continued success. Think about thousands of other people and hundreds of companies who depend on the airport, many of them located far away from Heathrow. If the airport were to disappear, the economy of much of west London would collapse and cause untold harm to millions. Yes, the airport is noisy and causes countless problems for many – it always has done – but this is the price we have to pay for having such an important economic driver and major employer on our doorstep.'

Another airport veteran, Keith Hayward, told me: 'Never forget, Heathrow didn't just happen overnight. It took years to develop and grow into what we know today as the world's leading airport. It touches the lives of millions of people – passengers, staff, and visitors – every year in some way. What other place in the country can make a similar claim?'

Mr Hayward was correct and as Heathrow enters its sixtieth anniversary year, it is time for its story to be told in detail for the first time. Most of that story is a human one and in this book, much of it is told by people who have been part of its history in some way during the last sixty years.

So now, ladies and gentlemen, boys and girls, it's time to fasten your seatbelt and prepare for take-off. Please be warned: as part of this journey you will experience some turbulence en route, resulting in a bumpy ride and the occasional rough landing. Have a nice flight . . .

ONE

1 JANUARY 1946

Time for Take-off 'From the Finest Runway in the World'

On this first day of the new year, this proving flight starts off from Heathrow which will be the future civil airport of London – and it takes off from the finest runway in the world.

Lord Winster, Minister for Civil Aviation at the opening of Heathrow Airport on 1 January 1946

THE FIRST PEACETIME CHRISTMAS for seven years had come and gone and the miserable winter of 1945/6 had wiped away all euphoria of victory from an exhausted Britain.

Rationing was still in force and would still be around for several years more. For thousands of servicemen and women returning to 'Civvy Street' and spending their first Christmas at home for what seemed like an eternity, the prospects for 1946 looked gloomy.

People in west London suburbs opening their curtains and peering out of the window on New Year's Day 1946 witnessed a bitterly cold and grey day with traces of fog left over from the day before. Most could go back to bed and pull eiderdowns and candlewick bedspreads over their heads and sleep on for another few hours. Some had stayed up late to welcome in the new year, but the drunken carousing that had regularly been seen on the last days of the year prior to wartime had still to return. Beer cost money, and there was not much of it around on the first day of the first full new year of peacetime.

Christmas had been a struggle. Turkeys were expensive, chickens were scarce and beef a lavish luxury – assuming you could find someone to buy it from and had money to pay for it. Thousands of people scraped together the contents of their Christmas from men in sharp suits and suede shoes, hair slicked back with Brylcreem and known to the world at large as 'spivs', to themselves as 'entrepreneurs' and to the police as black marketeers – people with the ability to get you anything you could not get for yourself, for a price and without coupons. They all looked the same and asked

Minister of Civil Aviation, Lord Winster (centre at microphone), bids Godspeed to passengers and crew travelling on the first flight to leave London's new airport, Heath Row on 1 January 1946. Air Vice-Marshal Donald Bennett, Chief Executive of British South American Airways and Captain of the first flight – an Avro Lancastrian called Star Light – stands to his left. John Booth, the new airline's Chairman stands between Lord Winster and Bennett. Standing to Bennett's left is Captain D.A. Cracknell (Navigator) and Star Girl Mary Guthrie. Captain Cliff Alabaster (First Officer) stands to Lord Winster's right (hands crossed in front of him). *(Keith Hayward collection)*

the same questions: 'Nylons? How many pairs? Tinned salmon? A box full will cost you £2 10s. A pork joint? Fifteen shillings. Meet me here tomorrow at six. I'll have the stuff, you bring the money. Don't ask questions. It fell from the back of a lorry, if you see what I mean.'

Products that could be bought over the counter were expensive to anyone fresh out of uniform. A pack of ten Churchman's No. 1 cigarettes would set you back 1*s* 3*d*, an ounce of pipe tobacco started at 2*s* 8*d* and new rubber hot-water bottles, back on sale again now the factory had reverted to manufacturing its original products after the government had requisitioned it to make rubber dinghies for the Navy, cost half a crown (2*s* 6*d*).

Post-Christmas sales sold 'utility' dress coats reduced from £11 to 22*s* but nylon stockings still cost 1*s* 6*d* and four precious clothing coupons. If you were rich and could afford a new car, a 1.5 litre Jaguar saloon would set you back £535 (plus £149 7*s* 6*d* purchase tax). Non-millionaires could buy a second-hand Austin 7 for £85 or a Coventry Eagle for £27 10s. New or old, rich or poor, car salesmen were hardly enjoying brisk business in the winter of 1945/6. Decent furniture, carpets, toys, bicycles, prams had not been seen in shop windows for years, or so it seemed.

To forget their new year troubles, people sought entertainment: dancing at the Palais, Locarno or Victory Ballrooms or going to the 'flicks' to see a newsreel, a second feature (usually a western) and then laugh at Bob Hope and Bing Crosby in *The Road to Utopia* or thrill to Cornel Wilde in *A Thousand and One Nights* – exciting, humorous, escapist fantasy entertainment designed to help folks forget their postwar domestic blues.

But things were changing for the people of London and its suburbs. For those not called up for active service or working in reserved occupations, civilian work in wartime had been relatively easy to find but not brilliantly paid. In the spring of 1944, just as thousands of children were being evacuated north to escape Hitler's flying bombs, hundreds of men were recruited to begin laying concrete for a triangular pattern of runways which would form part of a massive new development for the Royal Air Force (RAF). The triangular configuration would allow aircraft to take off in any wind direction.

The Ministry for Civil Aviation, created by Winston Churchill in 1944 to look at peaceful ways of using aeroplanes and airfields, and finding something worthwhile for aircraft factories to do after the war, said the new base would be used by RAF Transport Command aircraft travelling to the Far East. It was located in the middle of rich farmland 14 miles to the west of London, in the county of Middlesex and midway between the suburban towns of Staines and Hounslow, adjacent to a small hamlet called Heath Row.

By the end of 1945 one of the runways was completed, but signals that the war was ending meant that the RAF would no longer need a massive new base on the outskirts of its bruised and battered capital. By a roundabout route it was transferred from military to civilian use and designated 'the world's largest airport' and 'the country's largest postwar building scheme'. And on the first day of the new year of 1946 it was ready to be used.

Sixteen-year-old Keith Hayward was up early on that New Year's Day. He had gone to bed early the night before at his parent's home in Ruislip because he didn't want to oversleep and miss the big day that lay ahead.

Because it was a bank holiday, transport into central London was restricted to a limited service, although it had been ages since trains and buses had operated to any kind of timetable. It was cold and dark as the lad made his way past houses with curtains still tightly drawn, towards Ruislip's underground station and the Piccadilly line that would take him to Green Park and the offices of British South American Airways (BSAA) at 19 Grafton Street, London W1.

Keith Hayward, aged 16 – the 'new boy' at BSAA. *(Keith Hayward collection)*

With his company-issue greatcoat pulled tightly around his shoulders and his smart new uniform neatly pressed by his mother the night before, Keith could not believe his luck as he sat in the almost empty train rattling its way towards London. Just a few weeks before, he had been an aircraft-mad student at Harrow County School and a member of the Air Training Corps. Now, following a rousing talk to young scouts about the new peacetime Utopia that awaited Britain, given by the legendary head of the RAF's Pathfinder Force, Air Vice-Marshal Donald Bennett, CB, CBE, DSO, Keith was about to work for the man himself. Bennett had been appointed Chief Executive of a new airline, which that day would make the first flight from London's new Heath Row bound for Buenos Aires Airport. And Keith would be part of the team travelling to the airport later that day, to witness the historic departure, as one of BSAA's newest and youngest trainee traffic officers.

He had already 'done his bit' for the flight before Christmas, rushing around London to the Passport Office and various South American embassies, fixing documents and arranging visas for crew members and flight engineers who would today be flying down to South America on the company's first departure.

Mary Guthrie stayed in bed a little longer that morning. The 24-year-old former Air Transport Auxiliary pilot would be driving herself to Heathrow that day from her mother's flat in Basil Street, Knightsbridge and she did not need to be there until later in the morning. She hoped that she could remember the directions she had been given through London's streets and out of town towards the Bath Road running alongside

Mary Guthrie, Britain's first peacetime air hostess – or Star Girl as BSAA preferred to call its cabin staff – boards the first flight to depart from Heath Row. Thanks to her photograph appearing in national newspapers, Mary was a household name by 1 January 1946. *(Author's collection)*

the massive building site from where she would be taking off to South America at lunchtime that day. It was all very exciting.

By 1 January 1946, and to her great surprise, Mary had become one of London's best-known 'faces' after her photograph appeared in newspapers telling readers that the 'blue-eyed, fair haired former nurse will step onboard the Lancastrian airliner Star Light as first hostess of BSAA. But because the words "hostess" and "stewardess" are officially disliked, she will take her title from the Star class of airliners and be known as a "Star Girl".'

Mary had been well trained for the demanding job ahead of her – two whole days of it. She had landed the job by accident while visiting the airline's offices to talk to someone about a navigation course, and had been pointed in the direction of an airline executive who asked if she knew anything about nursing (yes), had any military training (yes, sir) and could speak any foreign languages (*oui, oui*). And now, after two days learning how to prepare hot meals from frozen food – known as 'frood' – at Joe Lyons' Corner House, Marble Arch, here she was driving towards an airport still under construction to become 'Britain's first postwar air hostess'.

Patchy fog still clung to the fields as she headed out of west London's built-up areas and towards smallholdings and market gardens surrounding the building site where a small plane, looking more like a bomber than a passenger plane, was waiting to take

By May 1946, BSAA's Lancastrian, Star Light, had already completed several round trips between London and Latin America. *(BAA (Heathrow) Archives)*

passengers and crew onboard. In the boot of her car was the suitcase she had carefully packed the night before. It contained her new woollen swimsuit, which she hoped to christen in the warm water lapping Copacabana beach at least once before returning to freezing Britain in 19 days' time after a round trip of 14,400 miles.

As she approached Harlington the words her stepfather had spoken over the Christmas holidays rang in her ear: 'I don't approve of this job you've been offered, Mary. You're likely to be captured by white slavers in South America and we'll never see you again. Buenos Aires is no place for a young girl.'

The mist was clearing now, but it was still bitterly cold as Mary turned left at the Magpies public house and into an area containing a two-storey square block building with a smaller structure on top, which looked like a cube-shaped greenhouse but which she immediately recognised as an RAF-style control tower. A row of other temporary prefabricated buildings, large tin sheds and ex-military caravans stood to one side and Mary parked her car in front of one of them. As she removed her suitcase from the boot, she could see the Avro Lancastrian on which she would soon be queen of the tiny galley in front of the passenger cabin and squashed between a pair of metal wing spars. She knew it would be an exhausting flight across the world to South America – someone had told her it might take thirty hours – and there would be no time for sleeping.

At some stage during his six-year-service in the Royal Air Force (RAF), Wing Commander R.C. Alabaster, DSO and Bar and DFC and Bar, from Willesden, north London, had mentioned to a friend that the next three decades would be a pretty interesting period for aviation – never thinking that he would be part of that exciting future.

On New Year's Eve 1945, the Wing Commander – better known to RAF pals as 'Alaby' (pronounced 'Ally-bee') – enjoyed a couple of celebratory drinks at home in Wembley before turning in to bed for a good night's rest; the last sleep he would enjoy for almost two days.

Passing a few New Year party stragglers on their way home to bed, Alaby headed in the direction of his office, 19 Grafton Street, London, and the top floor of the building where he had started a special school for ex-RAF pilots and navigators wanting to join BSAA now the war was over.

Under the peacetime 'command' of his former Pathfinder Force boss, Air Vice-Marshal Donald Bennett, Alaby had started the school at which airmen spent seven hours a day sitting at trestle tables in a purpose-built classroom being taught how to navigate civilian airliners for BSAA. By October 1945 more master bomber pilots had signed up with the airline than remained in the RAF.

During the war this elite corps of aircrew, with high navigational ability, flew at the head of thousands of Lancaster and Mosquito bombing sorties to targets in Berlin and the Ruhr. They flew through the flak to accurately pinpoint enemy targets with coloured flares that allowed the main bombing force to achieve more accurate bomb drops. Between 1943 and 1944, the Pathfinders made a vital contribution to the success of Britain's bombing offensive against Germany and to the D-Day preparations.

Sixty per cent of BSAA's crew were former Pathfinders looking for a new flying role in postwar life, including Alaby who was an experienced navigator and pilot. Working for their old boss and alongside RAF pals seemed like a safe bet in the uncertain world of civilian life. Ground staff attached to the Pathfinders was also drafted into the company in managerial and administrative jobs and 19 Grafton Street was more like an RAF station with staff still wearing their military uniforms and doors marked Wing Commander X and Squadron Leader Y.

Alaby would have liked a cup of tea in the basement canteen the airline shared with staff working for the fashionable ladies' hairdresser, Mr Teasy-Weasy Raymond, whose stylish salon had opened next door. But it was a bank holiday and the canteen was closed, so he made his way to the ground floor where a group of excited staff, including the company's youngest and newest staff member, Keith Hayward, had gathered to board a special bus transporting them to the airport to witness their new company's first departure.

Several others boarding the staff bus that day would be travelling on the Lancastrian – registration G-AGWG – which the company had christened Star Light. It was one of fourteen Lancastrians BSAA would operate during its short lifespan. Built by A.V. Roe & Company – 'Avro' – at Woodford, Cheshire, the design was a modified version of the famous four-engine wartime Lancaster heavy bomber. Gun turrets and other military fittings had been removed and an extended nose section fitted to carry cargo. Four Rolls-Royce Merlin engines powered the plane, which the British Overseas Airways Corporation (BOAC) had been operating successfully on long-haul 'kangaroo routes', from Bournemouth to the Far East and Australia, for the last year.

Fitted with up to thirteen single seats staggered on both sides of the aircraft, the converted bombers were designed as a 'stop-gap' commercial aircraft while British plane makers worked furiously to produce new passenger airliners for peacetime flying. They were far from perfect, with a tiny galley located between the Lancastrian's main spars, meaning that Mary Guthrie would have to clamber over the large angular metal girder every time she had to serve meals to her passengers and collect empty trays. Passengers sitting at the front would also have to negotiate the same angular metal spars as the crew whenever they needed to use the tiny and primitive chemical toilet at the rear of the aircraft. The Lancastrians were also unpressurised, noisy and forced to fly at low altitudes in all weathers across South America's great mountain ranges which blocked out all radio communications. While flying over the Andes, passengers and crew had to don oxygen masks. BOAC flying crews, used to travelling in luxurious flying boats, were not impressed with the Lancastrians and when asked to test

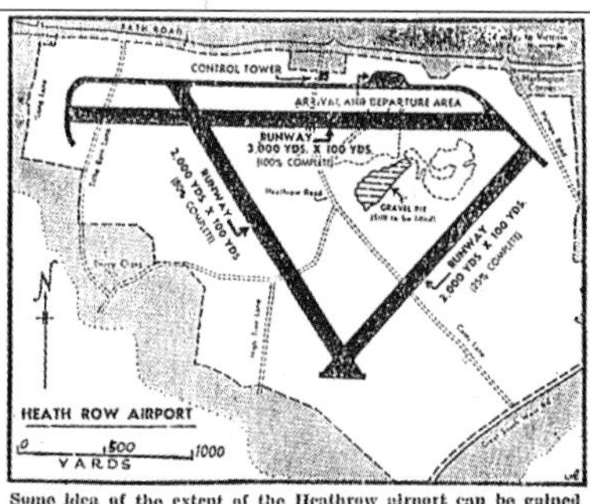

Some idea of the extent of the Heathrow airport can be gained from this plan, which we publish through the courtesy of the "Daily Express." The north boundary along the Bath Road extends from Harlington Corner in the east nearly to the "Peggy Bedford" in the west. The buildings and control tower in the top centre of the diagram are adjacent to the Magpies public-house. The site of the Celtic Shrine discovered during the excavations was towards the eastern end of the 3,000 yards runway.

HEATHROW WILL "SHOW THE WORLD"

First Civil Plane Takes Off from Huge New Airport

LONDON'S largest and costliest airport, at Heathrow, was officially handed over by the R.A.F. to the Ministry of Civil Aviation on Tuesday, and on the same day Air Vice-Marshal Donald Bennett, who formed and commanded the R.A.F.'s famous Pathfinder Force, took off from the terminus in the British South American Airways' Lancastrian "Starlight" on the first "proving flight" to South America.

Lord Winster, Minister of Civil Aviation, bidding God-speed to the plane, said that from now on things would begin to move and Heathrow would play a central and dominant part in the development of civil aviation.

Heathrow, which it is estimated unofficially will cost about £20,000,000, is at present a great plain of raw earth intersected by a 3,000-yard main runway and two incomplete runways. Situated 14 miles from the centre of London, it is outside the built-up area, and is capable of development without extensive demolition of private property. Lying between the Bath Road and the Staines Road, it is two miles from the Waterloo-Staines section of the Southern Railway and the same distance from Hounslow West Underground Station. It covers a total area of 1,500 acres. The airport was designed as a military airfield for the R.A.F. capable of handling the heaviest types of aircraft, especially in the closing stages of the war in the Far East as it was expected to develop.

In the planning it was taken into account that such an airfield could be subsequently developed for civil aviation as the main terminal airport for London. It was clear from the beginning, however, that the construction of the runways would involve many difficult engineering problems. The selected area included about 120 acres of ponds and disused gravel workings and a portion of the main runway would have to traverse these ponds. Special drainage problems were presented, as the discharge of huge quantities of water would have to be regulated so as to avoid flooding the surrounding land. These and many other problems were successfully solved, and in April, 1944, plans were complete for three runways, one of 9,000 and two of 6,000 feet, together with a perimeter track 25,000 feet long connecting the ends of the runways. The width of the runways was 300 feet and that of the perimeter track 100 feet. The runways are sited so as to be capable of extension, one to 15,000 and the others to 9,000 feet.

Regular Services next Summer

The main east-west runway of 9,000 feet is now complete. The second runway, extending from the north-west to the south-east, is expected to be complete in February. The arrival and departure apron, together with temporary terminal buildings, is also complete. The installation of apparatus and the completion of the third runway, extending from the south-west to the north-east, will proceed without delay, and the airport will be ready to accommodate regular passenger services in the summer. It will be the main London airport for trans-oceanic traffic. The internal and European services will make use of Croydon and Northolt, though eventually some of them also will be accommodated at Heathrow.

During the first summer and winter a total of two million tons of earth and gravel was excavated, 36,000 feet of multiple ducting for the electric cables were laid and 60 miles of wire laid through these ducts. On the main runway, 9,000 feet long by 300 feet wide, the concrete paving is 12 inches thick. The laying of this mass concrete paving was begun in April, 1945, and the bulk of the work was completed in three and a half months. When the three runways are complete, more than 1,114,000 square yards of 12-inch thick concrete will have been laid.

The results have been possible only because of the high degree of mechanisation developed on other construction projects during the war with the consequent heavy reduction in the numbers of heavy navvy labourers required. At no time has there been more than 700 men in this category employed at Heathrow, the general average being about 400. Some 200 lorries, 40 mechanical excavators, 50 bulldozers and tractor-drawn excavators, besides many other items of plant of the most modern type, have been used in addition to the elaborate concreting equipment. Over a thousand men were housed and fed on the site in a workmen's camp, and attractive indoor and outdoor recreational facilities were provided. Considering the magnitude of the engineering problems and the existence of war-time restrictions and control of labour and materials, all of which was complicated by flying bombs and rockets, the successful completion of this work is a credit to British engineering skill.

Finest in the World

Mr. Ivor Thomas, M.P., Parliamentary Secretary, and Sir William Hildred, Director-General of Civil Aviation, were among the big crowd at Heathrow to see Air Vice-Marshal Bennett, take off. The Lancastrian carried a crew of eight and 10 passengers, including officials of British South American Airways, who are to operate the service. The plane is travelling via Lisbon, Bathurst, Natal (Brazil), Rio de Janeiro and Montevideo.

Wishing the passengers and crew bon voyage, Lord Winster said that the Lancastrian was taking off from the finest runway in the world, and when Heathrow was completed neither Idlewild (the new airport for New York) nor any other aerodrome would have anything on Heathrow; in fact they would have something to show the world in airport design. It was a happy omen that yesterday's fog had cleared and that the Air Vice-Marshal was taking off in fine bright weather. This aeroplane, with its beautiful

How the *Middlesex Chronicle* reported the airport's opening day in January 1946. *(Author's collection)*

fly one of the aircraft a pilot wrote in his report: 'Unsuitable as an airliner but, with a few modifications, will make an efficient bomber aircraft.'

Star Light would soon be joined by other BSAA Lancastrians also carrying the 'Star' name along the front-nose section – Star Dust, Star Land, Star Glow and so on.

In addition to Alaby, also travelling on the bus that day was Air Vice-Marshal Bennett himself, the Australian-born former Imperial Airways flying-boat captain and mastermind behind the RAF Pathfinder force. Bennett would be in command of the flight and for the journey had taken his best pinstripe 'civvy' suit, a 'civilianised' version of his RAF greatcoat and a new black Homburg hat. Alaby would be in the seat next to Bennett as First Officer, flying the Lancastrian over one of the world's longest water crossings, often by stars in the night sky and frequently popping up into the aircraft's Perspex astro-dome to get a star fix with his sextant.

Other bus passengers included the airline's Chairman, John Booth, former bomber pilot Wing Commander D.A. Cracknell, DSO, DFC and Bar (First Officer), First Radio Officer J. McGillivray, Second Radio Officer R.W. Chandler, First Engineer T. Campbell and Second Engineer G.S. Rees.

As the bus cruised to a halt at the edge of the airport taxiway, the passengers could see a large crowd gathered on the apron around Star Light. Three large saloon cars with newsreel cameras mounted on top were positioned beneath one of the wings and a posse of pressmen, armed with cameras and notebooks, stamped their feet on the concrete and blew on cupped hands in an attempt to keep warm. Earlier that morning, reporters, photographers and newsreel cameramen had been taken on a joy ride around the new airport in a DC-3 Dakota to give them a better idea of the great length and width of the runways and Heathrow's general layout.

Alaby saw that the Lancastrian's front nosecone section was open and assorted boxes and parcels were being passed from a lorry to men at the top of a wooden tower with a ladder running up one side. It looked more like something used in a medieval siege than a simple aircraft loading device which had been hastily assembled days before and built high enough to allow ground staff to load goods into the forward freight compartment.

No sooner had staff climbed from the bus than a black motorcade swept onto the apron and stopped a few feet away from Star Light. A driver from one of the cars quickly jumped out and ran around the vehicle to open the back door, out of which climbed two men – one a small middle-aged man wearing a Homburg hat, thick black overcoat and round spectacles and the other a man dressed in similar clothing but standing about 6in taller. They obviously recognised Bennett and the men walked towards each other, warmly shook hands, wished each other a happy new year and agreed that it was, indeed, a very cold day. The smaller man was Lord Winster, Clement Atlee's Minister for Civil Aviation, who just a few days before Christmas had bowed to pressure and agreed to take the wraps off Britain's new showpiece airport to allow Bennett to operate a series of 'proving flights' to South America on behalf of the British government. The taller man was Ivor Thomas, MP, and Parliamentary Secretary at the Ministry of Aviation who was joined on the tarmac by Sir William Hildred, Director-General of Civil Aviation.

The men were desperate to counter negative media stories about the new airport, its cost (estimated at £25 million), when it might open for business and how successful it might – or might not – be. Anxious to demonstrate that his ministry was keen to get on with things, Lord Winster let Bennett launch his fledgling airline from the airport on exactly the same day that it passed from military to civil aviation ownership. Not only would it provide newspapers and newsreels with a great home-grown new year story on an otherwise 'slow news day', it would also win his ministry full marks for initiative in allowing a new British airline to use the airport's only runway in service within days of being completed.

Those flying in Star Light that day surrendered their luggage before Ministry of Aviation officials who shepherded the freezing crowd into a large informal group under the Lancastrian's starboard wing. The group included government officials, a handful of passengers travelling onboard to Buenos Aires, BSAA staff, their wives, a few airport staff who had been recruited to work in the control building, a delegation of construction workers engaged in building the second runway and an army of pressmen impatient to get on with the story. Three microphones had been positioned on the apron – one for each newsreel company – and at 11.45 a.m., the crowd was brought to order.

With hands thrust deeply into his overcoat pockets, Lord Winster told the crowd in a carefully modulated voice and without the aid of a prepared speech:

> On this first day of the new year, this proving flight starts off from Heathrow, which will be the future civil airport of London – and it takes off from the finest runway in the world. I think it's a happy omen for the flight that yesterday's fog has cleared away and Air Vice-Marshal Bennett, who leads the flight, will take off in fine, bright, clear weather. To me this aeroplane with its beautiful name, Star Light, is a symbol of the determination of our country to regain our place in the markets of the world and to use the air as a means of cultivating good relations with other nations and cultivating with them the arts of peace. Air Vice-Marshal Bennett . . . during the war, pioneered the transatlantic delivery of aircraft. Today he starts off on another pioneering job and this flight is the first step towards the establishment of a swift and regular British air service to South America. Air Vice-Marshal Bennett and all who fly with him today are truly ambassadors, representing the spirit and determination of this country to play the same leading part in the air that it has always played at sea. I wish them all Godspeed and a pleasant and successful journey.

There was a round of genuine applause before Bennett was invited to say a few words.

> We are about to take off on our first flight and about to do so with a fast four-engine airliner of proven quality. It has those things that are necessary for an airline – safety, speed and comfort. Our service will start within a few weeks, immediately following this proving flight. We hope to offer the peoples of this country and South America a service of which we will be proud and they will be happy to use. On this, the first day of 1946, we propose to take the first practical steps in getting that going.

There was more applause and cries of 'hear, hear' which was broken by the sounds of an air-raid siren, no longer used to announce the terrifying arrival of Luftwaffe bombers overhead but now used by peacetime factories across the country to signal that 12, midday, had arrived: time for lunch – and, today, time for the first official departure from the capital's new airport.

The siren also signalled that it was time for Mary Guthrie to climb up the Lancastrian's steps to welcome her boss, his crew and BSAA's first passengers onboard. In total, Mary would have seventeen people to look after on the thirty-hour flight – ten passengers and eight members of crew. Press photographers, however, had other ideas. They wanted 'just one more shot, Mary', but Mary had a job to do and quickly ran up the steps where the aircraft door was already open to admit the airline's first flyers.

First to board was BSAA's fare-paying passengers, who had each paid £190 2*s* to fly one-way to Montevideo or £192 6*s* for the single fare to Buenos Aires. Mary's passenger manifest told her that travelling on the plane would be Signor Falcao, the Brazilian Consul General in London; Colonel Stirling Wylie, British Military Attaché in Uruguay; Mr Donald Edwards, a BBC foreign correspondent and Signor and Signora Marroquim, a Brazilian couple who had spent Christmas in London and were now returning home to Buenos Aires. Also onboard were five BSSA staff who would be 'dropped off' en route to South America to represent the new carrier as managers at various stops along the 7,200-mile journey, including Lisbon, Bathurst (Gambia), Natal (on Brazil's eastern Atlantic seaboard), Rio de Janeiro, Montevideo and Buenos Aires.

Alaby, Cracknell and Bennett were next up the steps, the latter leaning out to shake hands with scores of well-wishers wanting to give the famous Pathfinder and skipper of Heathrow's first departure their good wishes.

It was time to depart and as soon as Bennett, Alaby and their crew had gone quickly through their pre-flight checks, and Mary had made sure that all the passengers were settled and had their seat belts buckled, Star Light was ready to taxi out towards the airport's brand new 3,000yd-long runway. A Union Jack flag, which had been poking out of the cockpit window was taken inside as the Lancastrian accelerated and its nose-wheel lifted 1,000yds along the runway, using just one-third of its length. As it rose further into the air, it banked towards the south and soon disappeared into low cloud covering Middlesex.

No sooner had Star Light disappeared into the early afternoon murk than the world's newest airport was officially closed again, to reopen eighteen days later when the Lancastrian returned from its long journey over cities, oceans and mountains. It would be nearly five months before it was declared 'officially open'. All subsequent BSAA flights flew from the new airport.

The crowds dispersed, many to board buses taking them to witness how work was progressing on the second runway, now 80 per cent completed, and gaze at the enormous concrete mixing and pouring machines used to create it. Afterwards, they would return to one of the temporary buildings along the Bath Road to enjoy a buffet lunch hosted by Lord Winster.

Young Keith Hayward was not invited to lunch. After all, he was only a 16-year-old new starter in the topsy-turvy world of peacetime civil aviation, yet thrilled to be part of the history that had been made that day. And he had also been given permission to go home early, where his mum had promised to have his new year tea waiting on the table back in Ruislip.

TWO

HEATH ROW 3000 BC TO AD 1919

Time Flies Backwards – An Historic Flypast

On Hounslow Heath as I rode o'er,
I spied a lawyer riding before.
Kind sir, said I, aren't you afraid
Of Turpin, that mischievous blade?

From an anonymous poem written in 1793

IT LIES ON 4½ SQUARE MILES of flat gravel plain between Staines and Hayes in Middlesex and 14 miles by road from Charing Cross. If the River Thames had not receded from its original bed over 15,000 years ago, to leave a vast flat stretch of gravel subsoil known geologically as the Taplow Terrace on its northern banks, Heathrow Airport might never have been built on its present site.

Archaeological research conducted prior to the start of construction work on the airport's new Terminal 5, in 2002, shows that Heathrow has been a 'take-off' point since the Stone Age. Druid high priests, 5,000 years ago, are understood to have used the site as a spiritual runway to travel to the spirit world or to communicate with ancestors.

Archaeologists discovered that a 2½-mile long and 23ft-wide site stretching from the Terminal 5 site towards where British Airways' Heathrow maintenance base now stands, was once artificially raised 6ft above the surrounding countryside and flanked by 9ft-deep ditches. It was almost as if the area had been made ready to receive the arrival of a prehistoric flying machine piloted by Neolithic cavemen working for Jurassic Airways.

There is little doubt that the Heathrow site was once a substantial religious centre used for sacred processions, possibly associated with fertility and funeral rituals. During the 1944 construction of Heathrow's runways, remains of a small rectangular building, possibly a Celtic temple with a surrounding colonnade, were uncovered. It was clear from pottery found nearby that this dated from the early Iron Age.

Evidence was also uncovered confirming that Heathrow had been visited by early Roman settlers. The remains of a 300sq. ft Roman camp, discovered where one of the

A cargo of newspapers, leather, several braces of grouse and some Devonshire cream is loaded onboard the world's first international flight – a de Havilland DH-4A owned by AT&T flying between Hounslow Aerodrome and Paris–Le Bourget Airport on 25 August 1919. *(Author's collection)*

runways is now located, had probably been one of Caesar's stations after he marched towards the nearby River Thames during his second invasion of Britain in 54 BC in pursuit of Cassivellaunus, the region's earliest known ruler.

Nobody knows how Heathrow – or Hetherewe (fifteenth century), Hetherow and Hitherowe (sixteenth century), Hetherowfeyld and Hedrowe (seventeenth century) and Heath Row (eighteenth century) – got its name. A fourteenth-century document refers to a man named William Atte Hethe, a tenant of some standing whose dwelling later became the site of Heath Cottages, one of several picturesque residential buildings in the village of Heath Row on the route from Colnbrook to Stanwell. They were demolished in the 1940s to make way for what we know today as Heathrow Airport.

The next known ruler to show interest in the site was King Henry VIII who hunted stag, deer and wild boar on the vast open plains and forests of Hounslow Heath, a large area to the west of London covering thousands of acres of open parkland and oak forests stretching from Brentford to Staines. The King's chief minister, Cardinal Thomas Wolsey, originally paid for a watercourse to be dug from the River Colne at Longford to Hampton Court, on a route skirting around what today is the airport's western perimeter. When finally completed, in the reign of King Charles I, it would reinforce water supplies to the ornamental waters and fountains of Hampton Court and Bushey Park. The watercourse, known by a collection of names including the Cardinal's River, the Hampton Court Canal, Queen's River and today as the Longford River, is still owned by the Crown, managed by the Royal Parks Agency and feeds the same fountains it fed over 360 years ago.

A second man-made water channel was also built in the reign of Henry VIII to provide power to a watermill in the grounds of Syon House at Isleworth. The Earl of Northumberland bought the river and stately home from King James I in the seventeenth century and the watercourse, known today as the Duke of Northumberland's River, still supplies water to the ornamental lake at Syon Park.

These twin rivers, which originally ran parallel to each other along Heathrow's boundaries, were both diverted along new courses to make way for Terminal 5 and are the airport's oldest visible landmarks.

In the early seventeenth century, a stagecoach journey from London to Bath took three days. Queen Anne had helped to re-establish the popularity of Bath as the nearest health resort to London and the only way to get there was by road. By 1784 the journey time had been cut to sixteen hours with relays of horses stationed along the route. The villages of Longford and Colnbrook, and their coaching inns, shared the boom of the prosperity that followed.

By the early years of Queen Victoria, the settlement and surrounding area of Heath Row – a hamlet at the western end of Hounslow Heath, without a church and with a population of less than 100 – was a desolate wasteland occupied by beer houses and flocks of greyhound-like sheep, described by an early observer as 'pitiful and half-starved looking animals subject to rot [presumably foot rot, a disease common among farm animals that are not properly cared for]'. But, thanks to the underlying gravel which provided excellent drainage, the land was extremely fertile, producing enough

Captain Gerry Shaw who piloted the second international service between Hounslow and Paris prepares to board his DH-4A. *(Author's collection)*

crops to allow market gardeners and smallholders to take their produce into London by cart to sell. They returned with wagonloads of manure from the many horses coming into the city, which Londoners were glad to be rid of. It was then dug into Heath Row's gardens and smallholdings, producing rich and fertile soil, which eventually transformed the wasteland into excellent growing and pastureland.

The Bath Road has always catered for travellers and 170 years ago was lined with coaching inns where passengers, horses and coachmen would rest on their horse-drawn journeys between the east and west. A pub named The Magpies was built in 1765 and was one such place put up to cater for this trade. It still stands today surrounded by modern twenty-first-century coaching inns – Hiltons, Sheratons, Marriotts and Holiday Inns – catering for passengers travelling between eastern and western continents.

Hounslow Heath, the land on which Heathrow Airport now stands, was once the notorious hunting ground of highwaymen, including Dick Turpin. *(Author's collection)*

The notorious Dick Turpin, Claude Duval, Moll Cutpurse, Ned Wicks, John Hawkins, George Simpson, John Everett, William Parsons and William Page (the 'Dandy') were all active along the Bath Road and hid in small hamlets, such as Heath Row, until a dense cloud of dust on the horizon signalled that another unfortunate mail coach was on its way.

Hangmen's gibbets lined roads approaching Hounslow, from which executed malefactors were hung in chains as a warning to all who passed by. They did little to deter the violent activities of desperate highwaymen and footpads at large in the area, who preyed on passing travellers and merchants.

Highway robbers were eventually put out of business when Hounslow Heath was enclosed, licences refused to publicans known to harbour criminals and mounted police patrols formed to introduce law and order to the area. Stagecoach traffic along the Bath Road further diminished when the Great Western Railway put them out of business in the 1830s. The railway also punctured the lucrative business traditionally enjoyed by the coaching inns along the Hounslow Heath section of the Bath Road, including those in Brentford, Hounslow, Longford and Colnbrook, who lost 80 per cent of their regular trade overnight, plunging many into bankruptcy within the year.

By the mid-1930s, Gordon S. Maxwell in his book *Highwayman's Heath* described the Heath Row settlement as 'little more than a few cottages and the village pub, the Harrow. There are two fine old farms in this village (Palmer's Farm and Perrott's Farm, both built in the seventeenth century) both on the right of the road; the first notable for its large stockyard, is Heathrow Hall on the old maps, and the second farm, a little further on, reminds me strongly of one of those delightful old farmsteads met with in the Weald of Kent, minus the oasthouses. . . . In Heath Row are some old cottages which might be in the heart of Devonshire, for their antiquity, their picturesqueness, and lonely situation. Very few people ever see them, for so few go along this road, which leads only, and by a roundabout way, to Stanwell, which is far easier to reach by other routes; no motorist would waste his time (thank heaven!) on this mere by-road with the arterial horrors so near.'

Betty Richardson, who has lived in the Heathrow area all her life recalls: 'As a schoolgirl I remember watching the airport's development, from market gardens and fields and isolated houses, and a tithe barn – all gone now. With my friends, we would cycle across the fields to Staines from our house at Harmondsworth and sometimes we would go along Tithe Barn Lane – now the site of an airport animal quarantine centre – to watch the ducks on some small lakes. It was very quiet and peaceful, a lovely area.'

Next to Heath Row was an even smaller hamlet, now occupied by a massive community of builders creating Terminal 5. This was called Perry Oaks, described by Maxwell as 'a few scattered cottages, a delightful old farm and some orchards and meadows . . . it is hardly a hamlet, even, but it is never-the-less a beautiful spot. Few have ever heard of it, and if you ask the average person if they know it, they look at you as if you were enquiring for a place in Cumberland, or some equally far away place, instead of one hardly a dozen miles from London. In fact Perry Oaks, though certainly on the map (and not all of them), is only just so; and therein lies its charm.'

In the fourteenth century Perry Oaks was known as Pyrye and Pury and is thought to derive its name from Robert de Pyro, an early tenant. The word Oaks was added later after timber from oak trees growing there was used to repair the Baber Bridge on Hounslow Heath during the reign of King Henry VIII.

Land around Heath Row and Perry Oaks became the site where accurate map-making in England started life. In 1738, Major-General William Roy was commissioned to survey part of southern England in order to establish the exact relative positions of the observatories of Greenwich and Paris. Roy spent three months measuring a base line on Hounslow Heath, the first operation of its kind undertaken in England. Work commenced at an area known as King's Arbour, a short distance from Heath Row, where soldiers cleared surrounding ground and guarded Roy's precious instruments.

To ensure accuracy, Roy made his measurements with a steel chain, deal rods and long glass tubes. It took him two years to complete his work from Hounslow Heath to the English Channel and Roy's work became the basis of the General Ordinance Survey of the British Isles. For many years a cannon could be seen at Heath Row, embedded in the ground and enclosed by railings, close to the site where the Harrow inn would have provided sustenance to Roy and his men. The weapon marked the one end of Roy's base line and a second cannon, 27,404ft away at Hampton Hill, marked the other end. The gun was removed when work commenced on building the first runway.

The Heath Row hamlet continued to be a prosperous place throughout the eighteenth century. In addition to agriculture, the tiny settlement was a thriving centre for trade in lamperns – eel-like creatures with suckers in place of mouths. An observer, Edward Ironside, wrote in 1797: 'Hethrow [*sic*], has a very considerable fishery for lamperns, a small kind of lampreys, which are used as bait by the English and Dutch in the cod and turbot fishery barges. Large quantities are fetched by the Hollanders during the demand for the fisheries from November to June. The usual price is 6/- per hogshead; afterwards they are sold for as many pence.'

'In Heath Row are some old cottages which might be in the heart of Devonshire for their antiquity, their picturesqueness and lonely situation', an observer wrote in the mid-1930s. Heathrow's Terminal 3 now stands where these cottages once graced the countryside. *(Author's collection)*

Between the sixteenth and eighteenth centuries, a small number of large barns had been built at Heath Row to store agricultural produce and equipment, and shelter animals. One of these barns had once been part of the Great Barn of Harmondsworth: one of the largest surviving barns from the medieval period and still standing today close to the edge of the world's largest international airport. The cathedral-like timber structure had once included a projecting wing which had been removed when the old manor house nearby was demolished in 1774. Made from oak and standing on sturdy columns, it was rebuilt at Heath Row, measuring 128ft long by 38ft wide, and was divided into two floors. A rough roadway running alongside was called Tithe Barn Lane.

At Perry Oaks Farm, just a mile down the lane, stood another large timber-frame barn, which began life in the sixteenth century and by the end of the eighteenth century had been extended to contain seven separate bays.

People living and working at the twin hamlets of Heath Row and Perry Oaks lived in relative contentment until the outbreak of the First World War in 1914. Some local lads went off to fight the war in France and Flanders and, like every other village, town and city in the country, the hamlets had their share of boys who failed to come home again. But at around 9.15 a.m. on a wet and gloomy morning on 25 August 1919, those working on the land heard a sound in the sky coming from the east and looked up to see a small aeroplane banking around in a westerly direction under the low clouds towards London and the coast. All eyes were focused on the tiny machine – a de Havilland DH-4A – which had taken off from a bumpy grass runway at the former Royal Flying Corps aerodrome 3 miles away on Hounslow Heath.

Ever since the armistice, aerial movements from the aerodrome had been reduced to almost nil, but the small aircraft, piloted that day by Lieutenant Eardley H. Lawford and carrying just one passenger in the single seat behind him – Mr George Stevenson-Reece of the *Evening Standard* – was making history as the world's very first international flight. The newspaper had paid 20 guineas for the privilege of being the first journal to go aloft on a peacetime aerial journey between one country and another. The wood and canvas biplane was flying 220 miles from Hounslow Aerodrome to Le Bourget Aerodrome, near Paris, and Lieutenant Lawford of the new civilian commercial airline company AT&T (Air Transport and Travel) expected to cover the distance in under three hours. In addition to the gentleman from the *Evening Standard*, Lawford was also carrying a cargo of newspapers, a quantity of leather, some Devonshire cream and several braces of grouse destined for the table of discerning Parisians.

As the small plane disappeared from sight, and Heath Row and Perry Oaks farmers returned to their chores in the rain, Stevenson-Reece was penning notes in the tiny makeshift cabin of the former wartime aircraft. He wrote:

> The world has watched in astonishment as the confines of our country, protected until now by the waters of the English Channel, have been swept aside by today's daring advance in aerial transport. No longer can these islands of Great Britain assume inaccessibility from other shores as civil aviations adopt the mantle of their military brothers with the commencement of regular air services to the continent.

Once the aircraft had reached an altitude of 1,000ft over London, Lawford admitted that he was having 'a pretty sticky time' flying over the outskirts of the city, hanging on to his compass which was swinging freely above his controls. By the time they were flying over the Crystal Palace at Sydenham 'which showed like a child's toy', the aircraft had reached 2,000ft. Stevenson-Reece continued to scribble notes as he gazed down on London:

> For a moment the Thames appeared like a varnished zinc strip and unexpectedly close. Thus was the course of history changed with the inauguration of a regular London–Paris service and the world's first commercial international civil air service.

The trailblazing flight took two hours and thirty minutes with Lawford finding his way to the coast by following railway tracks and locating train stations and landmarks along the way. By 2.45 p.m. that afternoon the plane was again flying over Heath Row's fields on return to the aerodrome on Hounslow Heath. 'When you consider that the single journey by train and steamer takes seven hours or slightly more, it is a sufficiently remarkable indication of the speed of aerial transport', wrote Stevenson-Reece.

Later that day another AT&T aircraft took to the skies over Hounslow Heath, this time carrying four passengers. Mr Holt Thomas, one of the airline's directors commented: 'If anyone had seriously announced forty years ago that our businessmen would in a few years be able to have their lunch in London and their tea in Paris and be able to work in the morning at their office, transact business in Paris and return to London in time for dinner, they would have been laughed at.'

If farmers stacking soaking-wet beetroot and cabbages in the muddy fields around Heath Row and Perry Oaks had time to read the next day's newspapers, they would probably have been just as amazed as the rest of the country. But they were also glad that their own feet were firmly on the ground instead of up in the clouds. For them, flying was for the birds.

THREE

1919–44

Mr Fairey's Flying Machines

Never take a machine into the air until you are familiar with its controls and instruments; before beginning a landing slide, see that no machines are under you; pilots should carry hankies in a handy position to wipe off goggles; riding on the steps, wings or tail of a machine is prohibited; hedge-hopping will not be tolerated; aviators will not wear spurs while flying; do not trust altitude instruments; if you see another machine near you, get out of its way; don't take a machine into the air unless you are satisfied it will fly; if flying against the wind and you wish to turn and fly with the wind, don't make a sharp turn near the ground – you might crash; it is advisable to carry a good pair of cutting pliers in a position where both pilot and passenger can reach them in case of an accident.

Flying rules found in the Fairey Aviation hangar at the Great West Aerodrome, Heath Row, 1920

IT WAS ASSUMED THAT following the pioneering London–Paris flight Hounslow Heath Aerodrome would become the main airport for London and its surrounding counties – but it was not to be.

AT&T began operating daily weekday services to Paris–Le Bourget using one- and four-seat aircraft depending on demand; business was brisk for the first six months. At weekends it was even possible to take joy rides over London on fifteen-minute-long hops following the railway line from nearby Feltham up to Waterloo station before turning back over Big Ben and returning above the Thames to Teddington and then descending to Hounslow Heath. One passenger even paid AT&T an extra fee to fly him under Tower Bridge and the airline nearly had its wings clipped by the Air Ministry for agreeing to the stunt, which was enjoyed by hundreds of onlookers.

Unfortunately the bumpy turf covering Hounslow Heath turned into mud fields during the winter months. In January 1920, a Hounslow local newspaper reported: 'The use of Hounslow as an airport is to cease, the government has let it be known. The place is not suitable for the purpose because of bad communication with London and is subject to mists. A plateau near Croydon is to be developed. Hounslow is now to be used by the military authorities for the training of cavalry.'

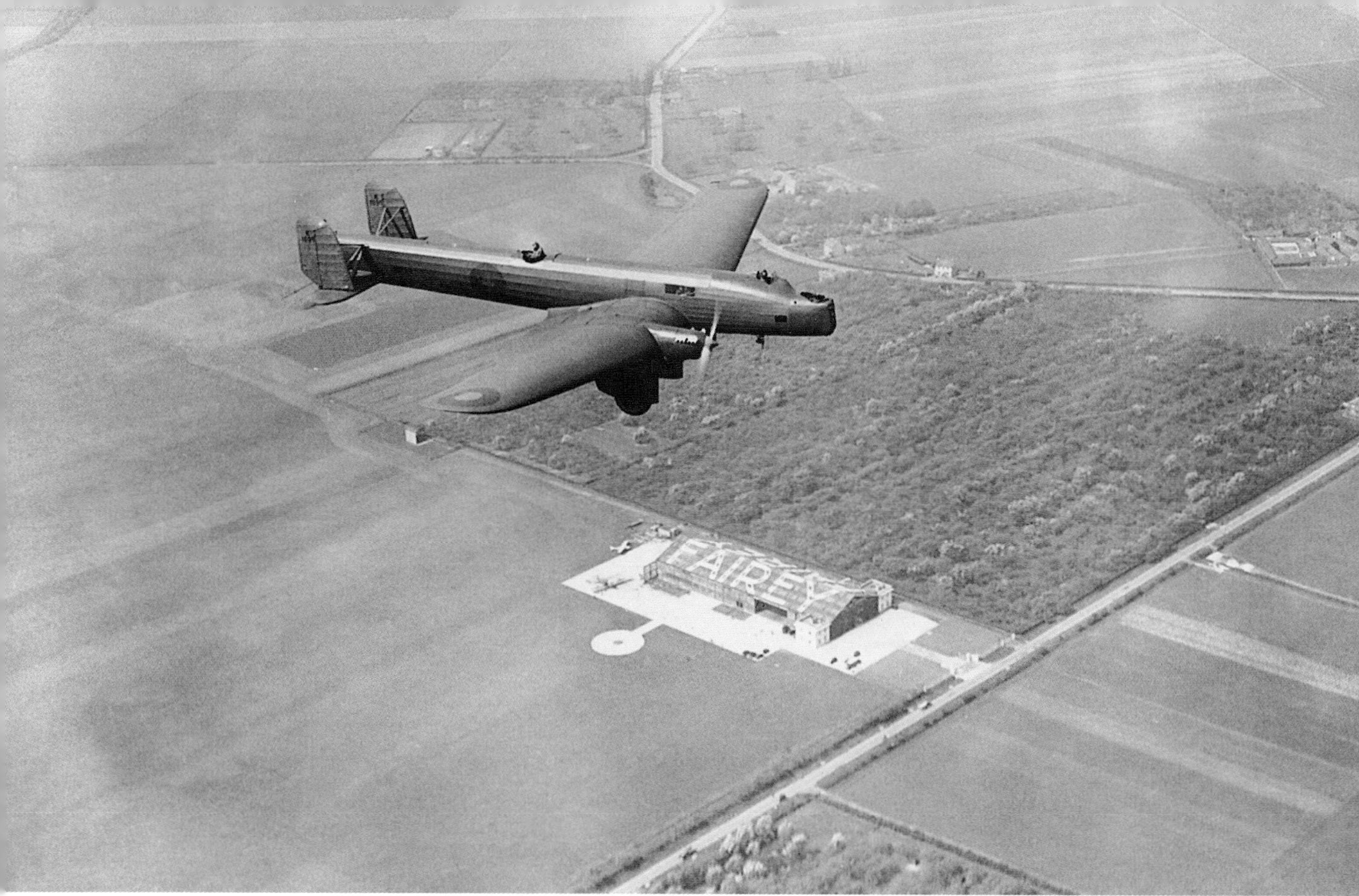

Croydon Aerodrome, 10 miles away from central London, had been in use since 1915 when it was established as part of the Air Defence of London. Military aircraft from Croydon were used to attack raiding Zeppelins in 1916 and enemy aircraft threatening the capital during daylight in 1917. The National Aircraft Factory had also been built on the site and in March 1920 the aerodrome was adopted as the Customs Air Port of London, putting Hounslow Heath out of business and forcing AT&T to move operations to Croydon. The site, once occupied by the airfield from which the world's first international service was inaugurated, is today a mixture of residential streets, industrial properties and green land.

The skies above Hounslow Heath remained silent for the next decade until 1930 when a 46-year-old aero engineer and aircraft builder called Charles Richard Fairey paid the vicar of Harmondsworth £15,000 for a 150-acre plot on which to build a private airport to assemble and test aircraft. The site was perfect. The land was flat, with no buildings, trees or railway lines likely to get in the way of aircraft taking off or landing. Fairey's company, manufacturing both private and military aircraft, had been operating from leased premises owned by the Air Ministry at nearby Northolt Aerodrome, where runway length and hangar space was limited. Fairey needed a testing site of his own from which to put aeroplanes designed and made at Hayes, Middlesex and Hamble, Hampshire through their paces.

People living at Heath Row, Perry Oaks and along the Bath Road were unhappy when news was leaked that aircraft would soon be buzzing over their hedgerows and rooftops – many of them thatched – creating noise and pollution. But Fairey assured

The first aircraft to 'christen' Richard Fairey's Great West Aerodrome was a new twin-engine bomber called the Hendon, built for the RAF. It took to the skies for the first time on 25 November 1930 with the company's chief test pilot, Norman Macmillan, at the controls. *(Heathrow Visitors Centre)*

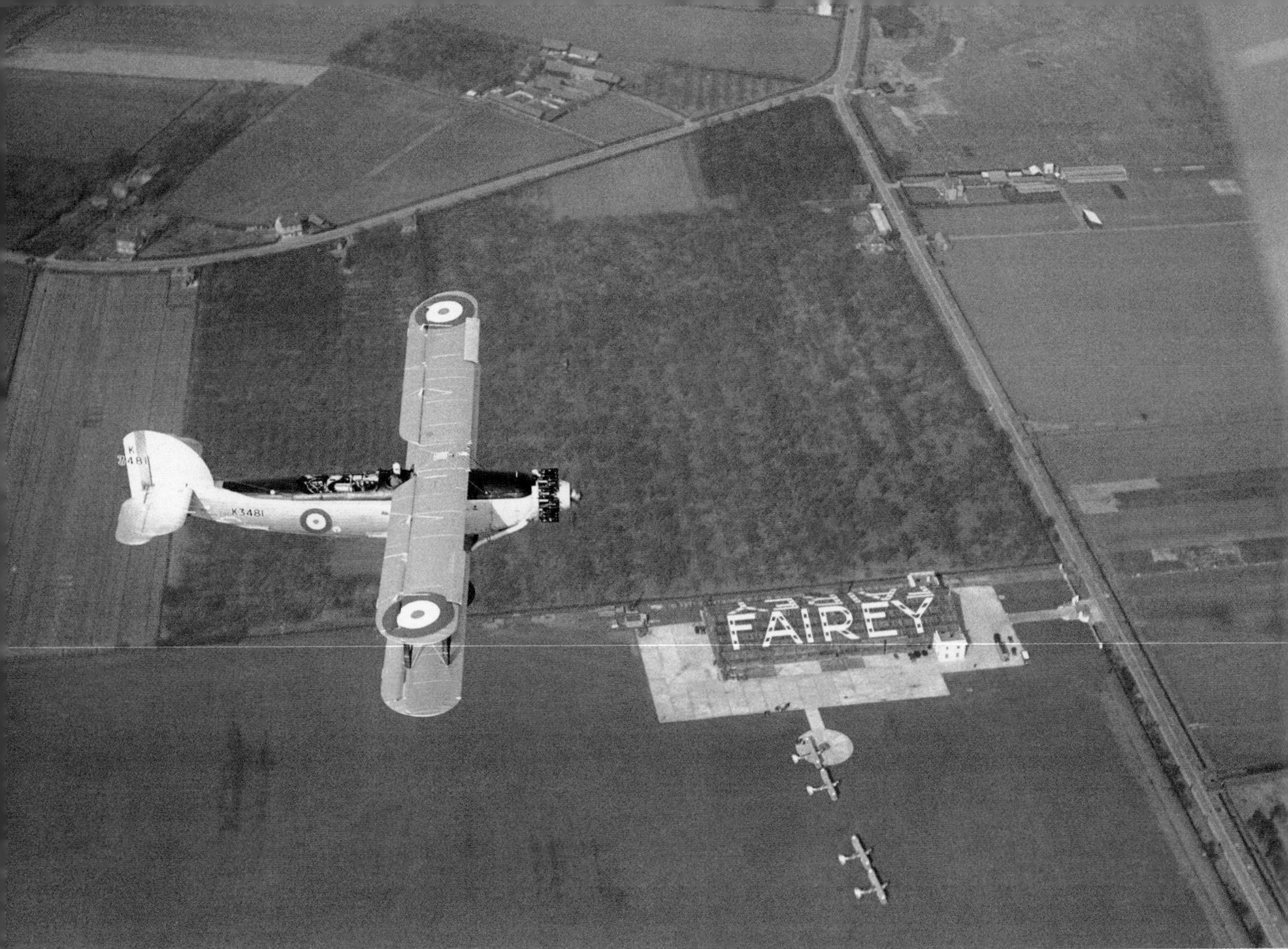

Local people enjoyed watching the occasional Fairey aircraft soar overhead. One of the most popular planes tested at the Great West Aerodrome was the Fairey Swordfish, photographed here above the flight hangar in March 1933. *(Quadrant Picture Library (Flight International collection))*

them that aircraft building was a slow process; components had to be brought to the site by road to be assembled and his company could only produce two aircraft a week. Noise would be kept to a minimum and all aircraft start-ups, take-offs and landings would take place in an area well away from homes.

Fairey finally managed to win local approval by informing residents that once opened his private airport would host summer events, including garden parties for British aviators and flying displays organised by the Royal Aeronautical Society – and they would be able to watch free aerial demonstrations from the comfort of their own garden chairs or bedroom windows. They were also told that a number of VIPs would be attending, including the society's patron, HM the King.

Over the next ten years Fairey's private airport would be given various names, including the Great West Aerodrome, Harmondsworth Aerodrome and even Heath Row Aerodrome. It was located midway between the Bath Road to the north and the Great South West Road (opened in 1925 and better known as the A30) to the south-east. Caines Lane – a quiet and narrow tree-lined road linking the villages of Bedfont and Hatton to Sipson – provided the easterly boundary while the village of Heath Row plus Heath Row Road, High Tree Lane and the Duke of Northumberland's River marked the western boundaries of Fairey's airport; originally sited where part of Heathrow's runway 27L and some of the airport's busiest taxiways are located today.

A disused section of Caines Lane, which once linked the Great South West Road with the Bath Road and ran past the entrance to Fairey Aviation's Great West Aerodrome, remains under the flight path at Heathrow Airport. *(Alan Gallop)*

In the north-east corner of the site, at the top of Caines Lane, Fairey built what was to become the biggest aircraft hangar of its kind at the time. A company called C.P. Hunter was commissioned to lay down a large stretch of smooth turf along the full length of the site – known as 'Hunterised Greensward' – which would be used as a runway that would be as smooth as a bowling green for take-offs and landings.

The first aircraft to 'christen' the Great West Aerodrome was a new twin-engine bomber called the Hendon, built for the RAF. The aircraft was delivered in a fleet of lorries from Fairey's aircraft factory in Heaton Chapel, Stockport for final assembly. It took to the skies for the first time on 25 November 1930, with the company's chief test pilot Norman Macmillan at the controls and leader of the design team, D.L. Hollis Williams, as a passenger. The flight, powered by two 525hp Bristol Jupiter engines, was a total success and another took place the following day. Both flights indicated that modifications needed to be made before the bomber could enter service, but Fairey's new airport had been inaugurated and his latest aircraft tested on the site.

The Hendon was the only heavy bomber conceived and built by Fairey Aviation. Fourteen were eventually delivered to the RAF and used extensively until Wellington and Whitley aircraft were ready to leave their production lines.

Local people enjoyed watching the occasional Fairey aircraft soar overhead, until March 1931 when the Hendon prototype overshot the aerodrome, crossed over a road and ended up in an orchard. The accident caused so much damage that the aircraft had to be dismantled and rebuilt in the giant hangar. Fortunately there were no injuries to farmers or Fairey people.

In 1935 a junior draughtsman joined Fairey's staff. His name was Peter Masefield and to supplement his small salary he began writing freelance articles for the *Aeroplane* magazine. Masefield stayed with the company for two years, going on to become a distinguished war correspondent, flying with the US 8th Bomber Command based in Britain and was later an adviser in civil aviation matters to wartime and postwar cabinets. In later years he was appointed an executive with leading airlines and aircraft manufacturing companies, finishing his career as Chairman of the British Airports Authority – owners of Heathrow Airport where his career had begun thirty years before.

Meanwhile, business was booming at Croydon. A number of small British airlines, including AT&T, were operating flights to Paris, Amsterdam, Rotterdam and Berlin, and by 1924 they had merged together to become Imperial Airways. The world's first purpose-built air terminal had opened in 1924 and services were extended to all parts of the British Empire and beyond. But not everyone was satisfied. One passenger described a flight to Paris as follows: 'They put you in a box, they shut the lid, they splash you all over with oil, you are sick and you're in Paris.'

A 1945 advertisement recording some of the aircraft put through trials at Fairey Aviation's Great West Aerodrome and Hayes, Middlesex testing centres. *(Author's colledtion)*

However the mid-1920s and 1930s marked the truly great days of flying, when passengers wearing tropical clothes would turn up at Croydon on a winter's day, already dressed for their destination. It would take 1 week or longer to fly to the other side of the world in an Imperial Airways Handley Page 42, equipped to carry twenty to thirty passengers depending on the route.

During the aerial adventure, passengers would be joined by the Captain to dine on fine china and drink from crystal cut glass. On routes to India, Africa, the Far East, Australia and New Zealand they would stay overnight in special luxury air-transit stations in deserts and jungles and while aircraft were refuelled and made ready for the next day's flight, sleeping in comfortable beds, taking baths and enjoying sumptuous meals before flying off on the next stage of their air odyssey to far-flung places coloured red on the world map. In some desert locations, armed tribesmen on horseback would line landing strips, firing rifles into the air to welcome the arrival of British aircraft. The art of intercontinental air travel really began at this time, courtesy of Imperial Airways.

By the mid-1930s there were dark clouds on the horizon. Everyone was talking about war, and how any conflict might affect commercial life and the way people lived and worked in Britain. When war was finally declared, on 3 September 1939, Croydon was closed to civil aviation and became an RAF fighter station, a major player in the Battle of Britain and the London base for RAF Transport Command.

Over in Westminster, civil servants were preparing to draft a document with the working title of 'A plan for London' seeking to examine how London might cope with expansion in the decades that would follow. It would address issues such as population, housing, industry, use of land and transport issues. The war brought a temporary end to research for the document, but it would reappear in 1944 and become a major force in identifying a number of things the capital and its surrounding areas might require in peacetime, including sites for civil airports.

At the Great West Aerodrome, Fairey Aviation was busy testing a new combat aircraft called the Battle, built to carry a crew of three and up to 1,500lb of bombs. As the early years of the war progressed, increasing numbers of aircraft were brought to Fairey's private airport for assembly and testing as part of the country's massive rearmament programme. Aircraft sections were made at Austin Motors' factory in Birmingham and then rushed to Harmondsworth, where they were quickly pieced together in the massive hangar before being wheeled out onto the green turf and taken into the air. The first squadron to fly them was No. 63 based at Upwood. The Fairey Battle was not one of the company's most successful planes, but it served the RAF well during the early years of the conflict and the period known as 'the phoney war'.

Fairey wanted to expand his business at the Great West Aerodrome but met with resistance from the Air Ministry. Nobody was prepared to give him a reason why. He argued that he was helping the war effort by churning out aircraft built to RAF specifications and delivered on time. If he could expand his Harmondsworth facilities, Fairey Aviation would increase productivity and deliver twice as many aircraft.

In 1944, a bomb was dropped on Richard Fairey's private airport – not by Göring's Luftwaffe but by the Air Ministry who coldly informed him that he must quit the Harmondsworth site and make way for a new RAF Transport Command airfield to be used by long-range B-29s from the Tiger Force taking troops and reinforcements to help defeat the Japanese and win the war in the Far East.

The explanation given was an outright lie and it took Fairey Aviation until 1964 to receive compensation from the government for having to leave his private airfield during its busiest and most productive phase. By then Richard Fairey was dead and the company only existed on paper.

Fairey transferred flight-testing operations to nearby Heston Aerodrome and White Waltham in Berkshire and people living around the Great West Aerodrome held their breath to see what would happen next.

FOUR

1946–9

Professor Abercrombie's Timely Vision and How Harold Balfour Hijacked Heathrow for Civil Aviation

> *Almost the last thing I did at the Air Ministry of any importance was to hijack for civil aviation the land on which London Airport stands under the noses of resilient ministerial colleagues. If hijack is too strong a term, I plead guilty to the lesser crime of deceiving a Cabinet Committee.*
>
> *Harold Balfour (Lord Balfour of Inchrye),* Wings Over Westminster

EVEN IN WARTIME, plans for civil aviation were being studied. Politicians knew that once the hostilities were over there would be a need for commercial air travel by people appointed to the task of getting the country back on its feet, restoring relations with foreign nations and rebuilding trade with the rest of the world.

The Port of London Authority began lobbying the government for a combined sea and air port to be built south of the Thames near Woolwich. Word came back that they should wait until the return of peace before such a radical idea could be considered.

By 1943, civil servants were revisiting the document they had put to one side in 1939 and attempting to define London's future growth. In charge of the project was Professor Patrick Abercrombie, a distinguished town planner and Vice-President of the Royal Institute of British Architects. The need to refocus on a London severely damaged during the Blitz was now a major priority for the government and Abercrombie was brought in to mastermind the creation of the Greater London Plan, eventually published in 1944.

In his introduction to the section dealing with civil aviation, Abercrombie wrote:

> There is little doubt that air transport will in future play a vastly larger part than it did before the war. Under the stress of warfare, air movements in methods of flying and types of aircraft have been accelerated, inventions have been tested, devices

have been perfected, and with the return of peace we may anticipate a greatly increased demand from people who are ready and anxious to travel by air. . . . But when civil flying becomes permanently established as a normal means of communication and an enormous centre of population is concerned, the planning of a system of airports becomes of first importance.

Abercrombie rejected the idea of a single airport within the boundaries of London itself and – with some foresight – advocated a need 'for a ring of airports from which the centre and the region may be more or less equally accessible. And this question of accessibility by other means than by flying becomes one of the important aspects of the internal communications plan by road and rail.'

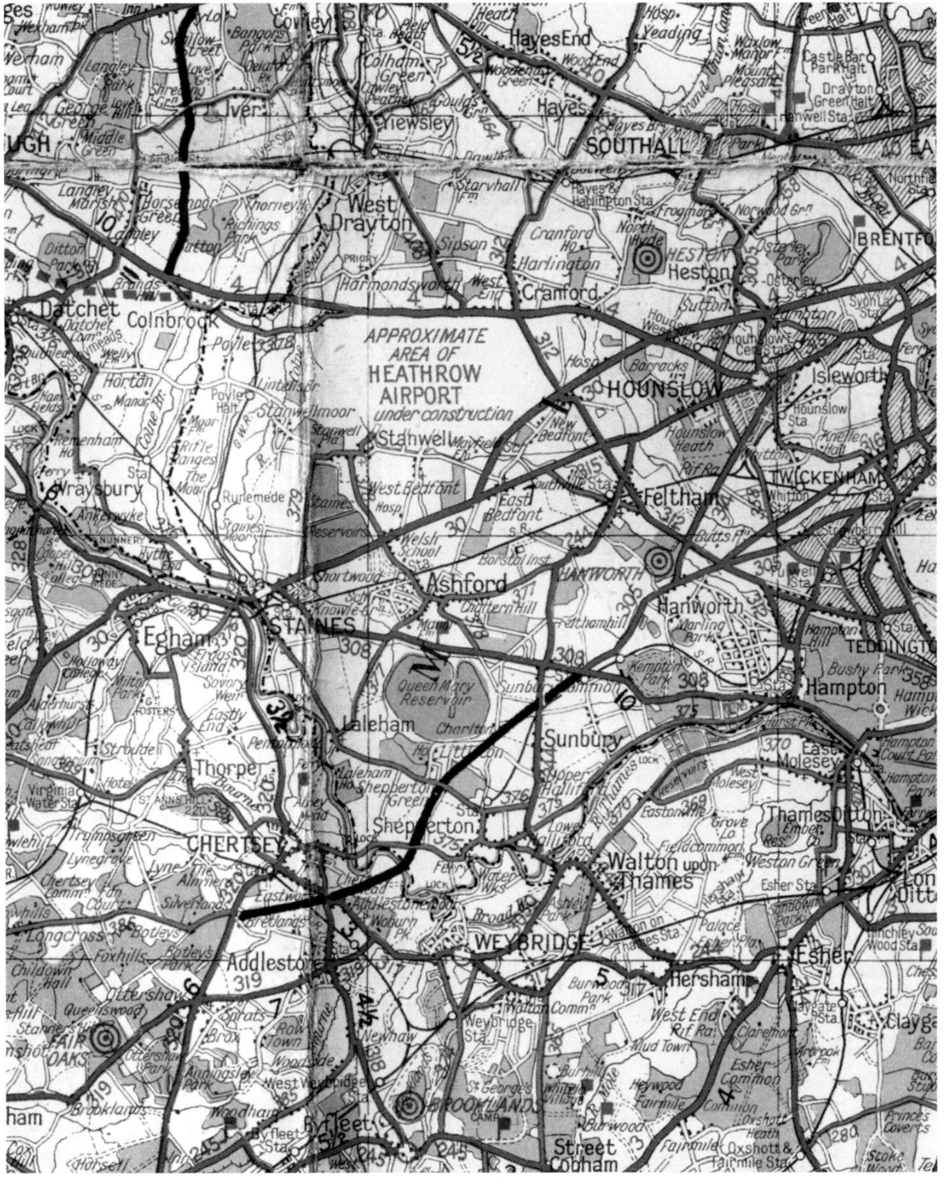

Section from a 1945 map '35 miles around London' showing 'the approximate area of Heathrow Airport under construction'. *(Reproduced by permission of Geographers' A–Z Map Company Ltd. © Crown Copyright 2005. All rights reserved. Licence No. 100017302)*

The document pondered on the possible use of vertical take-off and landing equipment being used to transport passengers from his ring of airports and landing 'on the flat roofs of some of the great terminal stations'. There was even a plan for BOAC's flying boats – soon to be phased out of operations – to land on some of the large reservoirs being built to the west of London near Staines, Middlesex. When completed, they would be large enough to allow flying boats to take-off and land with ease, but the idea was abandoned because flying boats were slow and the government of the day wanted to encourage the manufacture of faster aircraft using traditional runways in the postwar years.

Abercrombie predicted that London needed as many as ten different airports to serve intercontinental and international routes. One of these would be 'one airport of trans-ocean type, which requires extremely careful siting; its demands as to size, etc., are great and it must not be too far out'.

Boldly, Abercrombie stuck his neck out and stated: '*Now* is the moment for London to prepare a plan for its air terminals, of different types of service, when it is possible to articulate them to the road and rail plan which is being worked out at the same time ... [as a result] the capital of the Empire will take its rightful place among the cities of the world as one of the greatest centres of civil aviation.'

Among the airports Abercrombie had in mind would be one single airport 'capable of dealing with distant traffic from all parts of the world. While such an airport should be conveniently near to the centre, it must also be of a size to accommodate the largest aeroplanes. As there is no open space of this order within the built up area, it will be necessary to find a site further out. . . . Within this area one airport of this character will, it is considered, meet the needs of world wide traffic; an alternative airport will no doubt be required for use in different weather conditions, but this would be much beyond the area of Greater London.'

Fifty-two sites around London were considered and forty of them rejected as unsuitable, for a variety of reasons. Many were operating as RAF stations and offered possibilities for peacetime use. Top of Abercrombie's list of locations was an area '12 miles west of Victoria Railway Station, on level land with a gravel sub-soil and measures three and a half miles by three miles'. It was called Heathrow (one of the first times that the two words making up the name of the tiny agricultural hamlet had been joined together to make a single place name).

It is interesting to note that Abercrombie's plan included land north of the Bath Road because 'it is desirable to provide for possible future needs; it would be unfortunate if a major airport was developed and later had to be abandoned because land in its vicinity had not been kept open; but the portion north of the Bath Road would remain in its present agricultural state, together with various groups of houses on it, for some years to come, if not permanently'.

The report noted that 'although the site of this whole airport is on land of first-rate agricultural quality, it is felt that after consideration and thorough weighing up of all the factors, that the sacrifice for the proposed purpose of the part south of the Bath Road is justified. Parts have already suffered impairment of agricultural value through urban encroachments, gravel digging and sludge disposal.'

Professor Abercrombie envisaged the airport being connected to central London via new express roads and by 'electric railway to Waterloo and Victoria by means of a short branch to Feltham. A 2-mile extension of the tube railway from West Hounslow would also give direct connection with the Underground system.'

He also suggested that the nearby Grand Union Canal 'provides a means of bringing by barge the large supplies of petrol which will be required, but it may be found desirable to use a pipeline'.

As for the terminal buildings, Abercrombie predicated that they 'will be extensive, including control rooms, booking halls, waiting rooms, customs halls, restaurants, hotels, hangars, workshops, repair shops, staff accommodation and canteens, while in addition there will be a railway station, a coach station and car parks. It will also be necessary to provide room for the large numbers of the public who may be expected to use the airport. It will be desirable to provide shops, cafés and perhaps a cinema for the entertainment of passengers and their friends awaiting the arrival or departure of planes.'

As a final note the professor added: 'Apart from the central area actually occupied by the aerodrome, it is important to prevent any further building development on the surrounding fringe. The existing market gardens on this good fringe land can accordingly be left undisturbed.'

Other airports on Abercrombie's list of possible sites were:

Heston, Middlesex – 'The future of this existing airport may be mainly in connection with goods traffic. It is near road, rail and canal facilities.'

Bovingdon, Hertfordshire – 'This site adjoins the express arterial road leading inwards to London and outwards to Birmingham, Lancashire and Carlisle. Weather conditions are more favourable here than any of the other sites.'

Hatfield, Hertfordshire – 'It has good road and rail facilities. . . . The existing railway line between Hatfield and St Albans will be duplicated and electrified and will thus afford direct rail communication between the airport and London.'

Matching, Essex – 'The site will be provided with a spur road about 5 miles long to the express arterial road, leading inwards towards London and outwards to Cambridge.'

Fairlop, north-east London – 'The area of the prewar proposed site would have to be considerably increased. . . . Careful planning will be necessary at the intersection of two express arterial roads to keep them well below the angle of flight from the north-east corner of the airport.'

Lullingstone, Kent – 'This site, like Heston, may be mainly used in connection with goods traffic.'

West Malling, Kent – 'This site is near the Maidstone branch (electrified) of the Southern Railway and the main road from London to Folkestone.'

Gatwick, Sussex – 'The outstanding advantage of this site is its direct connection with the electrified main line of the Southern Railway from London to Brighton. . . . The London to Brighton road (A23) will have to be diverted westwards. The surface drainage of the site may be difficult, as it is only slightly above the River Mole, which has very flat gradient.'

Croydon, Surrey – 'This existing airport is without rail connection and is surrounded by built up areas.'

By 1944, Harold Balfour, a former Royal Flying Corps pilot who had been shot down over Vimy Ridge in 1917, was Under Secretary of State for Air, working closely with Lord Beaverbrook, Prime Minister Churchill's Arms Minister. Throughout the war Balfour had often pondered on what lay in store for civil aviation once peace had returned. Like many others, he knew that there would be a huge demand for air transport to and from the London area and over the years had kept a close watch on developments taking place at Richard Fairey's private Great West Aerodrome.

At the same time as Professor Abercrombie was drafting his Greater London Plan, Balfour was quietly working behind the scenes to cut through miles of red tape in order to find a suitable site for a major civil airport which could be ready as soon as peace was declared. Balfour was more than familiar with the workings of civil airlines and recognised the pre-war shortcomings of Croydon Airport. He was determined to do something about it.

In his memoirs, *Wings Over Westminster*, Balfour makes a frank admission:

> Almost the last thing I did at the Air Ministry of any importance was to hijack for civil aviation the land on which London Airport stands under the noses of resilient ministerial colleagues. If hijack is too strong a term, I plead guilty to the lesser crime of deceiving a Cabinet Committee.

Balfour states that others like him, who had studied the needs of postwar civil aviation, were aware that surrounding Fairey's grass aerodrome was land ideal for London's main airport. He also knew that any attempt to grab land for civil purposes would mean having to go through long and complicated civil procedures, including a public inquiry. It would also mean that other government ministries, including agriculture and housing, would almost certainly raise objections.

To get around the problem, Balfour worked towards acquiring Fairey's aerodrome and land surrounding it by using emergency wartime powers, allowing him to ride roughshod over almost anything within reason.

Like everyone else, Balfour knew that German defeat was only a matter of time and Churchill's government was deep in planning the next part of the war, including British efforts for the final conquest of Japan alongside American allies.

To win this part of the war, Britain was prepared to supply long-range air transportation of troops and supplies from the UK to the Far East. In the six years since war was declared, aircraft had greatly increased in size, requiring landing strips of extended length.

Balfour put together a powerful document for Churchill's Cabinet stating that, by requisitioning Fairey's private aerodrome and a large area beyond under wartime powers, Britain could create an RAF station from which all of its future needs could operate. Several other bomber airfields in the Home Counties could have done the job just as well, but Balfour was fixed on the Harmondsworth site.

Balfour's paper was discussed by Churchill and his Cabinet colleagues, who appointed a committee to take the matter forward. Balfour discovered that Lord Beaverbrook was to be a member and he took the aging politician and newspaper baron into his confidence as to the real reason he was pressing 'for what we were sure was London's best chance for a great civil airport'.

As expected, the Minister for Agriculture fiercely objected to sacrificing acres of grade-one farmland to aircraft and concrete runways. The Minister for Housing joined in the protest, claiming that Balfour's plan would take away fringe land earmarked for future housing schemes.

Balfour made an impassioned speech about the importance of finding a suitable site to help Britain in the next phase of its war effort in the Far East: 'I did not dare to breathe the words "civil aviation"', Balfour recalled. 'I put this right out of my mind so effectively that I really convinced myself of the priority of our case.'

The Cabinet came down on Balfour's side and the Air Ministry duly evicted Fairey Aviation from its aerodrome. Hiroshima killed the next planned stage of the war – and the massive site, which Balfour never intended to use for military purposes, passed into his hands.

At around the same time, Churchill created the Civil Aviation Ministry to act separately from the rest of the Aviation Ministry. This continued to concentrate on military matters until Churchill was evicted from office on 23 May when a Labour government toppled him and his government from office, including Beaverbrook and Balfour.

Attlee's new government was keen to win public plaudits as soon as possible and his new Conservative Aviation Minister, Lord Winster, announced that a new airport for London was right at the top of his agenda and that construction and operations would take place simultaneously. He failed to mention that it was likely to cost £25 million – the largest sum ever allocated to a single government-funded project, originally intended for military movements and due to pass into civil use as soon as practicable.

The press demanded to know where this new airport might be located, but the Air Ministry insisted on following official wartime advice to civilians for the time being: 'Be like Dad – keep Mum.' The papers sought the opinion of Brigadier-General Alfred Critchley, Director General of BOAC, whose wartime operations had been severely curtailed and centred on airfields at Whitechurch, near Bristol, and Hurn Airport, near Bournemouth – a tedious, 100-mile, three-hour road journey from London. He told the press that while driving from his home in Sunningdale to his office at the Victoria Air Terminal he had discovered 'an excellent site for the future London Airport', but claimed that the Air Ministry could not be persuaded to consider it. He said that his airline's transatlantic services from Hurn were 'particularly impractical' because passengers were forced to bypass the site on their three-hour-long journeys from London to the south coast. But Critchley declined to name the precise location.

On 31 May 1946, the Air Ministry finally disclosed its plans to Middlesex County Council. Using emergency wartime powers, under the Defence of the Realm Act 1939 which prevented an appeal, the government drew up a compulsory purchase order for 2,800 acres of land, including Heath Row, Perry Oaks and the Great West Aerodrome.

Shortly afterwards the *Middlesex Chronicle*, a local newspaper read by everyone living in the Hounslow and Bath Road area, reported:

> The announcement was made this week of plans for the postwar establishment in south-west Middlesex of the world's largest airport, capable of accommodating the biggest airliners and transport planes likely to be used in the next quarter of a century. The scheme provides for the finest equipment and the port will have a link with London by District Railways. The necessary land covering a wide area in the borough of Heston and Isleworth and urban districts of Feltham, Staines, Hayes and Harlington, Yiewsley and West Drayton had, it is understood, been acquired. Although the location had been reduced to a specific district, the exact site still remained undisclosed. The public was told that 'one of the reasons that led to the siting of the airport in this district was that it could be done with the minimum disturbance to householders'.

A news blackout was thrown over the project and it would be almost two years before anything further could be officially disclosed about the world's largest airport postwar scheme taking place in south-west Middlesex, to be built while the war had still to be won.

FIVE

1945–6

Wimpey's Workforce Rolls Out the Runway

PEOPLE LIVING AT THE VILLAGES of Heath Row and Perry Oaks feared the worst. Many had noticed increasing numbers of strangers wearing suits and carrying clipboards driving to the area, parking, walking up and down their normally quiet lanes, and making copious notes. Occasionally one of the strangers would drop into the Harrow pub for a pint of beer, but no amount of friendly probing over the bar could coax information about the purpose of their visits. Some thought they had something to do with a sewerage disposal works about to be built in fields close to Perry Oaks. Others thought that the men had something to do with gravel-raising schemes: extracting sand and ballast on fallow land close to the village.

And then the official letters began arriving, stating that under emergency wartime powers people's homes, gardens, farms, orchards, barns and smallholdings would be acquired by a government compulsory order for military use. Villagers were told that they would be compensated at current market rates and the Ministry of Health (working with local councils) had been charged with providing assistance, where required, to relocate them elsewhere. Displaced people were forced to accept alternative accommodation at higher rents and for many agricultural workers genuine hardship lay ahead. Compensation was based on 1939 property prices plus 30 per cent. Additional compensation would include payment for crops or produce grown in 1944 and payments based on proof of the previous year's income. Farmers or smallholders unable to produce paperwork confirming sales from crops, fruit, vegetables, livestock or poultry sold in 1943 would have a problem on their hands.

Orders to vacate homes lived in and land worked on for generations were politely worded, yet firm and irrevocable. Within weeks, an army of workmen and their vehicles had moved into the area, felling trees, digging up bushes and ancient hedgerows, pulling down fences and demolishing walls. Work on wiping the ancient villages of Heath Row and Perry Oaks from the map had begun in earnest; creating the world's longest runway on the same site was about to get under way. There was no going back.

At the same time, Fairey Aviation – with a full order book of military aircraft to assemble, test and deliver – had to vacate the Great West Aerodrome and relocate to

Heston Airport and its totally inadequate air traffic control facilities as a flight test centre. Two years later the company was forced to relocate again to White Waltham, near Maidenhead. These disruptions cost the company dearly by way of reduced productivity and profits.

Heath Row and Perry Oaks villagers were rehoused in ordinary suburban homes in Heston, Hayes and Harlington. Some went further afield. None of them was offered any growing or pasture land. The Ministry of Health, desperate to find accommodation for hundreds who had lost homes in the Blitz, had little time for a handful of farmers who through no fault of their own had got in the way of an airport development. It would be years before they were properly compensated and many claimed that they were never paid the sums expected.

By May 1944 George Wimpey & Company, from Denham near Uxbridge, was a household name in building and civil engineering when it was awarded a contract to construct three new runways for the airport scheme. The runways would be built in the regular RAF triangular 'Shield of David' pattern, permitting aircraft to take off and land in any possible wind direction with a 4mph crosswind. The runways would also allow simultaneous take-offs and landings so as to achieve optimum utilisation.

Wimpey's workforce takes time out from constructing a 'new runway for the RAF', on the site of the former village of Heath Row, to smile for the camera in 1945. *(Heathrow Visitors Centre)*

Above and overleaf: A large workforce was recruited to work around the clock to lay the airport's east–west runway. During the first seven months of construction, 2 million tons of earth and gravel was excavated. A huge travelling spreading machine was brought in to produce enough concrete to make a runway 9,000ft long, 300ft wide and 12in thick – enough to build a new road from London to Edinburgh. *(Heathrow Visitors Centre/Author's collection)*

A large workforce was recruited to work around the clock to complete the task, working Mondays to Saturdays, with Sundays being the only day when work stopped. Each man recruited was instructed to remain silent about the work he was engaged to perform. If challenged about their employment they were to say that they were clearing and preparing the site for a large peacetime housing scheme – and nothing else.

Wimpey's airport army was a motley collection of men. Experienced surveyors, engineers and builders in reserved occupations worked alongside young and inexperienced lads awaiting military 'call-up' and drafted in to work as labourers. Middle-aged and elderly members of the Local Defence Volunteer force – better known as the Home Guard – who had worked in pre-war building jobs offered their services, while Labour Exchanges across Middlesex sent every available man on their books to help remove for all time the traces of former farms, market gardens and disused gravel pits. A small number of German prisoners of war and Land Army girls were also brought in to assist.

From 6 June 1944 onwards, daily convoys of buses and lorries collected runway gangs from town squares, railway and underground stations and drove them to the giant building site. At the end of the day they drove them back again before collecting another contingent of Wimpey workers to labour on the next shift, working in all weathers by the light of hurricane lamps and headlights from 200 lorries, 40 mechanical excavators, and 50 bulldozers and tractor-drawn excavators.

Hundreds were housed and fed on the site in a temporary village split into two sections – 'Tintown', made up of Nissan hut-type, half-circle-shaped dwellings made

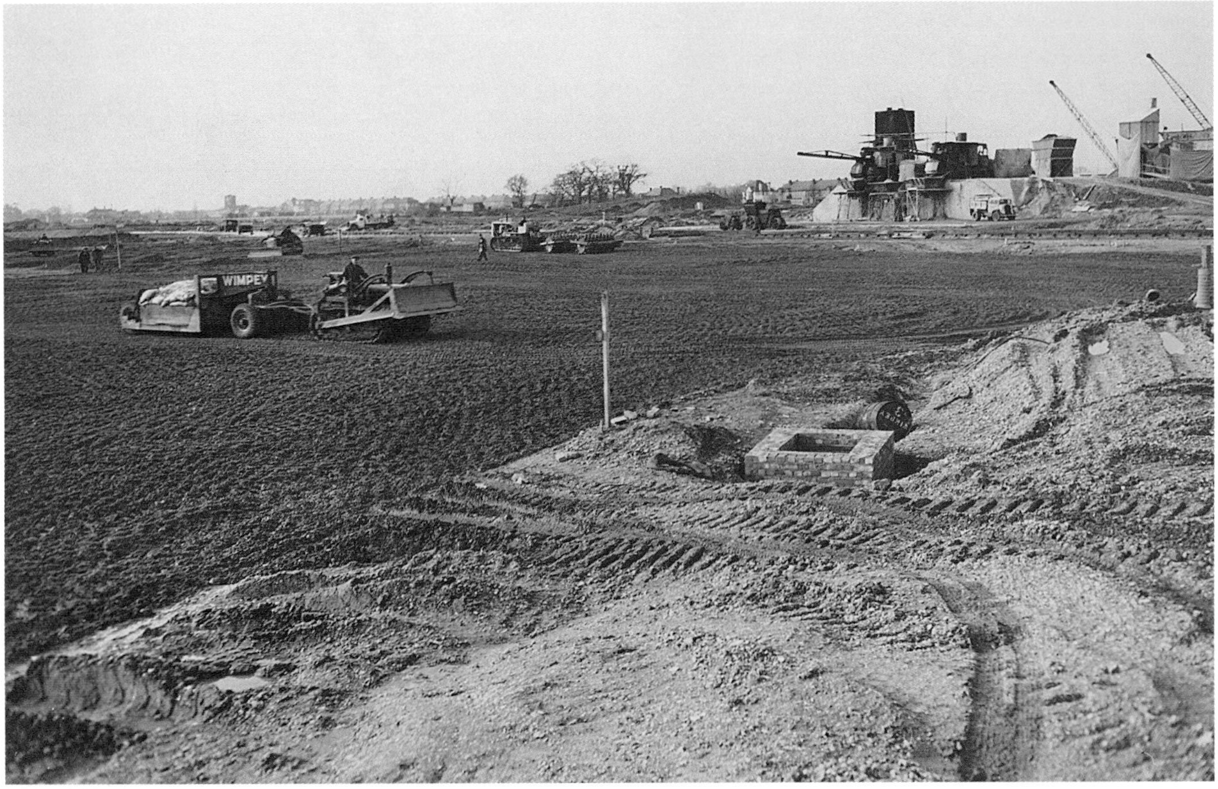
WIMPEY

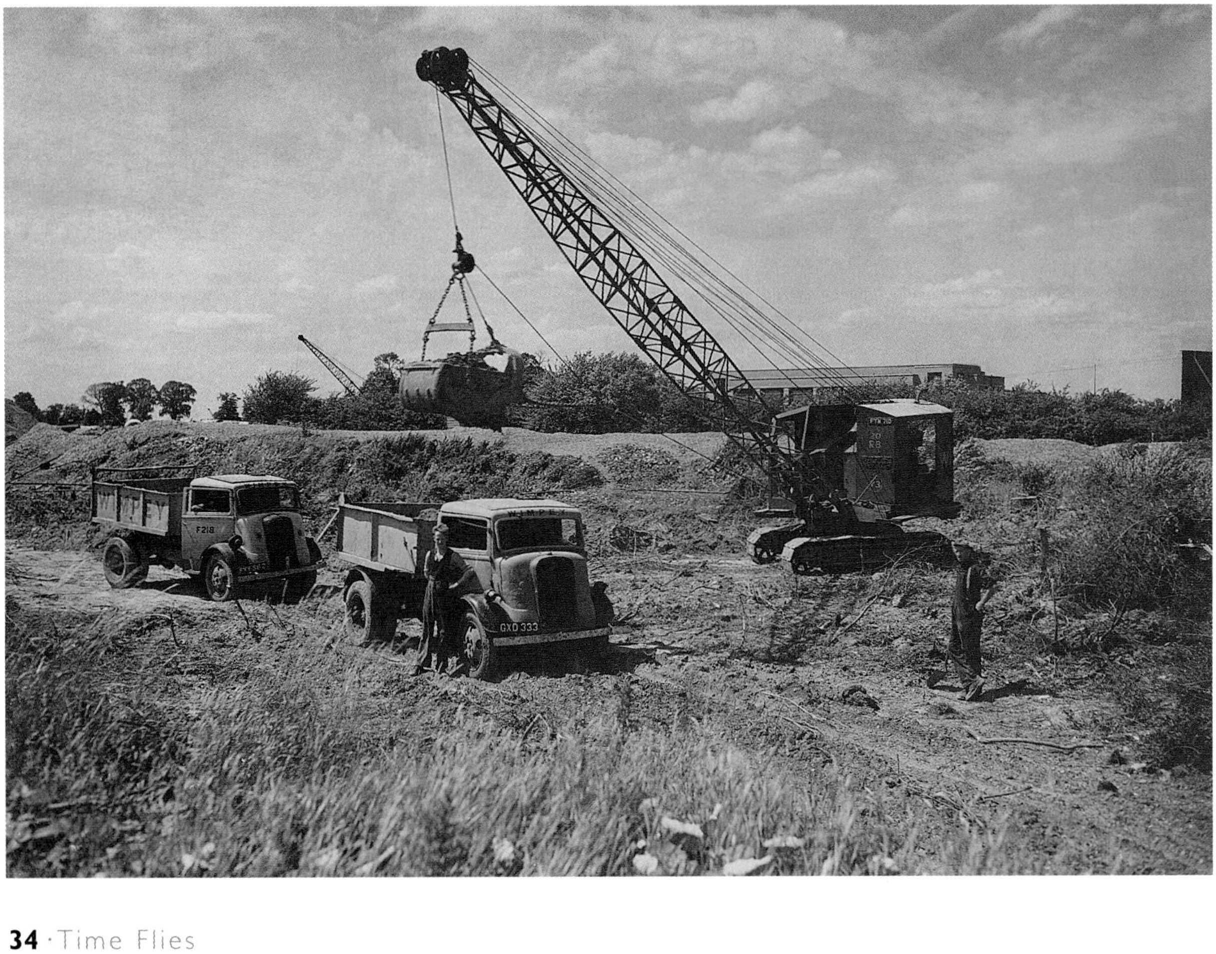
WIMPEY
F218
GXO 333

from corrugated tin, and 'Timbertown', constructed from wood and taking on the appearance of an Army barracks. Tintown offered indoor recreational facilities including table tennis and card tables. A room was included where workers could listen to their favourite radio programmes while enjoying a smoke and a cup of tea. Outside there were a football field and a cricket pitch. A Timbertown hut was turned into a makeshift theatre where films were screened and concert parties performed.

Residents were encouraged to help 'Dig for Victory' and create wartime gardens growing vegetables for the work camp's kitchen. Anyone wanting to drink beer could easily walk or cycle to one of the many pubs in Stanwell, Longford or along the Bath Road, but George Wimpey & Company did not tolerate drunkenness; anyone returning to the village the worse for wear was immediately sacked. The company argued that many people still lived close to the building site and were exposed to enough disruption during building without having to put up with drunken navvies keeping them awake all hours of the night.

Runway gangs worked a forty-eight-hour week and were paid £5 16s whatever their trade or profession. Workers signed up by Wimpey until all airport runways were completed – expected to be towards the end of 1946 – were given one week's paid holiday a year.

It was clear from the beginning that laying the east–west runway would present a raft of engineering problems. The area included 120 acres of ponds and disused gravel workings which needed to be drained without flooding the surrounding area. To get around the difficulties, a pair of temporary pits were dug at either end of the runway site into which 100 million gallons of water and ½ million cu. yds of silt were discharged. At a later stage, a large drainage scheme was incorporated into the plan to collect rainwater which would normally have soaked into the ground, but would soon sit on top of a 300ft-wide expanse of concrete runway. The water was directed through 13 miles of 54in concrete piping towards a pair of balancing reservoirs located on either side of the A312 road. Sixty years later it is still in use as part of a nature reserve dedicated to the conservation of plants and wildlife species that surround Heathrow Airport.

The Wimpey workforce then had to fill in the former ponds and gravel pits, making sure that the elasticity and resilience of the filled ground was similar to natural surrounding land to ensure the runway would absorb the shocks transmitted by the wheels of thousands of aircraft as they thudded down to land from all parts of the world.

During the first seven months of construction, 2 million tons of earth and gravel were excavated, 36,000ft of multiple ducting for electric cables and 60 miles of wire were laid through ducts.

When searchlights picked out German bombers in the night sky over Middlesex, the hurricane lamps and vehicle headlights were quickly turned off, leaving a large dark area over which the Luftwaffe found nothing worthy of dropping their deadly cargo. The bombers, however, found plenty to destroy nearby. Residential areas were a key target along with the railway depot at Feltham, just 4 miles away and a prime target thanks to its goods yards and main line running directly into central London. The King George VI reservoir on Staines Moor – to the west of the airport building works – was completed in 1939 but remained unfilled during wartime. Local people claim that a mock-up of Clapham Junction railway station was built on the reservoir's sandy floor to lure enemy bombers away from the real thing. This has never been proved, but the Ministry of Defence still uses the reservoir – which now contains millions of gallons of drinking water for Londoners – and it is closed to the general public.

Flying bombs were another hazard and several found their way into the streets and homes of people living in communities around the runway building site, forcing hundreds of families to evacuate their children to safer communities in countryside areas of the Midlands and northern England. Betty Richardson's dad had other ideas. Betty, from Harmondsworth, recalls: 'My parents moved to Harmondsworth from north London at the outbreak of the war. I had two older brothers and had just started going to school. I don't think our parents wanted us to be evacuated so they moved to what they thought would be a safer area. I remember my dad telling me that I would become a country bumpkin.'

Betty remembers that during the London Blitz 'we could see London burning from our bathroom window and that gives you some idea of how flat the area was [and still is] without all the buildings which have subsequently been erected'.

Work on the runway progressed in 1945 when a giant mixer and a huge travelling spreading machine were brought in to produce enough concrete to make a runway 9,000ft long, 300ft wide and 12in thick. Daily quality tests were conducted to ensure an average strength of over 30 per cent above the standard demanded in the original specification. It took fourteen weeks to mix, spread and compact the concrete runway and half of Wimpey's workforce was laid off during this period when mechanisation took over from manpower.

In addition to the runway (known as runway No. 1), a 100ft-wide taxiway and apron also had to be laid adjacent to the Bath Road. As soon as this was completed, men were laid off while the concrete-spreading operation got under way and were re-engaged to begin clearing the site for two more runways: both 2,000yds long and

100yds wide, one running north-east–south-west (runway No. 2) and the second north-west–south-east (runway No. 3).

All three runways were built with a view to being extended as soon as the Air Ministry saw fit to do so – the main one by a further 6,000ft and the two smaller ones by an extra 3,000ft. By mid-July 1945, 1,114,000sq. yds of 12in-thick concrete had been laid on the largest civil engineering project ever undertaken in Britain and by Christmas 1945 work on runway no. 1 was complete, no. 2 was 25 per cent completed and 80 per cent completed on no. 3.

Writer Paul Townend was allowed to inspect the runway building site for an article which could only be published once the war was over and the airport in use. He recorded:

> Concrete is made by the lorry load in giant mixers at various strategic places on the aerodrome. Watching these mixers, I was reminded of a huge cake-making machine; the ingredients of stone (graded to various sizes), sand, water and cement are loaded like a cake mixture into the tall towers and churned around until the concrete is ready to be disgorged down a chute into a waiting lorry. From there it is driven and dumped in front of the concrete spreaders, astonishing power-driven machines which advance on rails spreading and levelling the piles of concrete as they jerk inexorably forward. On a blistering hot day a 3,000 yard long runway presents an amazing sight. Heat waves dance along the shimmering surface, and before the eye has succeeded in reaching the end, the runway has been transformed into a long band of glistening water. This, of course, is only the optical illusion one gets from standing at one end; a pilot's view when he approaches in his aircraft will be totally different.

Many claim that the RAF never used the site later to be known as Heathrow Airport. This is untrue. In 1940 when the Battle of Britain was at its height, Hurricane aircraft from 229 Squadron, based at nearby Northolt, were diverted to Fairey Aviation's grass airstrip for safety while their home base was under the threat of enemy attack. In 1945, RAF Lancasters, Halifaxes, DC-3s, Ansons and Yorks were also diverted to land and take off from a runway still under construction. Although the site received military aircraft, it was never formally adopted as a traditional RAF base, complete with hangars, maintenance sheds and living quarters.

By Christmas 1945, enough concrete had been mixed and poured onto the runways to build a new road from London to Edinburgh – a distance of over 370 miles. Now all that was needed was a peacetime commercial aeroplane to christen it.

SIX

1945–6

Star Light and the Pathfinders

ONE MORNING SHORTLY BEFORE CHRISTMAS 1945, Air Vice-Marshal Donald Bennett CB, CBE, DSO and newly appointed Chief Executive of British South American Airways (BSAA) was driving from his home in Farnham Royal to the BSAA offices in Grafton Street, Mayfair. His route usually took him along the Bath Road in the direction of Hounslow and Hammersmith and past the site where a new airport was taking shape.

Instead of driving past the site, Bennett, who in his early 30s had been the RAF's youngest Air Vice-Marshal, swung into the building site and asked to speak to Wimpey's chief foreman. After a few moments Mr Steer, the building company's resident engineer, appeared from one of the many building huts lining the Bath Road.

Cliff 'Alaby' Alabaster, who worked alongside Bennett in the RAF's famous wartime No. 8 'Pathfinder' Group and was now running the navigational school for BSAA at Grafton Street, takes up the story:

> Bennett had ended his RAF career and had been appointed Chief Executive for a new airline which planned to operate services from the UK to South America. He had to deal with people at the Air Ministry who didn't have half of his experience and knowledge and were getting in the way of him starting up the new airline. So he by-passed them. On the day before we were due to take delivery of our first Lancastrian airliner from Avro's factory in Waddington, Lincolnshire, he called into the airport building site and had a quiet word with someone from Wimpey and told him that he wanted to land a Lancastrian there the following day. He asked if they could move all of their building barrels and equipment off the runway and out of the way. I don't think for a moment that he had to grease any palms because Bennett was – how shall I put it – careful with his money.

Captain Cliff 'Alaby' Alabaster in 2004 with a model of a Lancaster bomber, from which the commercial version – known as the Lancastrian – was based. Captain Alabaster was a crew member on the first service from Heathrow. *(Alan Gallop)*

So sure enough, next day he landed the Lancastrian at the airport and tucked it away in a corner before going up to the Air Ministry to discuss the new passenger proving flight BSAA had been licensed to operate from the UK to South America. The Air Ministry demanded to know what proving flight and what passengers he was talking about. They told him that if he wanted to fly passengers he could only do it from Hurn (Bournemouth) Airport from where BOAC was conducting long-haul operations. Bennett said he would do no such thing and was going to fly from the new airport at Heathrow. They told him it was impossible and still incomplete, covered in building equipment. Bennett informed them that he had already landed there and that's where his plane was parked ready for its first operational flight. And because he'd already landed there he might as well take off from there. The Air Ministry was aghast because, of course, they knew nothing about it. But Bennett got his way. That's how he always got his way, by being one step ahead of everyone else and going straight to the top. He didn't care who he had to climb over to get his own way.

Captain Cliff Alabaster's logbook entry for 1 January 1946 – the first flight from Heathrow – listing the names of his fellow crew members, routings and sector timings. *(Alan Gallop with thanks to Captain Alabaster)*

Following the end of the war, Lord Beaverbrook was influential in creating three new state-owned airline corporations: British Overseas Airways Corporation (BOAC) serving Commonwealth, Far East and North American destinations; British European Airways (BEA) flying short-haul European and UK domestic routes; and British South American Airways (BSAA) operating to Latin America.

BSAA had originally planned to trade under the name of British Latin American Airways. Founded by a consortium of private shipping companies under the leadership of business tycoon John Booth (of Booth Shipping Line) the company was founded with a start-up capital of £1 million. Bennett, who had briefly flirted with politics as Liberal MP for Middlesbrough after leaving the RAF in 1945 and lost his seat at the General Election shortly afterwards, needed a high-profile job; he liked the idea of being in charge of a new British airline.

The same election that had ousted Bennett from his parliamentary seat also booted out Churchill's Conservative government to make way for Attlee's Labour Party and their plans for nationalising just about everything in the country – including airlines.

There were rumours that Australian-born Bennett was to be offered the job of Governor General of his home country, but Bennett wanted a job that would keep him in the air and in charge of a major British organisation with international prospects.

BOAC, however, had other ideas. As the country's flag-carrying airline, it felt it was entitled to have the South American routes to itself and had, in fact, already operated its own proving flight to Buenos Aires using an Avro Lancastrian, flying from its main operational base at Hurn – a three-hour drive from London. Air Minister Lord

The crew of Star Light arrive at Rio de Janeiro after an exhausting twenty-eight-hour and eighteen-minute flight from London. Left to right: First Radio Officer J. McGillivray, Air Vice-Marshal Donald Bennett, Star Girl Mary Guthrie, Wing Commander D.A. Cracknell and Captain Cliff Alabaster. *(Mary Cunningham collection)*

Flight engineers – and a BSAA Star Girl – prepare Avro Lancastrian Star Land for another service from London to Latin America. *(Heathrow Visitors Centre)*

Winster called an airline showdown with BOAC who was represented by its Director General, Brigadier-General Alfred Critchley while John Booth and Bennett appeared for BSAA.

Critchley claimed that his company was ready to begin regular flights to South America within three months, as soon as it had taken delivery of new aircraft. Bennett responded that he was ready to start flying almost immediately. He had paid A.V. Roe & Company £30,000 for each of the twelve Lancastrians which were almost ready for delivery and in the advance stages of being converted from 20,000lb payload bombers into comfortable passenger airliners with thirteen reclining seats. He informed Lord Winster that he had already recruited over forty ex-Pathfinder crews to his new airline's staff, including twelve Captains and fifteen First Officers, and he had personally negotiated bilateral route agreements with Brazil, Argentina and Uruguay.

The BOAC Chairman accused Bennett and Booth of having nowhere to base their aircraft, warning them that BOAC was using every inch of space at Hurn. 'Surely, you can spare one hangar for BSAA?' protested Lord Winster, but Bennett informed the meeting that he had already made his own 'very satisfactory arrangements'. Asked to provide details he told Lord Winster that he had created a maintenance base at an airfield on the outskirts of London under the direction of Group Captain Sarsby, ex-Chief Engineer of the Pathfinder Force who knew every inch and rivet on a Lancaster. When Winster asked for the name of the airfield, Bennett replied that he would rather not reveal its name in front of Critchley 'because he will do everything he can to stop me'.

After the meeting was adjourned, and Critchley had left the building, Bennett told Lord Winster that the Chairman of Wimpey & Company was a fellow Australian who had loaned him four small buildings at London's new airport that was taking shape to the west of London and had been given use of its runways. Maintenance and hangars were located at Hawker Aircraft's private airport at Langley, near Slough, just 4 miles away from the new airport which was still awaiting hangars, a completed control tower and passenger facilities.

Lord Winster told Bennett and Booth that the new airport was to be named Heathrow Airport, after one of the small villages that had disappeared under the bulldozers to make way for the runway. And although the RAF still – technically – owned the airport, there were pressures to turn the site over to the Ministry for Civil Aviation (a new division of the Air Ministry) for commercial use. 'How soon?' asked Bennett. 'How soon would you like it?' replied Winster with a smile. Bennett quickly replied, 'How about January 1?' 'Good God', said Winster, 'that's only a couple of weeks away!'

By 1945, British aircraft manufacturing company Handley Page was preparing the market for the arrival of its new propliner, Hermes. The company was hopeful that airlines using London's new airport would purchase the planes. *(Author's collection)*

The *Aeroplane* for 11 January 1946 reported:

> Whoever thought of introducing the press to Heathrow and staging a coincident departure of a British South American Airways proving flight to South America on 1 January, the day on which the Air Ministry handed over Heathrow to the Ministry for Civil Aviation should be sent straight to the top of the class. It made it possible for Lord Winster to say in his ceremonial speech that his Ministry 'gets on with things'. It gave him the opportunity to allay fears of the daily press that all was not well with Heathrow; and it gave him the chance of showing that he was making use of the nucleus organisation built up by Messrs Booth and Bennett to get the British South American Airways service started. Full marks, therefore, to the Ministry for Civil Aviation for its initiative and for the opportunity of seeing London's embryonic airport, and an air liner using it, soon after the first runway was completed. Bennett has actually used it before, so it was not the first take-off. Anything else we say on the subject of Heathrow, therefore, must not be allowed to detract from this fully merited praise and the excellent press which the occasion received.

The magazine then went on to probe into the airport's construction and layout 'and here the picture is not as propitious as the hopeful augury suggested by the departure of Star Light, the BSAA Lancastrian to South America'. It criticised the lack of airport buildings stating that

> at present there is a small temporary central building which could accommodate only a very limited number of radio, meteorological, operations and other essential personnel. The number of aircraft handled will be limited accordingly. As for customs, immigration, passenger rooms and facilities, offices, freight sheds, maintenance hangars, technical stores and all the other requirements of a civil airport, there is nothing but a few huts at present to serve this purpose. Obviously temporarily buildings will have to be built if, as is apparently planned, the airport is to be put into service gradually as and when each of the three runways is completed. All three runways should be finished in June.

Lodge Plugs were pleased to advertise the fact that its products had been used on the first service from Heathrow. *(Author's collection)*

The magazine attacked the proximity of airport's taxi track to the Great West Road and the future need to spread airport buildings along the road, instead of locating them in one key area. It predicted that either the 12in-thick taxiway would be dug up and relocated or the Great West Road diverted.

The magazine then mentioned 'the unholy union' between the military and civil authorities regarding the airport's creation, stating: 'It seems clear that the original idea for developing this site was with the object of making it the major civil airport for

London.' The 'political difficulty of allocating millions of pounds on a civil vote in wartime had to be circumvented, a position we are convinced could, and should, have been openly faced and overcome. . . . The only way to get the money allocated was on a military vote. That is why the explanation is now put out that Heathrow was built for Transport Command and the Japanese War; as if there were not hundreds of perfectly good runway aerodromes all over England for this purpose! Why choose one of the few places in this country suitable for the main London Airport?'

Sixteen days after Star Light's historic departure from Heathrow (which some newspapers still referred to as Heath Row), the BSAA Lancastrian returned to London – and the media were again out in force to welcome its crew home, including the country's best-known air hostess, Mary Guthrie. The following story from the *Daily Express* dated Wednesday 16 January 1946 with the headline 'I had £25 but could have spent £2,500 – Ocean hostess sees glamour shops' by the newspaper's air correspondent, Basil Cardew, provides wonderful insight into immediate British postwar needs and aspirations:

> The world's first trans-ocean air hostess, Miss Mary Guthrie, of Knightsbridge, SW, stepped on to the Heath Row tarmac at 1.15 p.m. yesterday with bananas, tangerines, pineapples, cream cakes and a still damp swimsuit in her suit case. She had collected these and also a tropical bronze on the first all British airline flight to Buenos Aires – a 14,400-mile trip that started only a fortnight ago.
>
> She attended to the passengers disembarking from Star Light before telling the story of this milestone flight for British air transport. Captained by AVM Donald Bennett, the Pathfinder ace, the Lancastrian arrived from Lisbon after an up-to-the-minute journey from South America in which a record was set up between London and Rio de Janeiro in the flying time of 28 hours 18 minutes.
>
> Even the American airlines have not employed hostesses on long sea crossings, so it was news to find out how Miss Guthrie, a 24 year old former ATA pilot got along and she said: 'I had four swims – one in West Africa and the others at Rio, Montevideo and Buenos Aires. We flew from winter to the glamour of high summer in South America. As it was a proving flight we did not go fast and I have lost some sleep, but I had to be on duty at night. The South Americans were very pleased to see a British plane with a British crew on the new air service. I suppose it's because we did so much in the war that the whole crew of nine were to find such genuine joy on our arrival. And the shops . . . they were a dream. I saw everything that a woman has wanted in England for the last 6 years of war – piles of fully fashioned silk stockings at 16/- a pair, nail varnish, evening gowns,

Fly with the Stars
to
South America
Central America
and
The West Indies

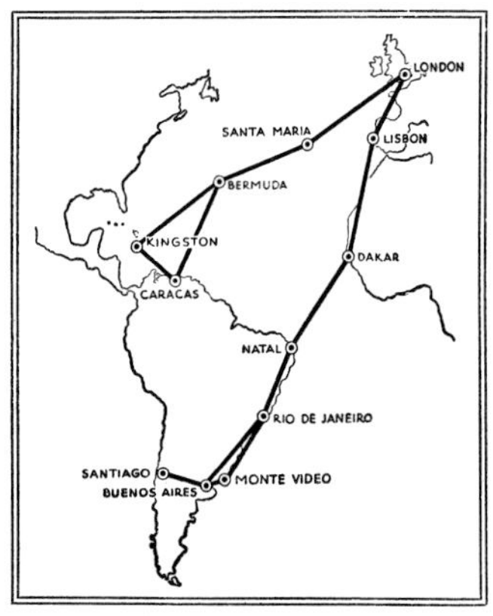

Regular Services for
PASSENGERS, FREIGHT and MAIL
as follows:
Tuesdays and Fridays to **LISBON, DAKAR, NATAL, RIO DE JANEIRO, MONTEVIDEO** and **BUENOS AIRES.**
Saturdays to **LISBON, DAKAR, NATAL, RIO DE JANEIRO.**
Wednesdays to **SANTIAGO.**
Mondays to **AZORES, BERMUDA, JAMAICA** and **CARACAS.**
For further information apply to LEADING AGENCIES, or to
BRITISH SOUTH AMERICAN AIRWAYS
19, GRAFTON STREET, LONDON W.1.
Telephone: REG. 4141. Telegrams: AIRWAYS, TELEX, LONDON.

British South American Airways were quick off the mark advertising passenger and cargo services from London to Latin America and a chance to 'fly with the stars'. *(Author's collection)*

★ FOR AIR-MINDED CHAIRMEN AND DIRECTORS

Immediate action impresses your South American customers

IF AN URGENT PROBLEM arises in one of your South American markets, nothing will put matters right as effectively as a flying visit by you or one of your senior representatives. Immediate action of this sort enormously enhances prestige and goodwill with South American customers.

British South American Airways operate the most frequent, and therefore the most time-saving, service to important South American cities.

Specimen fares:

From London to	*Fares Single*	*Return*
Rio de Janeiro . . .	£171 . 4	£308 . 3
São Paulo	£174 .19	£314 .18
Montevideo	£190 . 2	£342 . 4
Buenos Aires . . .	£192 . 6	£346 . 3

Subject to alteration

Fast services also to Natal, Santiago, Lima, Barranquilla and the West Indies.

Emergency shipments — emergency treatment:

B.S.A.A. give shipments of urgently needed goods — spare parts, for example, or consignments to meet seasonal sales — emergency speed of handling.

It's often *cheaper* to ship by air

Lower insurance charges and lower packing costs (most freight can be packed in cardboard cartons) mean that it is often *cheaper* to ship goods to South America by air than by sea. Other economies are lower warehousing costs — you need not maintain large stocks overseas, since you can deliver immediately on order—and quicker turnover, which frees working capital.

Business by Air - by

BRITISH SOUTH AMERICAN AIRWAYS

Reservations and Information, at no extra charge, from travel or freight agents, or from British South American Airways Corporation, 9/11 Albemarle St., London, W.1 (Regent 4141).

An early advertisement designed to attract business travellers on services from London to South America. *(Author's collection)*

stacks of toeless shoes and even the two-way stretch girdles that are never seen here. I was allowed £25 for the trip but I could have spent £2,500. Most things are expensive compared with prewar prices here.

AVM Bennett said they had now got some sort of organization for the airline at every stop. He confirmed that Star Light had achieved speeds of 240mph – the fastest cruising speed of any airliner. 'We have started up first and we intend to keep British aviation right ahead on the British–South American run', he said.

SEVEN

Tented Terminals and the Race to be First as Time Flies onto the Front Page

THREE WEEKS AFTER STAR LIGHT had inaugurated the world's newest airport, newspaper stories began appearing about advanced plans to expand Heathrow. The *Middlesex Chronicle* reported the story on 19 January 1946 with the page one headline 'Heathrow Airport to Double its Size'.

The story claimed that a Bill would shortly be introduced through Parliament identifying land and houses it planned to purchase to aid the airport's next phase of development, allowing expansion to spill across the Bath Road and increase Heathrow's size from 1,500 acres to 4,000 acres.

'People living in East Bedfont, Cranford, Stanwell, Sipson, Harmondsworth and Harlington – areas all affected by the proposed extensions – have been much alarmed in recent weeks by rumours and London newspapers' reports of proposed wholesale demolitions of houses, historical monuments, etc.', the paper reported.

A *Middlesex Chronicle* reporter, who made enquiries at the Ministry for Civil Aviation, learned that although Sipson village 'is doomed by the proposed development' it was hoped to save about one-third of Harlington, including its historical church and sixteenth-century Dawley Manor Farm, once owned by the Earl of Tankerville.

Asked about the total number of houses likely to be demolished, the paper learned that the number would be about 1,000. An official told the paper: 'We have done our best to avoid demolition of houses and historical monuments, but of course some will have to go. Over 100 alternative plans were examined and an enormous amount of care taken.'

Readers were told that the expansion plan would be spread over seven to ten years 'and the majority of people affected will be able to retain possession of their houses for the major portion of that time, although a few individual houses on the Bath Road might have to go before then'. Parts of the ancient village of Stanwell, on the airport's south-west side, were expected to be affected and its historic church likely to be demolished. Large numbers of new houses would be constructed in Harlington 'to provide accommodation for airport officials and employees'.

Communities around the airport held their breath and feared the worse. Sixty years later, many of the same communities are still holding their breath as similar plans to those first mooted in 1946 resurface like a ghost from the past.

Opposite, top: 'A complete plan of London Airport' originally produced in June 1946 shows how the Ministry for Civil Aviation planned to expand the airport's boundaries north and south of its existing site to create new runways and taxiways. Sixty years later the same idea has resurfaced. *(Author's collection)*

Opposite, bottom: Heathrow from the air, 1946/7. *(Author's collection)*

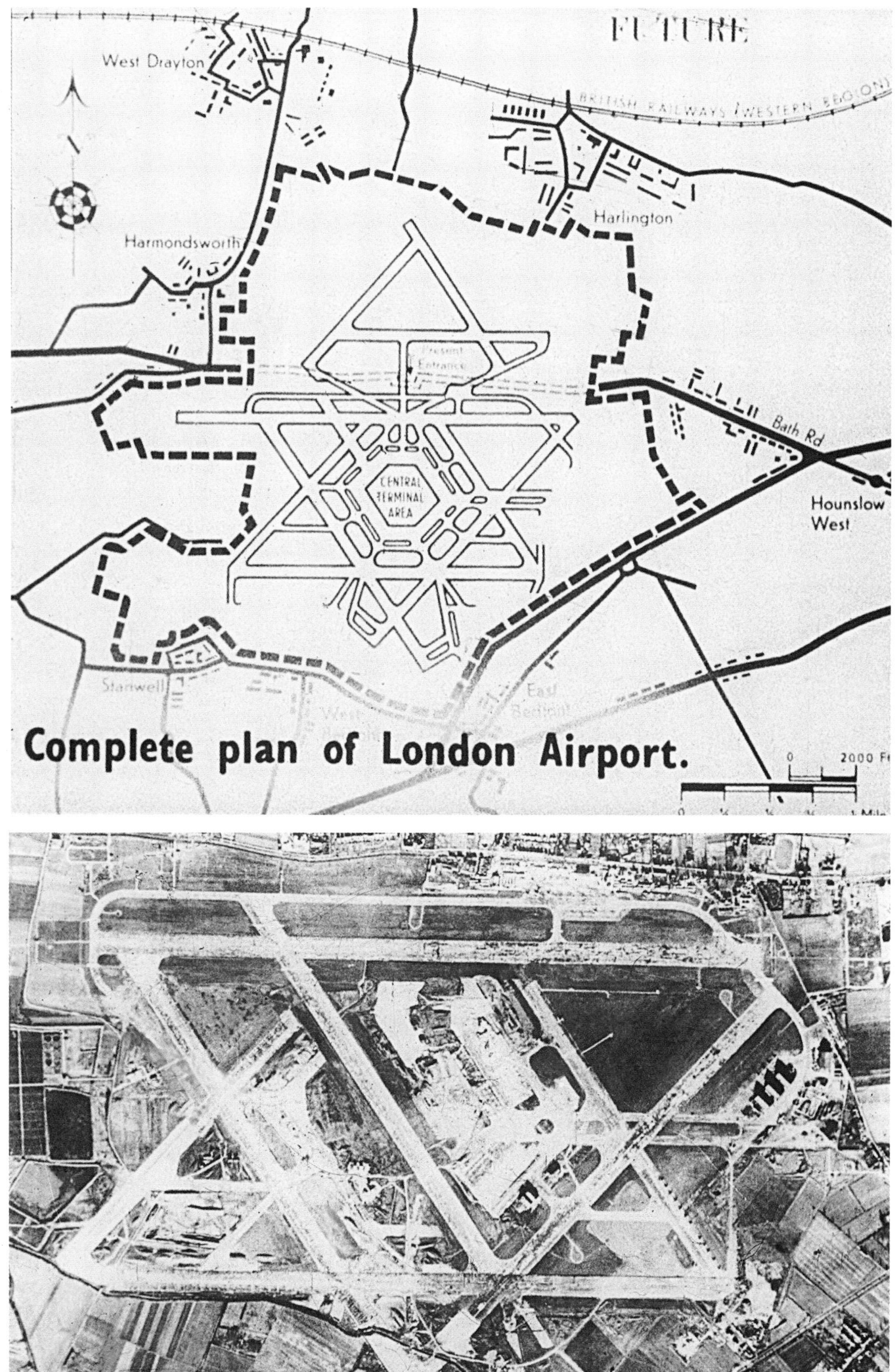
FUTURE
West Drayton
BRITISH RAILWAYS WESTERN REGION
Harlington
Harmondsworth
Present Entrance
Bath Rd
CENTRAL TERMINAL AREA
Hounslow West
Stanwell
Complete plan of London Airport.

The airport's first buildings took casual observers by surprise. One could be forgiven for thinking that it was a Bedouin encampment or an Army outpost. Ex-military marquees were used as temporary terminals in 1946. Duckboards were laid down so passengers would not sink into the mud as they walked to waiting aircraft. Outside were three telephone boxes, a pillarbox and a mobile post office. *(BAA (Heathrow) Archives)*

BSAA operated five more 'proving' flights to South America between February and March 1946 and Mary Guthrie was the Star Girl in charge of three of them. The airport was 'officially opened' to airline traffic on 25 March, by which time work on the 38ft-high control tower had been completed and a series of prefabricated huts constructed alongside to accommodate meteorological, teleprinter and radio operational staff.

Other buildings were of a less permanent kind; in fact casual observers, unaware that an airport had been built, might be forgiven for thinking that they were looking at an Army outpost or Bedouin encampment. A tented village had been thrown up next to the main apron, near the Bath Road, using ex-military brown marquees which would double as waiting rooms and arrivals and departure terminals for the remainder of the year until more permanent – yet still temporary – buildings were ready for use.

The 'waiting room' marquee, complete with windows overlooking the apron, was equipped with long rolls of coconut matting on uneven floors made from clinker and sand. It contained comfortable armchairs and settees (many of which were stolen during the dead of night) and small tables containing vases of fresh flowers. Passengers could buy tea and coffee from a small refreshment stall at one end, while those wishing to send telegrams could use facilities provided by Western Union which operated from a dining-room table along one side of the marquee.

Passengers knew when it was time to depart because take-off times would be chalked on a giant blackboard next to the exit flap. Airline staff would also call across the marquee to passengers asking them to assemble before being escorted out across the duckboards to their waiting aircraft. Passengers filed past customs and immigration officers, who occasionally inspected luggage on wooden tables. A cardboard sign indicated items that were to be declared and likely to incur a tax payment.

Another marquee contained more armchairs and tables, a cashier and the newest branch of booksellers, W.H. Smith & Sons, that had moved to London Airport from Strawberry Hill station in Twickenham. Ted Carpenter, who was assistant district sales promoter at the time, recalls that the bookstall was painted green. 'I was paid £6 a week – and no commission – at the time', Ted recalled in 1996. 'The floor of the bookstall used to get soggy underfoot at times, despite a covering of coconut matting.'

The marquee shop was so popular that it generated over £2,000 in sales between July and December 1946 and over £6,000 during the same period the following year, making it one of the company's most successful – and smallest – sales outlets. In addition to books, newspapers and magazines, it also sold cigarettes and tobacco: sales were split between 'print and smokes'.

Inside the 'terminal' marquee, passengers could relax in comfortable chairs, buy tobacco and newspapers from the newest branch of W.H. Smith & Sons, send a telegram from a Western Union cable station and find out about arriving and departing flights from information chalked on a blackboard. *(BAA (Heathrow) Archives)*

The circus has come to town? No, it's just Heathrow Airport's first temporary terminals, as seen from the forecourt of the Bricklayer's Arms public house (later renamed the Air Hostess), in the summer of 1946. *(BAA (Heathrow) Archives)*

In hot weather the walls of the tented terminal could be taken away to allow fresh air to blow through. In winter weather the temperature in the marquees often fell to nearly freezing. *(BAA (Heathrow) Archives)*

When it rained, the marquees leaked and dozens of buckets and bowls had to be brought in to catch water seeping into the 'terminal'. To reach aircraft parked on the apron, passengers walked over wooden duckboards, which protected their shoes from the sea of mud that existed underneath. The boards extended from the marquees to the concrete apron.

There was no heating in the marquees and it was often cold as well as damp. But Britain had only recently come through six years of wartime discomfort and a 'blitz spirit' still prevailed across the country, which made allowances for an airport still going through its birth pangs. When the weather was warm, the canvas marquee walls could be removed to allow a cool breeze to blow through. Fire buckets full of water and sand were positioned outside every entrance and exit in the event of a careless match, cigarette or cigar butt setting the 'terminal' alight.

Outside the marquees were three bright-red telephone boxes, a pillarbox and a mobile post office. Dozens of former RAF mobile caravans doubled as staff offices for airlines, customs, immigration and retail employees.

Airport toilet facilities were primitive, to say the least. But there was one flushing toilet – located in a police guardroom tucked away between two marquees. If terminal porters spotted a wealthy-looking passenger, they would direct them towards the flushing toilet and more often than not be rewarded with a tip for their trouble. Porters called this little perk their 'piddle pennies'.

To transatlantic visitors everything looked a mess. They called it 'Tent City' and couldn't believe how primitive London's new airport looked. Back home they had 'real airports – like La Guardia – with real buildings which had bars and restaurants, car parks and viewing areas'. British travellers were content to wait. Lord Winster had told them that London would eventually have the best airport in the world – and they believed him. Like everything else in postwar Britain, it would come – eventually.

The date that Heathrow 'officially opened' is covered in confusion. BSAA's Lancastrian, Star Light, with Bennett, Alabaster and Cracknell at the front and young Mary Guthrie looking after the passengers at the back, had been the first departure on 1 January 1946. Five more flights had followed. Yet, despite the nationwide publicity that this service generated in newspapers and newsreels in both Britain and South America, it was always regarded as a 'proving flight' and never an 'official' service, despite the fact that some passengers paid to travel on the journey.

On 28 May 1946, another Lancastrian took off into heavy skies over Heathrow – G-AGLS – operated jointly by BOAC and the Australian airline, Qantas. This was known as the 'kangaroo service' and BOAC claimed that passengers flying down under that day were the airport's 'first fare-paying passengers to depart from the airport'. The airline had inaugurated the service from Hurn four months before and established a record flying time for the journey – forty-nine hours. Today it would be carrying just six passengers who would sleep in special bunks installed for the long route and sit in armchairs positioned next to a table and a window. The flight would also be the airline's first from Heathrow, from which it now planned to operate, winding down operations from Hurn.

And then, on 31 May 1946, the airport was 'officially opened' and three rival airlines raced across the world hoping to be the 'first' to land at Heathrow. Pan American's Constellation service, London Clipper, appeared in the skies above Heathrow after a fourteen-hour flight from New York's La Guardia airport at the same time as American Overseas Airways' Constellation flagship, Great Britain, from the same city announced its arrival in London air space. And then a third aircraft requested permission to land – the BOAC–Qantas Lancastrian returning to Britain from Australia, in the air traffic zone two hours earlier than planned thanks to strong tailwinds. It had covered the 12,000-mile

Passengers and crew make their way out to the 'first official' flight to depart from the airport – a Lancastrian flying on the 'kangaroo route' operated jointly by BOAC and Australian airline Qantas – on 28 May 1946. This date is generally regarded as the airport's first operational day, although many disagree. *(BAA (Heathrow) Archives)*

The BOAC Lancastrian takes off into heavy skies over Heathrow on the first leg of its long journey to Australia on 28 May 1946. The aircraft – G-AGLS – is seen flying over the giant concrete mixer used to produce concrete for the airport's remaining runways. *(BAA (Heathrow) Archives)*

journey in sixty-three and a quarter hours. All three airlines had been operating from Hurn while European carriers operated from Croydon, which the RAF had handed back for civilian use earlier in the year. BOAC's flying-boat fleet continued to fly to Africa and the Far East from its base at Poole, Dorset.

Who would be allowed to land first and lay claim to the title of being 'first commercial airline' to land at Heathrow? Would it be one of the American airlines, in recognition of that country's support for Britain during the recent war and acknowledgement of the United States' achievement in civil aviation with the development of the sleek triple-tailplane, Lockheed Constellation? Or would it be the British service operated by a British carrier with a British-built aeroplane and carrying British passengers?

The British won the day on the grounds that the Lancastrian had travelled the furthest distance. But which American airline would be first over the boundary fence? The race was won by Pan American (just) but both Constellations were allowed to taxi onto the apron, switch off their engines and discharge their passengers at the same time. To save face, both airlines were given the distinction of being 'first overseas airline' to land at London's new airport.

On seeing the ex-Army marquees waiting to welcome arriving passengers, an American was heard to remark: 'Say, what time does the circus start?' When foreign passengers saw airport staff scurrying around in their brown overalls, many thought that German prisoners of war had been drafted in to help out at Britain's new airport.

Readers may choose their own preferred airport opening date: 1 January, 28 May or 31 May 1946. Air Vice-Marshal Bennett went through the rest of his life claiming that his Star Light Lancastrian had been the airport's first service. BOAC – now British Airways – claims 28 May as the airport's opening date, while Heathrow's owner, BAA plc, claims 31 May as its 'May Day' – even though by that time at least thirteen aircraft had either taken off or landed at the new airport.

Waiting to greet passengers on the 'first day' (31 May) was Lord Winster with a delegation of parliamentarians and air attachés from all countries whose airlines were expected to use the airport. An impressive array of aircraft lined the tarmac for the VIPs to inspect, and demonstration flights took place using a BOAC DC-3 and an RAF York; aircraft which would become regular users of the airport in months to come.

Winster knew that waiting pressmen wanted another good story about the airport – and he had one for them. He told the media that he planned to alter the airport's name from Heathrow to London Airport 'because the name Heathrow was extremely difficult for many foreigners to pronounce'.

Winster had more information to convey: 'Because the airport will be the first piece of England on which thousands of foreign visitors will land, I attach great importance to the design of the terminal buildings, which will be among the finest of their kind in the country. The layout of the airport will also be improved so as to be capable of handling 160 aircraft movements an hour in good weather and 120 in bad.'

He told the media that he envisaged the airport eventually having six runways made up of three parallel pairs arranged around a central terminal building. The two runways

The race to be the first 'foreign' commercial airline to land at Heathrow ended in a tie between Constellation aircraft operated by Pan American and American Overseas Airways. Although the Pan American plane was the first to touch down (just), both aircraft were allowed to taxi towards the tented terminals at the same time. *(Author's collection)*

still to be completed would be ready for use in June 1946 and he expected them to be capable of handling the world's largest aircraft, including the Bristol Brabazon, a giant British-designed passenger aircraft still in the planning stages.

Lord Winster said that the tents and mobile caravans would soon disappear, to be replaced by more substantial buildings which would in themselves also be temporary 'because they will be superseded at a later date by permanent buildings in the centre of the airport, between the triangular runways. Access to these buildings will be by way of a tunnel extending from near the Staines Road entrance to near the Bath Road entrance.' He also stated that 'both the Minister of Transport and I are fully alive to the necessity of developing access to the airport. Rail transport is being examined in conjunction with the main railways and the London Passenger Transport Board. For airport employees, access will be provided by extending the Underground Railway beyond Hounslow West and the airport itself.' It would be over twenty-five years before the tube finally pulled into the airport, first with a link to Hatton Cross and, in 1977, into the newly built Heathrow Central station.

Lord Winster confirmed that further airport extensions were planned 'but there will be no substantial demolition of houses or other property before 1950. One of the reasons for siting the airport in this district was that it could be done with a minimum of disturbance to householders.'

Plans published three weeks later triggered off mass alarm in communities surrounding 'London Airport'. As suggested in Professor Abercrombie's original vision, they showed the airport extending north of the Bath Road towards Harlington and West Drayton. The villages of Poyle and Sipson would be engulfed and the airport extended south-east to where Terminal 4 now stands. It was estimated that up to 1,200 houses would have to be demolished, over 11,000 people displaced and a massive project undertaken to rehouse families elsewhere in south-west Middlesex. The airport was expected to provide employment for up to 10,000 people in the next few years and there was talk of a new airport satellite town being built exclusively for the personnel. The Ministry for Civil Aviation predicted that 1,450 staff would work for the organisation by the end of the year, rising to 8,000 in 1950 and 10,000 by 1954.

The airport was now about to become a major newsgathering centre. News about airport developments, airlines and passengers resulted in regular visits from air correspondents attached to London-based publications, which in turn gave birth to a resident news reporting and photographic agency, working day and night to feed stories to daily and evening newspapers.

The agency was founded by Squadron Leader William 'Bill' Brenard, a larger than life winner of a Distinguished Flying Cross, whose father had run a similar news reporting operation at Croydon Airport before the war. Using one of the former military caravans as his newsroom and darkroom, Brenard Air News Services – 'Brenard's' for short – was at the airport from the beginning. In appearance Brenard himself looked like Frans Hals' portrait of the laughing cavalier, complete with a large round and open face, Van Dyke beard, twirling moustaches and an obvious zest for life. And, like the painted cavalier, Brenard could laugh up a storm; a loud and generous 'Ha! Ha! Ha!' of a laugh that could be heard outside his caravan-newsroom and across airport aprons. In the early days he came to his 'office' still wearing his RAF flying jacket and quickly won new friends, many of them former armed forces personnel like himself, to whom he gave jobs as reporters and photographers. He remained one of the airport's best-known personalities until his death in the early 1980s.

The airport's first temporary-permanent buildings were open by the winter of 1946. Built from materials similar to those used to construct postwar prefabricated homes, they were larger, more spacious, warmer and more comfortable than the tented terminals. Pictured is the cosy lounge in the final departures area. *(BAA (Heathrow) Archives)*

The airport's original control tower was built by the RAF on familiar military lines. *(Author's collection)*

The aerodrome control glasshouse situated on top of the control tower. *(Author's collection)*

One of Brenard's first reporters, Ray Berry, recalls the airport and the news reporting agency's early days:

> My first impression of London Airport was of nothing but a vast expanse of mist. From the top of my number 81 bus on the Bath Road, there wasn't a single aircraft to be seen, but my view hardly extended beyond the concrete of the north side parking apron. The immediate foreground seemed to be smothered by row upon row of camouflaged vehicles, military and RAF caravans. At their centre stood a handful of prefabricated, single-storey buildings like barrack blocks with flat roofs. This, I discovered a few days later, had recently succeeded the muddy brown tents, which had served as the airport passenger terminal for most of the past twelve months.
>
> The caravans I had glimpsed from the bus were the temporary offices of airlines, other services and private companies. One was the head office of Brenard's. It resembled a khaki painted, box-shaped removal van on an Army truck chassis, with two similar size 'winged' annexes. The annexes were served by single doors directly from the centre van, which was accessed through a similar door at the rear. This central office, some 15ft long and 6ft in width, became a 'news room'. One of the annexes served as a copy room and the other, draped in wartime black-out material, as a dark room for the company's two photographers.
>
> Two fitted desks were provided on opposite walls in the newsroom with three or four folding chairs. Two more chairs were available in each annexe, which also boasted long, portable folding tables. The maximum number of people to be accommodated overall comfortably would not have been more than six. The average was usually three.

Young airport reporter Ray Berry (front row, holding notebook) interviews Herbert Morrison (centre, wearing glasses), Labour Foreign Secretary. *(Ray Berry)*

In summer the temperature inside the central caravan was unpleasant, to put it heatedly. The entrance and/or annexe doors often had to be left ajar as the main windows [in the roof] were fitted, wired glass frames. The annexes, on the other hand, allowed wind to blow in from most points of the compass summer or winter, as here the walls consisted only of heavy, opaque green canvas draped between the floors and the ceilings. The prime source of winter heating was three paraffin oil burners [Aladdin Valor stoves] supplemented occasionally by unofficial low-wattage electric heaters. No one, as far as I can recall, ever took responsibility for trimming the wicks of the stoves, so the fumes were frequently suffocating in their intensity. And, of course, we all smoked incessantly.

The floors, too, were cold to the feet, as there was nothing between them and the ground, about 2ft below. Coconut matting helped slightly in the news room, but the lino in the annexes was always icy to the touch.

I met Bill Brenard within fifteen minutes of my 'interview' with his then news editor just inside the caravan. He 'crashed' through the door wearing both his RAF sheepskin flying jacket and calf-length fur boots, which he proceeded to kick across the floor. First impression was that he was abrupt and apparently didn't suffer fools gladly. But when in answer to one question, I concluded by addressing him as 'sir' he laughed after snapping back 'and don't call me sir'.

Bill Brenard's news agency made a major contribution to the success of London Airport by keeping it in the public eye for the next forty years. There was little that went on at the airport that Brenard's didn't know about. Here is a selection of some early news stories from London Airport, each one packed with the kind of facts, figures and gossip that postwar newspaper readers expected and which eventually made the airport the second most important newsgathering centre in Britain after Westminster:

3 June 1946: The first British land plane [rather than sea plane] service between London and New York, competing with two American airlines over the world's most profitable route, is to start on the first of next month. On that day a BOAC Constellation – one of five built in California for £1 million – will take 40 passengers, a crew of five and three stewards from London Airport to La Guardia Airport, New York in under 20 hours. Calls will be made at Eire and Newfoundland on the 3,445-mile trip. Fares will be £93 single, £168 return (£5 7s per hour). The new British service – the first since flying boats were withdrawn in March – will run twice weekly. Within a fortnight there will be tri-weekly services, speeding up to four per week and then daily. Flying at 20,000ft 'above the weather', the four-engine 8,800hp planes will have cabins 'pressurised' at 8,000ft. Hot and cold meals will be served onboard at 300mph.

5 June 1946: The eight tons of peaches brought in London Airport from France on Monday sold at Covent Garden yesterday from 6*d* to 1*s* 3*d* each wholesale. Shop prices are at least double. The best English peaches cost 5s to 10s each and a wholesaler said yesterday that French fruit cannot be compared with the best of English. 'They are smaller, have large stones, less flesh and coarse skins', he said.

2 July 1946: At 13 minutes past 10 tonight, BOAC's new Constellation aircraft left London Airport to open BOAC's regular commercial service between London and New York. At 10-o-clock the 42 seat aircraft had only 22 seats filled and of those three were occupied by non-paying priority government passengers, including Lord Knollys, BOAC's Chairman. In the 20 empty seats were rugs, pillows and newspapers. Excuse for the wasted space was: 'Because of headwinds, which sometimes reach 70mph on the east–west run, additional petrol has to be carried for safety reasons. So we decided to take only 22 passengers. At 11 p.m. an American Overseas Airways Constellation took off from the same 3,000-yard airstrip with 39 passengers bound for New York. Total for the BOAC trip tonight will amount to £1,679; for the American Constellation $3,697.

Crowds turn out to welcome Sir Frank Whittle (extreme right next to cameraman), the inventor of the jet engine, on an official airport visit in 1949. The building behind is the airport's main passenger terminal. The photographer shooting cine film is the legendary Brenard's press photographer, Tony Hewson. *(Heathrow Visitors Centre)*

MINISTRY OF CIVIL
TELEPH
HOUS
TELEPH

4 July 1946: Three bags full of women's model clothes containing everything from swimsuits to evening gowns complete with matching accessories lay on the floor of the customs tent at London Airport this morning. Three girls, whose clothes they are, are sitting in their rooms at a London hotel wearing garments borrowed from a fourth. And on the question of whether or not the girls and the clothes will get together again today depends on whether one of the girls, Jean French from New York, tennis star and model, will go to France to take part in the national tournament next week. Whether the three girls, professional models who put on a 'flight of fancy' show in a transatlantic Clipper yesterday, will put on the show again for television picture page programmes today remains to be seen. Will three of the girls keep their promise to show off their fashions to English designers and go to Paris next week? Or will they take the next plane back to New York today? The girls, Jean French, Joy Fog and Frances Dyer with their chaperone, Evelene Wade, brought over 55lb of luggage each – about £250 of clothes, accessories and cosmetics, given to them by American designers and business houses. Explained Miss Wade: 'The clothes the girls have been displaying are not new and belong to the girls personally. We brought them over just to show British and French dress houses our ideas for autumn fashions and we meant to buy some fashion creations over here to take back with us.' Customs estimate of duty payable is £350.

5 July 1946: A proposal to reduce the air fare from London to New York from £93 15s to £81 5s may mean that it will be cheaper to fly the Atlantic than to sail by liner. Airline operators believe that the £81 5s single fare will mean more than a saving of £8 15s on the £90 passage by sea. There is no tipping on the Atlantic air routes and at least two days of travel are saved.

On 11 July all airlines – including BOAC – using the gleaming new Constellation aircraft were forced to withdraw them from services following a fire onboard a Trans World Airlines model which crashed at Reading, Pennsylvania. BOAC's Lancastrians and Liberators, which had been taken out of long-haul service, were rapidly pulled out of their mothballs and reintroduced. But the Lancastrians only carried twelve passengers and the Constellations airlifted twenty-five, forcing the airline to operate twice as many aircraft – using twice the amount of fuel – until the American planes were re-introduced in the middle of August.

By the end of September over twelve airline companies were using London Airport. All three runways were in use and, although it would be years before the airport was complete (and sixty years later it is still under construction), regular users were impressed with the speed with which the new semi-permanent passenger buildings and offices were taking shape under the supervision of airport manager Mr R.C. Pugh.

The first terminals were ready by the end of 1946; buildings were constructed using similar materials used in creating postwar prefabricated houses. They were not perfect, but were larger, wider, warmer, more spacious, comfortable, colourful, more friendly and bustling than the marquees. They were inspired by American airline terminals,

Opposite: The airport's first aircraft marshals whose job was to skilfully direct incoming aircraft to parking stands – often with just inches to spare between wingtips. *(Heathrow Visitors Centre)*

which offered individual airline desks, seating areas, cafés and shops – although it would be April 1947 before a licence could be obtained to open a bar from which to sell alcohol.

Airport reporter Ray Berry remembers those early airport buildings:

> The airport's passenger buildings were primarily single-storey prefabricated structures with mainly flat roofs. The walls were made of asbestos-based fibre panels held in a skeleton of preformed reinforced concrete pillars. But the Ministry for Civil Aviation did their gallant best to brighten up the ersatz appearance with gallons of liberally and frequently applied salmon pink, biscuit beige and dove grey gloss paint on the interiors. One welcome touch in these potentially scruffy 'lounges' was the hundreds of square yards of carpeting on the concrete floors.

Before the end of the year, BOAC had transferred the remainder of its Middle and Far Eastern services from Hurn to London Airport and all of the airline's Lancastrians, Yorks – another aircraft from A.V. Roe's Manchester aircraft works – DC-3s and Liberators became familiar to staff working there and the increasing numbers of passengers using it.

Aircraft manufacturers on both sides of the Atlantic were busy courting both BSAA and BOAC in the hope of selling their new long-range civil aircraft for peacetime fleets. Air Vice-Marshal Bennett would not consider equipment built by an American or any other 'foreign' manufacturer. He was determined that his fleet would be British through and through and in addition to his ex-RAF Lancastrians (some of which he purchased from Avro at knock-down prices, eventually numbering fourteen), he bought a fleet of Avro Yorks: a high-winged and noisy monoplane which could carry up to thirty passengers. The first few Yorks each came with a £40,000 price tag, but Avro subsequently dropped its prices when they failed to sell as well as the company had hoped.

Now that the war was over, Britain could resume designing and manufacturing commercial aircraft again. A wartime agreement with the US government resulted in Britain concentrating its efforts on building military aircraft while America supplied transport aircraft. Although the agreement was successful, it gave the Americans a head start on designing and producing passenger planes that could be used in peacetime. By 1946, the DC-3, a military passenger and cargo plane, had been adapted for commercial use along with the four-engine DC-3 Skymaster and the Constellation. But Britain had civil aircraft on the drawing board, if not in the skies.

While BOAC and other foreign airlines agreed to purchase some American aircraft, Avro's future depended on the success of its new Tudor, a fully pressurised commercial passenger plane commissioned by the Ministry of Supply in wartime and now rapidly taking shape at the company's factory near Manchester. The Tudor was a four-engine low-wing monoplane able to carry thirty-two passengers and a crew of four. Bennett liked the plane and Avro looked to BSAA to help make their first postwar passenger plane a success. After putting a Tudor prototype through its paces, BOAC demanded major modifications to the aircraft and began losing interest in bringing it into the fleet. Bennett took the same aircraft on his own trials and flew it around the Caribbean, later stating that this was the perfect plane for his airline and that he failed to see why BOAC had rejected it. He ordered six enlarged versions of the aircraft, which would be known as the Tudor IV.

By November 1946, the Ministry for Civil Aviation began receiving the first complaints about aircraft noise at London Airport from local residents. All correspondents received the following pompous reply: 'With the development of air traffic, which is proceeding rapidly, it is regretted that it is not possible to encourage any hope that the arrivals and departures at London Airport could arbitrarily be restricted to particular hours, solely on the grounds that some local inconvenience be caused to residents by aircraft arriving or leaving the airport during those hours when the residents may usually be sleeping.' Noise complaints still continue to pour in to Heathrow – and every other commercial airport in the country.

During the same month, the airport experienced its first industrial unrest when lorry drivers working for Wimpey & Company came out on strike 'because of alleged dictatorial attitudes [by the company's management] and non-union membership' of two foremen. Wimpey said that the strike was settled amicably following joint negotiations between a strike committee and management 'and further negotiations would proceed through the official machinery which had proved so successful during the two and a half years in which construction at the airport had proceeded'. More – many, many more – industrial disputes would follow this little local difficulty.

In mid-December 1946, a Christmas party was given for 250 children whose parents worked at the airport. They stood on the tarmac to greet Father Christmas, who arrived in a Lancastrian 'Christmas special' carrying toys donated by nine airlines operating to and from London Airport. Children were told that Santa Claus had arrived a few days early 'owing to tail winds'. Airlines announced that they planned to serve Christmas dinners to all passengers travelling on 25 December – soup, roast turkey, creamed potatoes, Brussels sprouts and peas, Christmas pudding, mince pies and whipped cream. The food was prepared in new 'in-flight' kitchens opened at the airport and would be reheated onboard aircraft.

London Airport's first Christmas card was produced in 1946 showing a Hermes aircraft on the front. *(Author's collection)*

London Airport came to the end of its first year, stating that 63,151 passengers and 2,386 tons of air cargo had been handled travelling to and from eighteen destinations on 2,046 aircraft movements. Only one of the three British state airlines using the airport had made a profit that year – BSAA.

The prospects for 1947 looked better than good.

EIGHT

1947–9

An Air of Authority

THE COST OF CREATING London Airport and running it during its first year was so high that it would be years before the government recouped its £25 million investment. It needed more airlines, passengers, freight, commercial tenants and 'side shows' to help generate revenue. In 1947 a Ministry for Civil Aviation employee was prepared to predict the direction British airports needed to follow to be profitable. Under the headline 'Dance and Swim at the Airport', the *Daily Express* carried the following story on 3 October:

> Dance halls, swimming pools, band concerts and joy flights are being planned for state airports to give a holiday atmosphere – and to slash operating losses, now more than 50 per cent. The architect of the brighter airports scheme is 50-year old Lionel T. Scott, £1,330-a-year Director of Amenities to the Ministry for Civil Aviation. 'Courtesy is my number one priority', he says. He has plans for shops – including hairdressers – restaurants and even classrooms for children. Mr Scott expects the 'side shows' to pay for 40 per cent of an airport's total operating costs.

Sixty years later, most of Mr Scott's predictions had been realised decades ago. Hotels surrounding today's Heathrow Airport provide the swimming pools, music and dancing while the airport itself is now one of Britain's leading retail centres, with most of the country's best-known shops operating branches in the terminals. Rents paid by the retail and catering sectors generate millions of pounds for airport owner, BAA plc. Airports today must make a profit if they are to survive and, thanks to Mr Scott's foresight in 1947, London's major gateway to and from the world is the most profitable.

Mr Scott's ideas about joy flights at London Airport were short-lived. By 1947 the airport had become a magnet for visitors wanting to see planes landing and taking off. A day trip to the airport was a treat, a chance to rub shoulders with passengers checking in for flights to exciting destinations. Day-trippers were forbidden to enter the departure buildings, but many found a way to mingle with passengers posing as friends planning to wave them off at departure gates. This little plan often worked among adult airport day-trippers, but carried little weight with hundreds of children drawn to London Airport during school holidays who were duly ejected into the open-air public enclosure.

For 20s (£1) it was possible to take a joyride 'around the houses' from London Airport in an eight-seat wooden-built Dragon Rapide operated by Island Air Services (later renamed Birkett Air Services), which promised passengers aerial views of famous London landmarks – weather permitting. *(Heathrow Visitors Centre)*

But there was a way of experiencing a passenger-eye view of London and its new airport without having a passport or an air ticket. Mr Scott's suggestion that joy rides might be a way of generating revenue for airports resulted in a short-lived, but popular scheme that existed between 1947 and 1952 when a small company called Island Air Services (later renamed Birkett Air Services) offered thirty-minute 'flights around the houses' in eight-seat Dragon Rapide wooden biplanes.

A larger than life lady called Monique Agazarian ran the company. The daughter of an Armenian-born businessman, who, like Mary Guthrie had been a wartime Air Transport Auxiliary pilot, Monique was famous for flying a Spitfire at low level down Piccadilly on VE Day. She charged 12*s* 6*d* for a fifteen-minute circuit of the airport – including a flypast over Windsor Castle – and £1 for an hour-long journey over London and its docks. Her trips were enormously popular with families and made a wonderful – if expensive – birthday present. Monique was probably responsible for converting many boys away from wanting to be train drivers to becoming pilots when they grew up.

Sadly, the cost of a joyride in Monique's Dragon Rapide was too high for many people. Derek Rylatt recollects: 'As a small boy I remember being taken to the airport which was surrounded by grasslands virtually to the horizon in those days. I recall there were various displays and marquees everywhere, the purpose of which was lost on a young child. The Dragon Rapide offered pleasure flights and I recall being disappointed at not being able to take a flight as the fare of 12s 6*d* was a small fortune in those days.'

Later, Monique organised weekend gambling jaunts from London Airport to Deauville and Le Touquet (£4 return) and business was brisk until the day her Dragon Rapide got caught up in taxiway turbulence caused by the engines of a Constellation; being a wooden aircraft, it blew over causing several injuries. By that time the airport was becoming busy throughout the day and the Ministry for Civil Aviation called a halt to joyriding. Monique, by now married to a BEA pilot flying from Northolt Airport, began a charter operation flying flowers from the Scilly Isles. When London Airport became too expensive to use as a base, she moved operations to Ramsgate Aerodrome in Kent and reintroduced joyriding with limited success.

Overseeing the rapid growth of London Airport was Air Marshal Sir John D'Albiac, 53, who was given the title of 'Airport Commandant' and a brief to oversee all air traffic control, communications and general management duties. A former officer with the Royal Marine Artillery, D'Albiac was an observer during the First World War and sighted an enemy submarine near Ostend, making the first attack on a submarine in a British aircraft. The next war found him in Greece in charge of 80 British aircraft which had to face 800 German and 300 Italian machines. He was later posted to Ceylon at the time of the attempted Japanese invasion, which was repulsed by planes under D'Albiac's command. After that the Japanese never returned to that part of the Indian Ocean in any force.

Overseeing the rapid growth of London Airport was Air Marshal Sir John D'Albiac who was given the title of 'Airport Commandant'. He is remembered as 'one of nature's gentlemen'. *(Author's collection)*

A straight-backed authoritarian, and now remembered by former airport reporter Ray Berry as 'one of nature's gentlemen', D'Albiac would run London Airport with his own 'air of authority' and military style for the next ten years. He was expected to 'live on the job' in a special detached house with a garden, still referred to by some airport old timers as 'the commandant's house', at the junction of Caines Lane and the Bath Road. Today it is used by BAA as an office.

One of D'Albiac's first jobs was to oversee major changes to Heathrow's runway layout. The RAF-style runway triangle had been working well ever since the airport opened, but the Ministry for Civil Aviation quickly recognised that more runway capacity would be needed in the near future and plans were devised to create six concrete runways incorporating the original triangle. Each runway would be extended to 1¾ miles and form the pattern of a six-pointed star, allowing parallel take-offs and landings. During the runways' alterations the plan was slightly modified, limiting the number of runways to five and converting the sixth into a taxiway.

D'Albiac was also part of a team tasked with masterminding the next stage of the airport's development: planning the design and construction of a major airport city, complete with a terminal building, control tower, an office complex and a public viewing area in the centre of the runway complex, and linked to main roads leading to the airport by the tunnel Lord Winster had first mentioned in 1946.

Sir John D'Albiac encouraged competitive sports among airport staff and sponsored the annual D'Albiac Cup. He is pictured (right), in 1951, looking on while his wife presents the winning football trophy to airport fireman Rubin Lloyd. *(Brenard Press)*

There had been only one disaster at the airport since it had opened. Early in 1947, a nervous foreign passenger, who had just arrived in London, became distressed after being closely questioned by customs officers about how long he planned to stay in the country. They wanted to know if he carried enough money to support himself while in Britain – and they wanted to see his return ticket. The man decided to try to make a run for it, dashed onto the airport apron and right into the revolving propeller of an aircraft about to depart. Scores of passengers looked on in horror, unable to stop the poor man from meeting his untimely end in such a grim fashion.

There had been other close shaves – known at the airport as 'near misses' – in which aircrew had either misunderstood or failed to understand instructions from the Control Tower. Fortunately, air disasters had been avoided. This was to change shortly after 9.00 p.m. on 2 March 1948 when a DC-3 from the Belgian airline Sabena flying to London Airport from Brussels, crashed on landing and burst into flames. Of the twenty-two passengers and crew, all but three were killed.

The aircraft landed in a nosedive on the grass. There was an explosion and the aircraft burst into flames. The visibility was poor owing to fog and rescue squads worked to put out the fire and save lives using portable searchlights and vehicle headlamps. The

BSAA Avro Tudor IV, Star Lion, prepares to board passengers on its inaugural flight from London. *(Keith Hayward collection)*

While BOAC and other foreign airlines agreed to purchase some American aircraft, Air Vice-Marshal Bennett of BSAA bought the British-built Avro Tudor for his fleet. *(Author's collection)*

heat was so intense that firefighters were unable to get close enough to the crashed plane to make any further rescues.

The pilot had been warned about the foggy weather by radio while flying over the British coast and told that visibility was reduced to 20yds. The aircraft was 'talked down' until it was just a few feet away from the runway. What happened next was never ascertained. One theory stated that as the DC-3 touched down, the port wheel buckled causing the aircraft to lurch to one side and hit the ground, fracturing the main tank and starting a fire.

The crew of three were Belgian and of the nineteen passengers, fourteen were British, two were Italian, one was Russian, one from Poland and the other a Cuban.

A bizarre story surrounds this tragic air crash. Several firefighters and members of the police rescue squad battling to save lives that night claimed that a man wearing a pinstriped suit, bowler hat and carrying a briefcase and rolled umbrella was seen at the crash site. In the noise, heat and confusion, he was given little attention and it was assumed he was some sort of airport official. Nobody saw him arrive or leave. On several later occasions, and also in foggy weather, the control tower staff was alerted to something small moving out on the runway and several claimed to have seen a man in a pinstriped suit and bowler hat, carrying a briefcase and rolled umbrella, who disappeared just as quickly as he appeared. Although the last reported sighting was in the 1960s, some airport operational staff still talk about the spectre.

Everybody wanted to work at London Airport in 1947 and landing a job was not difficult – especially for ex-servicemen and women. Gordon Pankhurst, who by 1977 had become superintendent of Terminal 3, recalled: 'In those days Heathrow was

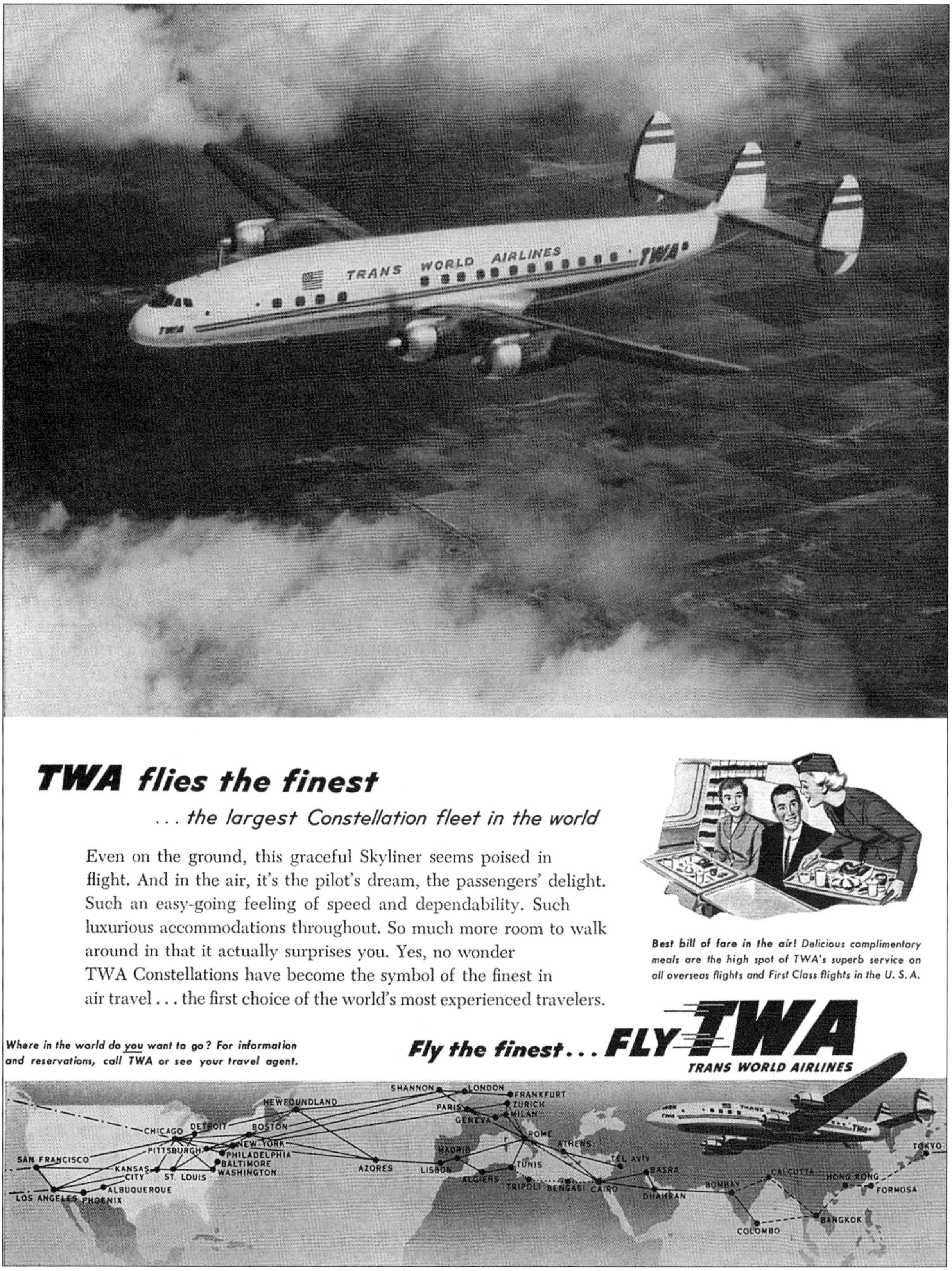

TWA flies the finest

... the largest Constellation fleet in the world

Even on the ground, this graceful Skyliner seems poised in flight. And in the air, it's the pilot's dream, the passengers' delight. Such an easy-going feeling of speed and dependability. Such luxurious accommodations throughout. So much more room to walk around in that it actually surprises you. Yes, no wonder TWA Constellations have become the symbol of the finest in air travel . . . the first choice of the world's most experienced travelers.

Best bill of fare in the air! *Delicious complimentary meals are the high spot of TWA's superb service on all overseas flights and First Class flights in the U. S. A.*

Where in the world do you want to go? For information and reservations, call TWA or see your travel agent.

Fly the finest . . . FLY TWA

TRANS WORLD AIRLINES

American airline TWA used sleek Lockheed Constellations to transport thousands of travellers across the Atlantic to London Airport throughout the late 1940s and 1950s. *(Author's collection)*

surrounded by fields and farms. I was in the police force at the time and one day just happened to be cycling past the new airfield. I shouted to an ex-RAF type to ask if there were any jobs going – and I've been here ever since.'

Another airport veteran was Leslie Green, a former Heathrow general manager, who joined the Ministry for Civil Aviation in 1946. Speaking in 1977, he remembered the airport's early years as 'great days, a time when everyone pulled together and helped each other'. According to Leslie

> the war had everything to do with it. We had all come through a great deal together. Everyone had lost someone close, had their home flattened by a bomb or been posted overseas for years at a time. We were all different people but, thanks to the war, we had something in common – the wartime experience. That's what made the airport work in its earliest pioneering days. It was the Blitz spirit. If anyone was ever in trouble, everyone rallied round to help them out of it. Everyone knew everyone else and had great respect for each other. Staff addressed their bosses as 'sir' in much the same way as they would have done in the armed forces. We even snapped to attention when someone senior approached us and some of us even saluted. For many airport staff, it had been their habit to do so for several years, so carrying this over into civilian life came quite naturally to many of us. When Sir John D'Albiac came into the old terminal just about everyone snapped to attention and he would walk down the length of the building turning left and right, telling us to 'carry on, carry on'. We all knew that we were taking part in something worthwhile. Every one of us was aware that air travel was the future, and anyone who worked at London Airport in the late 1940s was a witness to this each day. The place just grew before your eyes.

Stan Stern, a well-known airport personality in the 1970s and head of travel company Airport Assistance, recalls a twin-engine plane making an attempt to smash the London–Paris air record in 1946 in a Lancastrian fitted with jet engines. He recalls: 'A little way down the road from the runway was a well-kept garden full of flowers in full bloom. As the plane turned to move down the runway, the blast from the engine reduced the garden to a brown scalded patch. Not a flower left.' But the plane achieved the distance in fifty-five minutes and later went on to knock thirteen minutes from the record a few days later – by which time a large fence had been erected in front of the garden.'

Gordon Chubb from Weybridge, Surrey, recalls what it was like to arrive at London Airport as a passenger. He writes:

> I find it difficult to convey to present day travellers the basic nature of early postwar civilian air travel and its ground facilities and how completely domestic they were in scale. In January 1949 I arrived at London Airport from Nairobi on an ex-United States Air Force Skymaster operated by an airline called Skyways. This was a War Office charter flight via Khartoum and Tripoli. Having disembarked on the runway we walked to the concrete prefabricated buildings. It took but ten minutes to pass between officials sitting on Dickens-like high stools who dealt with immigration and foreign currency controls. The last official then invited each passenger to leave by a small door in the wall behind his desk. On stepping through the door and closing it

Daily life at London Airport in the early days, as captured by a photographer from the Central Office of Information for an educational film strip sent to schools across the British Commonwealth. *(Author's collection)*

in the normal way, one turned round to find oneself almost alone in a tiny car park directly on the Bath Road. That was it! One was back home in an unpainted, battered, postwar London to become, once again, one of its proud citizens dressed, for the most part, in equally drab and threadbare clothes.

Philip Gordon-Marshall recalls the airport's fire services during the late 1940s: 'We only had two sets of fire appliances. One was kept in a Nissen hut, which was the fire station, while the other stood out on the tarmac. The crash crews, dressed in full uniform, used to get jolly hot waiting there (the sun really used to beat down in those days). So Doug Lovegrove, sensible man that he is, thought it would be a good idea to take his trousers off. There he stood, overalls off, trousers off, just about to put his overalls back on – when the alarm bell rang! This meant that Doug had to climb up through the flap in the cabin roof to direct the hose – all of which he did in his underpants.'

Captain Cliff Alabaster (left) with Air Vice-Marshal Donald Bennett and Mrs Ly Bennett on the occasion of the first commercial flight by a Tudor IV to South America in 1948. *(Author's collection)*

By September 1947, the first of BSAA's Tudor IV aircraft – Star Lion – was ready to enter commercial service following a goodwill passenger-carrying proving flight to South America. Air Vice-Marshal Bennett planned to replace the noisy Lancastrians and cumbersome Yorks with the new thirty-two-seat planes.

Bennett had been unlucky with his aircraft. In August 1946 a Lancastrian had crashed in The Gambia without any fatalities. The following month a York had crashed at the same airport and twenty-four passengers were killed. Another York crashed in Senegal with six fatalities followed by the Lancastrian, Star Dust, which crashed in the Andes Mountains in August 1947. It would be over fifty years before its wreckage was located. The following month another Lancastrian hit a radio mast in Bermuda and, although there were no fatalities, the aircraft had to be written off. Then, on 14 November 1947, Star Light, the plane that had made history by becoming the first service from London Airport, crash-landed in Bermuda after its undercarriage collapsed. There were no deaths, but yet another BSAA aircraft had bitten the dust and was now unusable.

After piloting the new Tudor IV back to London Airport, Bennett declared that the Tudor would be economical to operate, allowing his company to run at a profit, and that 'from a passenger's point of view the greatest improvement in the Tudor is the increased silence which, I think, is greater than comparable aircraft currently in use. I am delighted with the Tudor from a technical point of view and can see nothing wrong with it.'

In October, Tudor IV Star Tiger commenced flying from London Airport to Bermuda following a fanfare of publicity at the airport. Twelve weeks later the aircraft disappeared without a trace over the sea north-east of Bermuda. No wreckage was ever sighted or discovered. Lord Nathan – who had replaced Lord Winster as Minister for Civil Aviation – ordered the Tudors to be grounded while a full inquiry took place.

The *Daily Express* invited Bennett to comment on the decision and the former Pathfinder chief took advantage of the opportunity to criticise the people running Britain's civil aviation interests. Under the banner headline 'I Contest Lord Nathan's Grounding of Tudor IV', Bennett told air correspondent Basil Cardew:

> There are two outstanding forces at work in civil aviation in Britain today. In the first category are those who are openly anti-British in aviation. In the second those who entered it either for selfish reasons or for other reasons – but are totally ignorant of aviation. These two categories are more influential than the professionals and those who have given their lives to it.

PATHFINDER BENNETT SACKED

For talking to Daily Express

By BASIL CARDEW

AIR VICE-MARSHAL DONALD BENNETT, chief executive of the State-owned British South American Airways, said last night: "I have today had the proudest honour of my life. I have been sacked for speaking my own mind."

PATHFINDER BENNETT

C.B., C.B.E., D.S.O. Thirty-seven. Air Vice-Marshal. Born Brisbane, Queensland. Creator of the famous Pathfinder Force of R.A.F.'s Bomber Command. Resigned commission 1945. Holder of world's long-distance seaplane record. A founder, as Flying Superintendent, of the Atlantic Ferry organisation (now Ferry Command). Chief executive for more than two years of the British South American Airways, only State-owned airline corporation to show a profit last year.

He was talking to Oxford students just after the board of the airline announced that his appointment had been terminated because of "differences on matters of policy."

My interview with 37-year-old Pathfinder Donald Bennett published in the Daily Express last Thursday, led to his dismissal.

Air Vice-Marshal Bennett was asked to withdraw his criticisms of Government interference with the management of the airline. He refused. Announcement of his dismissal came after a prolonged board meeting.

'Resign' threats

All employees of the airline are to receive immediate pay increases a staff meeting at the St. James's headquarters was told yesterday.

Many of the staff interpret this as a counter-measure to threats of mass resignation following the air vice-marshal's dismissal.

Resignations are expected especially from former Pathfinder pilots brought in to B.S.A.A. by Air Vice-Marshal Bennett. They make up more than nine in ten of the air crews.

Air Vice-Marshal Bennett said when his dismissal was announced: "A small team of professionals in British civil aviation two years ago started to create an airways system of vital importance to Britain.

"As the leader of that team, I have been proud of the result

Just over a year after flying the first service out of Heathrow, Air Vice-Marshal Donald Bennett was fired from his job as Chief Executive of BSAA, after a 'difference of opinion' with his airline's Board over the Tudor IV aircraft. *(Author's collection)*

Bennett went on to hit out at the way in which the government had interfered with how the state-owned airlines were run 'to such a degree that it has become increasingly difficult for an airline executive to be held responsible for the results he achieves'. He attacked the government for preventing airlines from dealing directly with aircraft manufacturers and Lord Nathan's decision to ground the new aeroplanes, stating that it was he who should make such decisions. 'I very deeply regret, therefore, that I should have been ordered to withdraw the Tudor IV from service, thereby inferring a lack of confidence in this type of airliner. . . . I have no lack of confidence in the airliner, nor in the ability of British aviation in general to achieve the success which British temperament and ability are bound to win if given the freedom.'

On 10 February 1948, the Board of BSAA announced that it had terminated Bennett's appointment as Chief Executive owing to 'differences of opinion over matters of policy'. In a page-one story, Bennett said: 'I have today had the proudest honour of my life. I have been sacked for speaking my own mind. . . . I granted an interview to a newspaper correspondent at which I expressed views concerning the obvious ills of British civil aviation in general, and concerning recent interference with the management by the Minister for Civil Aviation. It is because of this article that I have been forced to discontinue my appointment. I have been forced to take this course for exercising what I consider to be a right – namely freedom of speech.'

Lord Nathan claimed that Bennett's dismissal was 'not an isolated incident of its kind, but the culmination of a long series of differences between the airline's Board and its Chief Executive; that the Board had accordingly lost confidence in him, deciding that they had no option but to dispense with his services, that having refused the Board's

An early advertisement for BOAC long-haul services to Egypt, India and South Africa promoting flights 'without a government priority' to travel. *(Author's collection)*

suggestion that he should tender his resignation, the Board had been obliged to dismiss him and were making him a gratuitous payment of £4,500 in compensation for loss of office.'

There was talk of pay increases for BSAA staff to counter a rumour of mass resignations from the airline by Bennett's Pathfinder colleagues, but nobody walked out. Cliff Alabaster remembers:

Many of us were not surprised when Bennett finally left the airline. We knew that something, or someone, had to give and were not surprised when the Chairman, John Booth, said that the management was unable to support Bennett after what he had publicly said about them.

I personally felt let down by Bennett and his behaviour when he left the company. I was in charge of navigation for BSAA and worked closely with him. When he took issue with people at the Ministry for Civil Aviation, he told them he didn't care what they thought – this is what I say. He was very strong willed and wouldn't give in to these people. He was often disrespectful to them. Sometimes I would pop into his office and ask how things were going and he would start on about 'these idiots at the Ministry'. He would demand that they came to see him. He refused to go and see them.

Don Bennett never came around to say goodbye to us. He didn't write to anyone, either. After he had left, I met him from time to time at various reunions, once on the tenth anniversary of the first flight in 1956 and again in subsequent years. The last time I saw him was at the fortieth anniversary reunion. I learned of his death while I was away sailing in the Channel Islands and, although I missed his funeral, I went to his memorial service in St Clements Danes Church.

Bennett accepted an invitation to contest a forthcoming by-election at North Croydon for the Liberal Party, declaring that he 'would fight to the utmost against Socialist strangulation which has squeezed the spirit and strength of the people, restricting our production and impairing our trading efforts'. He was beaten by the Conservative candidate, then went back into civil aviation with his own private airline, using Tudor IVs to fly over 1,000 sorties during the Berlin Airlift in 1948–9.

In March 1949 the government announced that BSAA would be merged with BOAC. A statement said the merger 'is necessitated by the fact that the ban on Tudor IVs leave BSAA with York aircraft only, which are not competitive, and the obvious way of keeping BSAA routes in operation is to turn to BOAC, a complete merger with which (besides achieving efficiency and economy in other directions) will enable both corporations' services to be organised with a minimum of aircraft'.

Keith Hayward recalls: 'It was a sad day indeed for the BSAA staff, where *esprit de corp* was a matter of justifiable pride.'

The merger finally went through on 26 July 1949 – three years and seven months after BSAA operated the first flight from London's new airport, now being used by 394,000 passengers travelling on 36,675 flights and with a throughput of 12,629 tons of freight.

NINE

THE 1950s

Brabazon Flies in, and Breakfast at Ben's Café and the Green Dragon

EARLY IN 1951, Britain's most influential weekly news magazine, *Picture Post*, sent writer Brian Dowling to report on what was happening at London Airport. 'From whichever way you approach it, as a passenger, or a friend of a passenger, or just as a normal curious person, London Airport is a ragbag of fantasy,' wrote Dowling. He added:

> Everything is larger than life, and disturbing, though not unpleasantly so. There's its size; its impermanency, contrasted with its grandiose plans for the future; its huge working population, of whom so few seem likely to be connected with flying; the intricacies of its administration; its romance, deriving from the actual business of flying, and clashing all along the line with the airline companies' determination to sell flying as matter-of-factly as soap; its constant traffic of celebrities, surrounded by popping flashbulbs; its inherited nautical flavour, in whose context the jargon of practical flying is a constant irritation; everything about it appears as a jumbled mass of impressions which refuse to jell in the mind.

Dowling described the airport's early shanty-town buildings as

> tatty and mud-stained – the airport continually expands in a wen of temporary prefabs, above which aircraft rudders loom like ship superstructures in docks. Buildings push up like mothballs and disappear just as quickly; and even the newest ones are doomed to a very short life. Old houses, too, on the outskirts of the field, are suffering the fate of vanished Heath Row, and their shells, with old strips of wallpaper hanging from them, are perhaps the nearest thing to a symbol which London Airport has to show. Their steady destruction gives the feeling that here were those undisciplined and unorganised boxes where soft people, chock-full of 'human error' used to live; while the future only belongs to the great impersonal hangars, where perfect machines can live in perfect functional surroundings.

As far as passengers were concerned, Dowling reported that

> from the time when they hear the surrealist request to 'kindly take leave of your friends in the lounge and follow the green light' to the time when the aircraft door clangs to, departing passengers are jollied along by personable receptionists. There's a formula for each movement, a set of detailed, unambiguous instructions for every action.
>
> Those who remain, either waiting for friends or for aircraft, are left under discreet supervision in the lounge, where they can ask questions and buy buttered buns or 'genuine antiques' to their heart's content. . . . But all this careful insulation from shock, all these attempts to make them believe that the whole thing's a matter of course – the public will always see them as the smile on the face of the tiger. The uniforms that flit through the lounge on undeclared business, the bearded pilots in sober blue and mechanics dressed in birdman zoot-suits, the stealthily prowling newsmen who go to the airport each day as other men go to the office; such things don't pass unnoticed. They prove to the layman that flying still has its own mystique, that those who actually work it are initiators of a cult. And why shouldn't the layman believe it? It's nonsense to say that travelling through the air in a flying machine is merely the result of intelligent application of scientific laws. When, on a bright summer's day, a silver shell leaves the ground with a furious thunder of engines, not one of the 10,000 who watch from the public enclosure will deny there's magic in it. Even an engineer will sometimes look thoughtful. And whatever they do to London Airport, with steel and concrete and arty décor, they'll no more take the glamour from it than they could from a goods-yard at night.

The edition of *Picture Post* in which Dowling's article appeared in 1951. *(Author's collection)*

In 1953 over half a million people paid 6*d* to enter the public enclosure at London Airport to watch airlines from all over the world take off and land. *(Author's collection)*

Curious spectators descended on London Airport to get a close-up of Brabazon's one and only visit. *(Author's collection)*

The world's largest civil airliner (at the time), the 130-ton Bristol Brabazon I, made its maiden flight from the Bristol Aeroplane Company's base at Filton on 4 September 1949. It remained in the air for twenty-seven minutes, flying at an altitude of 4,000ft at a speed of 160mph. Brabazon was intended to be the great silver hope of Britain's commercial plane-making and publicity produced by the Bristol company announced that the luxury aircraft had been 'designed specifically as a trans-oceanic airliner to provide fast travel for a large number of passengers at one time and primarily intended for BOAC non-stop London–New York services and as such will set standards in comfort and amenities hitherto unknown in the history of air transport'.

Everything about Brabazon was big. At 177ft long, it was only 54ft shorter than one of today's Boeing 747s – but its 230ft-long wingspan was 35ft wider than the Jumbo Jet. It had a 25ft diameter fuselage (5ft greater than a Boeing 747), with upper and lower decks. It had sleeping berths, a dining room, a cinema for thirty-seven people and 'stand-up' cocktail bars with comfortable in-flight lounges. There was plenty of room for each passenger, too – 200cu. ft per traveller; about twice the interior room of a car. Leg room was not a problem and the seats, which reclined into full-length beds, allowed passengers to lie down and sleep as the plane rumbled its way across Atlantic night skies.

But the Brabazon's passenger capacity was small and only fifty to sixty passengers could travel in the big bird. It would also take twelve hours to cross the Atlantic to New York, roughly the same time taken by BOAC's American-built Constellations.

Like many commercial airport and aeroplane initiatives, Brabazon had been conceived in wartime to meet British postwar aviation requirements. The committee in charge of investigating the future needs of Britain's civilian airliner market met under the leadership of Lord Brabazon of Tara, after whom the country's new airliner, set to take the world by storm, was named.

Brabazon was not only big – it was also ugly, slow and noisy. After witnessing a flypast at the 1949 Farnborough Air Show, BOAC had serious misgivings about purchasing an aircraft that would clearly fail to meet its needs. The airline needed a plane that could carry more passengers in a quieter and more fuel-efficient machine, and Brabazon did not provide the solution. But the government put pressure on the airline, which had no option but to at least consider bringing a fleet of Brabazons into service to operate on prestigious London Airport–New York blue ribbon routes.

The 130-ton Bristol Brabazon was designed to be the saviour of the postwar British commercial aircraft industry, but the massive 177ft-long airliner was a massive failure. *(Author's collection)*

BOAC and the Bristol Aeroplane Company both agreed that Brabazon needed modifications and a second version – Brabazon Mk II – rolled out for its maiden flight in September 1949 and in June 1950 made its London Airport debut.

Prime Minister Clement Attlee would be the first VIP to fly from the airport in the massive plane, alongside twenty MPs, as it made a series of take-off and landing displays for the benefit of potential customers, local residents concerned about the noise it was reported to make and the thousands of tourists expected to flock to the airport to view Brabazon.

However, there was a snag. Although Brabazon was perfectly airworthy, having flown for 130 hours and had appeared at the 1950 Farnborough Air Show just a few days before, nobody at the Bristol Aeroplane Company had thought to obtain a passenger certificate allowing Mr Attlee and his fellow politicians to take a joyride around London Airport. The flight was permitted to go ahead – without the PM and his chums.

Brabazon appeared in the skies over London Airport on the afternoon of 15 June 1950. Cliff Alabaster was at work in his office next to the Bath Road and heard it approaching. 'I went outside to take a look as it arrived. It seemed to be travelling very slowly; so slowly in fact that I thought it was going to drop out of the sky. I suppose that was because it was much larger than other planes we were used to seeing and flying at the airport. It was noisy, too. Brabazon was a cumbersome old bird and I knew that no airlines would ever take it into their fleets. It was built to show the world what British aircraft technology was all about, but it became the white elephant that nobody wanted.'

John Boulding was on his way to work at BOAC engineering from his home in Hayes 'when I heard this racket in the sky and looked up and saw the Brabazon. It was a massive piece of engineering with lots of power. But it wasn't going anywhere. It just seemed to hang there in the sky over London Airport. No wonder it was a failure. It went nowhere – and very slowly, too.'

On 16 June 1950, the *Daily Express* reported: 'More than 4,000 people waited at London Airport last night for a trip round the 130-ton Bristol Brabazon, the world's largest airliner. They paid 6*d* to enter the public enclosure, then queued for seats in coaches at 1/- per head. The coaches were allowed within 50ft of the floodlit Brabazon, guarded by 49 policemen. No one was allowed within touching distance.'

The following day Brabazon made three practice take-offs and landings with Captain Bill Pegg, Bristol's chief test pilot at the controls. Thousands of people in the public enclosure along the Bath Road watched it lumber and roar its way down the runway and slowly rise into the air. Each time the plane landed, Captain Pegg reversed the eight Centaurus 18-cylinder engines which braked the giant airliner to a standstill.

Despite some stylish advertising designs used to help sell Brabazon to aircraft buyers, the massive aircraft was a spectacular commercial failure. *(Author's collection)*

The airport had expected 50,000 people to turn up, but in the end 13,361 spectators paid their sixpences to view Brabazon and most of them forked out an extra shilling to climb into the bus to view the big bird up close before it flew back to Filton for further modifications.

By the beginning of 1951, there were still no orders in place for Brabazon and BOAC had clearly lost all interest in the aircraft, knowing that something better and more economical was on the drawing boards of British aeroplane manufacturers. Bristol took their big bird – now looking more like a dodo – to the Paris Air Show where Captain Pegg took off again to put it through her paces in the hope of landing some orders. There were none.

Brabazon stood unused and neglected in a massive hangar at Filton for the next two years. Occasionally engineers tinkered around with the plane until they were told to put down their spanners for good in February 1952. In September 1953, Duncan Sandys, Attlee's Minister of Supply, told Parliament that the government had decided that 'further expenditure on the Brabazon project could not be justified' and gave directions that the plane should be dismantled. He said that the project, although costly, had made 'a most valuable contribution towards the progress of British aviation', despite the fact that £6.5 million had been spent on the project compared to the original estimate of £4 million.

The Bristol Brabazon was not a total failure. At least half of the investment poured into the project, including vast hangars and a runway extension at Filton, allowed Bristol to use its expanded facilities for other aircraft. The designers, plane-makers and engineers who had worked on Brabazon had all learned new techniques which could now be used on other aircraft and a few years later the Bristol Britannia, one of the world's most successful propeller-driven airliners – known as 'the whispering giant' – rolled out of the same hangar. A few years later, another aircraft would emerge from the same structure, developed as a partnership between England and France. It would be known to the world as Concorde.

By 1951 it was becoming cheaper to fly across the English Channel and the Atlantic Ocean from London Airport. British European Airways (BEA) had been formed as a state-owned airline in 1946 and had originally operated from Northolt Airport. It transferred part of its operations to London Airport in 1950 and by 1954, when Northolt was handed back to the RAF, had carried 3 million passengers and was operating over 100 aircraft.

Following the arrival of BEA at London Airport, passenger figures rose to 796,000 by the end of 1951 – the first time that the airport recorded more travellers than Northolt. London Airport was now on a roll which would continue for the next 50 years and beyond.

Prime routes from London Airport were competitive. The London–Paris sector was one of the most popular and BEA battled it out with Air France for their market share. In December 1951 both airlines announced that they were cutting London–Paris fares by up to 40 per cent, from £8 10s single and £15 6s return to £5 10s 6*d* single and £9 19s return. BEA's thirty-six-seat Vikings and Air France's thirty-three-seat Languedoc 161s would operate the services.

The cost of travelling by air became cheaper in 1952 when BEA slashed fares to Paris to as little as £9 15s return – a small sum by today's standards but a great deal of money to most people in the immediate postwar years. *(Author's collection)*

BEA, which moved to London Airport from Northolt in 1950, became Europe's largest passenger-carrying airline the following year. *(Author's collection)*

At the same time, BOAC and ten other airlines flying across the Atlantic announced that they were slashing fares between London Airport and New York, in order to make flying more affordable. BOAC reduced fares from £141 2s single to £96 9s.

A 'fly now – pay later' scheme was launched by BOAC and BEA in line with other postwar hire purchase programmes sweeping the country, allowing people to buy furniture and cars through a system better known as the 'never-never' – a seemingly never-ending trail of regular payments from one year to the next. The airline scheme allowed passengers to buy tickets for any service and pay in instalments, providing the total transaction exceeded £20. Airlines asked for 10 per cent of the full air fare up-front and the balance paid off in monthly instalments over a period of between six and twenty-one months depending on the final cost.

The hire purchase air fare scheme made a major contribution to BEA and BOAC's passenger-carrying figures in 1953. Together, London Airport's two busiest airlines accounted for 96.3 per cent of all British-owned scheduled services. BEA carried 1.6 million passengers of domestic and short-haul European routes, while BOAC carried 289,239 passengers. British independent airlines carried 238,673 travellers.

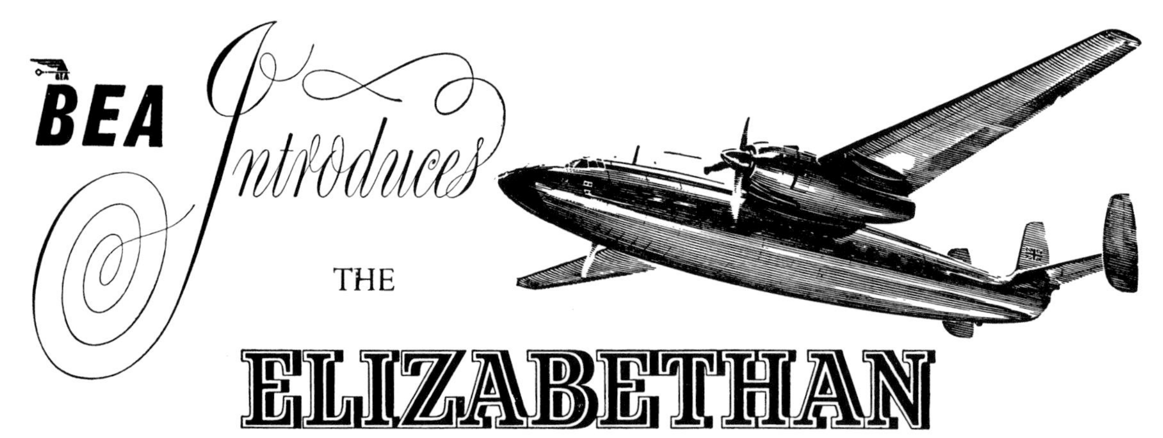

High-wing monoplane | beneath the wing, very large windows give you a wonderful view.
Cruising speed 245 m.p.h. | to Paris in 80 minutes; previous travelling time is cut by a quarter.
Pressurised cabin | you fly at fine-weather heights with ground-level comfort.
Length 81′ 1″, height 18′ 9½″ | the cabin is spacious — nowhere less than 6′ 4″ high.
Crew of five or six | includes two stewards *and* a stewardess to serve you.

So quiet you can talk in whispers. *Steady in flight* watch the cocktail in your glass stay level. *Air-conditioned* an atmosphere of luxury. *Superbly comfortable* armchairs . . . the Airspeed Elizabethan makes air travel a greater pleasure than ever before.

B R I T I S H E U R O P E A N A I R W A Y S

Pride of BEA's routes was its daily Silver Wing London–Paris service using Elizabethan high-wing monoplanes, which offered cocktails and a full lunch onboard the eighty-minute flight. *(Author's collection)*

Pride of BEA's routes was its daily 'Silver Wing' London–Paris service which offered cocktails and a full lunch onboard the eighty-minute flight. Following the demise of BSAA in 1949, Keith Hayward was transferred to BOAC and by 1951 he moved again to BEA at London Airport. He remembers:

> I was pleased to work for BEA because it meant that I got to work alongside a beautiful high-wing monoplane called the Elizabethan, one of my favourite aircraft. The cabin was quite spacious with room for only forty-seven passengers who enjoyed a superb lunch on the short crossing across to Paris. Sometimes they even slowed the flight down in order to have more time to serve the meal.
>
> We had a famous senior traffic officer called 'Bim' Kent whose job was to make sure the service got away on time every lunchtime. He was a military type who used to shout at us young fellows to make us move quicker and not delay the flight. We had to salute the aircraft away in those days. The plane flew a little pennant above the cockpit and, as it taxied away, staff working on the tarmac had to stop what they were doing, line up, snap to attention and salute it. The Captain would acknowledge it through the cockpit window and then haul in the pennant. This was a BEA flagship service calling for a great deal of attention to detail and a bit of ceremony as they departed. In cold and wet winter weather this could be a challenge as we still had to stand to attention while fumes from high-octane piston

engines, rainwater and de-icing fluid blew in our faces. The passengers probably wouldn't have been aware of it – but we certainly were!

In those days we also used huge and primitive walkie-talkie sets which were strapped to our backs. The batteries would often leak, leaving a nasty burn mark on our company-issue raincoats, which had to be replaced regularly. They also carried a tall aerial on top and if you had to go onboard the aircraft for any reason before departure and forgot about the aerial, there was every chance of ripping out a piece of the ceiling fabric.

BEA ground staff working on the tarmac used huge walkie-talkie sets strapped to their backs to talk to their control office. The batteries would often leak, leaving a battery burn mark in company-issue uniforms. *(Keith Hayward collection)*

BEA personnel were required to snap to attention and salute the departure of the daily Silver Wing service to Paris. *(Keith Hayward collection)*

I once went on board a Silver Wing service no more than a minute before departure because there was one passenger short and I needed to count heads. As I was doing this, the Captain suddenly burst into the passenger cabin furiously demanding to know what was going on. I told him what I was doing and he told me that if I wasn't finished in one minute he was going to take off with me onboard. Fortunately, I had miscounted the passengers and was out of the aircraft and down the steps before you could say Jack Robinson. Those Captains really knew how to rule the roost. There had to be a good reason for an aircraft not leaving on time. There was a leeway of three minutes and after that nobody – not even a young lad like me – was going to stand in the way of the flight departing. He meant it, too. If I hadn't shot down the steps he would have taken off with me onboard. It was their military mindset still at work.

Eric Driver, who used to work for a small British airline called Starways, recalls that airline passengers in the 1950s could sometimes be just as awkward as today's travellers:

There was an occasion when a passenger in a DC-3 was a little worse for wear and started to grope the hostess, who quickly called the Captain. 'Are you going to behave and keep your hands to yourself?' the Captain asked. 'Yesshir', said the passenger. So the DC-3 got underway and started to taxi out towards the runway. Suddenly, we noticed it was making its way towards a vacant stand, the door opened and the passenger was unceremoniously booted out of the aircraft. The door was shut and the DC-3 continued its taxiing, leaving a rather puzzled passenger standing in the middle of nowhere!

On another occasion a Starways aircraft was taxiing out to take-off without a passenger who had failed to check in for his flight. 'A few minutes later we received a call from our friends over at BEA asking us if we were missing a certain passenger', Eric remembers. 'We asked them how they knew such a thing and they told us they had picked him up walking around the tarmac and were bringing him to us. Once he was delivered, we asked him what he'd been thinking of, walking around a busy airport tarmac. "Well," he said, "I knew I was running late, so I thought I would head off towards the taxiway to wave the aircraft down as it taxied past".'

While Paris-bound passengers bolted down their lunch on BEA's Silver Wing service, passengers flying on BOAC's overnight New York service from London Airport were getting ready for a more leisurely aerial experience.

By 1951 three airlines operated the 3,500-mile blue ribbon Atlantic route – BOAC, Pan American and Trans World Airlines (TWA). BOAC's luxurious 'Monarch' service was described as 'the last word in luxury air travel'. Using the 'double-decked spaciousness' of pressurised Boeing Stratocruiser aircraft – a fifty-seat American-built bulbous aircraft powered by four propeller-driven engines – the Monarch service was famous for its in-flight 'extras'. These included seven-course champagne dinners served from a trolley brought to passengers' seats by white-jacketed stewards. During the meal, the Captain would visit the cabin to chat with passengers and explain the progress of their flight. After coffee and liqueurs in the lower-deck lounge, passengers settled for the night in either their reclining seat or retired 'to the privacy of a comfortable full size berth . . . available for a little extra' (£8 19s extra). As the aircraft approached the last stage of its journey, breakfast in bed was offered.

B. O. A. C. proudly presents . . .

THE Monarch

LONDON-NEW YORK DIRECT—OVERNIGHT!

It's the last word in luxury air travel! Relax in the double-decked spaciousness of a pressurized Stratocruiser Speedbird . . . meet congenial companions in the lower-deck lounge with its well-stocked bar. Three stewards and a stewardess study to please you.

Enjoy cocktails, a seven-course dinner with wine or champagne, then liqueurs . . . all served with the compliments of B.O.A.C. Finally, you may retire to the privacy of a comfortable full-sized berth (only £8.19.0. extra). Breakfast in bed, if you wish!

Complimentary "Speedbird Overnight Bag" for every passenger . . . an "Elizabeth Arden Beauty Kit" for every lady.

Yet, you pay no surcharge to travel by this luxurious new overnight service to New York — not a penny extra!

Free advice and information available on request from your local B.O.A.C. Appointed Agent, or B.O.A.C., Airways Terminal, Buckingham Palace Road, London, S.W.1. Telephone: VICtoria 2323. Early reservation advisable.

B.O.A.C. TAKES GOOD CARE OF YOU

FLY BRITISH BY B·O·A·C

BRITISH OVERSEAS AIRWAYS CORPORATION

The stylish way to fly across the Atlantic in the 1950s was with BOAC's luxurious Monarch service, described as 'the last word in luxury air travel'. During the flight in an American-built Stratocruiser, passengers enjoyed seven-course champagne dinners and slept in full-size beds, available for a little extra. *(Author's collection)*

Advertisements promised passengers opportunities to 'meet congenial companions in the lower deck lounge with its well-stocked bar. Three stewards and a stewardess are available to please you. There will be a complementary "Speedbird overnight bag" for every passenger, an Elizabeth Arden beauty kit for every lady.'

BOAC sold the flight for 'a little over £140 – roughly the same as the first class steamer fare, but the passage is four days faster than the fastest ocean liner' and it launched their famous slogan used for the next two decades: 'BOAC takes good care of you.'

Stratocruiser crews were known within BOAC as the 'Atlantic Barons', an elite group able to command the best salaries in the business for flying what was regarded as the toughest route of all across the Atlantic, calling for pilots with the most experience and skill when crossing vast stretches of ocean.

BOAC and Pan American competed for transatlantic passengers using comfortable Boeing Stratocruisers for flights between London Airport and New York. *(Heathrow Visitors Centre)*

On 31 January 1952, HM King George VI and Queen Elizabeth travelled to London Airport to wave goodbye to their daughter, Princess Elizabeth, and her husband, Philip, Duke of Edinburgh, travelling on the first leg of a five-month tour of Commonwealth countries. They planned to visit Kenya, Ceylon, Australia and New Zealand, travelling on the BOAC Argonaut airliner Atalanta.

It was a cold day, but hundreds of airport staff, passengers and onlookers turned out to see their King and raise a cheer for his young daughter and her dashing husband. Surgeons had removed one of the King's lungs four months before; he had been a heavy cigarette smoker all his life and he looked pale and drawn as he walked bareheaded across the windswept tarmac with his daughter and son-in-law, muffled in a heavy greatcoat, his hands thrust firmly into the pockets.

31 January 1952 – HM King George VI and Queen Elizabeth travelled to London Airport to wave goodbye to their daughter, Princess Elizabeth, and her husband, Philip, Duke of Edinburgh, travelling on the first leg of a five-month Commonwealth tour. They travelled on a BOAC Argonaut, called Atalanta. *(Barry Dix collection)*

The Duke shook hands with the King and was first to climb the steps into the Argonaut. Princess Elizabeth followed her husband and at the aircraft door turned and waved to her father. It would be the last time she would see him alive.

The King returned to his wife in the terminal and together they came out onto the chilly balcony of the Royal Lounge as the Argonaut began to taxi towards the runway. They watched as it gathered speed, rose into the air and soon became a small speck on the distant horizon before going back inside. This would be the King's final public appearance since he had reluctantly come to the throne in 1936 following the abdication of his brother, Edward VIII.

Six days later, at an exclusive forest hunting lodge near Nyeri in the foothills of Mt Kenya, Princess Elizabeth was told that her father had died of coronary thrombosis during the early hours of the morning. Plans were immediately made for her return and the young royal couple were rushed to Entebbe, Uganda, to where the crew of BOAC Argonaut Atalanta was on its way to collect the young Princess who would soon be their Queen.

The aircraft took off from Entebbe in a storm and completed the 4,444-mile journey in 19 hours and 43 minutes. It included a short stop in El Adem in Libya for refuelling and a change of crew. During the journey the crew maintained regular contact with BOAC's operations room at London Airport by wireless telegraphy, while the RAF and Royal Navy had taken precautions all along the route in case an emergency arose.

Over Sevenoaks, at 4.06 p.m. on 7 February 1952, the Argonaut descended to 4,000ft and began its approach to London Airport where the Atalanta touched down in England at 4.19 p.m. A small group were waiting on the tarmac, heads bare and wearing black overcoats and armbands. They included the Prime Minister, Winston Churchill, his Foreign Minister, Anthony Eden, and Leader of the Opposition, Clement Attlee. They bowed their heads as the door of the Argonaut opened and Princess Elizabeth began to walk down the steps. As her feet touched the tarmac they looked up to greet their new Queen.

The exact place where Princess Elizabeth first set foot on British soil at London Airport as the uncrowned Queen Elizabeth II is now the site of the Heathrow Renaissance Hotel's Brasserie Restaurant, where a striking wall plaque marks the historic spot. The large hotel, with the Bath Road at its front side and a busy airport perimeter road behind it, had once been part of the north-side airport tarmac. A special metal plaque commemorating the historic flight was later fitted on the inside door of Atalanta. The plane was scrapped over half a century ago. Whatever happened to the plaque?

By June 1953 and after the Queen's coronation, travelling to London Airport for the day to watch great airliners from all over the world take off and land was *the* favourite occupation for Londoners. The visitors' enclosure was expanded, a small funfair, complete with a roundabout, slide and miniature train ride, had been installed along with a children's sandpit and mock-up of an aircraft doorway where visitors could be photographed appearing to be departing or arriving from an exciting aeroplane trip.

A commentator was recruited at weekends and holidays to stand on the control tower balcony and tell visitors through his loudspeaker what was happening on the runways. Aerodrome control offices, housed in the 'glass house' at the top of the runway, fed information to the commentator who relayed it to the crowds below with the enthusiasm of a cinema newsreel narrator. In 1953, 527,000 people came to London Airport to watch aeroplanes take off and land.

There was also a refreshment bar, which began life – like so many airport buildings – in a marquee. Betty Richardson, from Heston, got a weekend job working in the refreshment station located on the Bath Road. She remembers:

> The whole of the north side consisted of prefab-type huts and marquees. I particularly remember the small fancy cakes that were delivered on bakers' trays and would be surrounded by wasps. We had to quickly cover the tray with an empty one and when we served a customer, had to carefully put a hand in and grab a cake hoping all the time that a wasp hadn't chomped at the icing. Eventually we were given sandwich bags – a new invention – to wrap the fancies in. I can still see the expressions on customers' faces as they looked with approval at fancy cakes

7 February 1952 – BOAC Argonaut Atalanta returns to London Airport from Entebbe with Princess Elizabeth following the death of her father. She set foot on British soil as Queen for the first time at London Airport on a site now covered by a large hotel. Waiting on the tarmac to greet their new monarch is the Prime Minister, Sir Winston Churchill, Foreign Secretary Anthony Eden and Leader of the Opposition, Clement Attlee. *(BAA (Heathrow) Archives)*

A line-up of planes and 1950s cars near the public enclosure at London Airport. *(Heathrow Visitors Centre)*

beneath a cellophane-type wrapping (rationing was still in force, so fancy cakes were a real luxury).

We served hot tea made in an urn and there was a deposit charge on every cup and saucer – something like 1*s* 6*d*. It was self-service with a lady at the end of the counter totting up the prices in her head and using an old-fashioned till. Crockery was washed up in an old-fashioned tin bath behind the scenes. We served ice creams kept in a fridge in small drums. The drums would be taken out as required but we had to ensure that most of the ice cream could be sold as once taken out and thawed, it could not be re-frozen. Sandwiches were made by ladies in the kitchen and bagged up, just like the cakes. It was all very basic but hygiene was always observed.

People flocked to the airport to see aeroplanes at that time and I enjoyed working there. In those days people would even stop along the Bath Road and picnic on the green grass verges. Imagine doing that today!

Edna Sparks, the mother of June Pearce from Northolt, worked in the airport's first official staff canteen. June says that her mother was employed in 'a pre-fabricated building with a very utilitarian interior. Part of my mother's duties was going to other areas of the airport with refreshments for staff and she moved around in a van. During the Berlin Airlift in the late 1940s she used to go out to the planes on the tarmac and assist in handing over supplies to the crews. Sometimes my brother Dennis and I would go to work with our mother and help out with some of the chores, clearing tables and washing up. There were no dishwashers then. Our reward, if we were lucky, would be a cream cake or a most wonderful apple fritter all hot and tossed in sugar. What a treat that was after all the rationing we had endured during the war and were still experiencing at that time.'

Edna Sparks worked in the airport's first official staff canteen, 'a pre-fabricated building with a very utilitarian interior'. Part of her duties was going to other areas of the airport with refreshments for staff. She is pictured here with other catering staff (in front, at the bottom of the aircraft steps) standing in front of an Avro York. *(Courtesy of Dennis Sparks and June Pearce)*

BOAC's maintenance hangar – part of its London Airport headquarters building better known to staff as the 'Kremlin'– on completion in 1954. For many years the building held the record for being the world's largest reinforced concrete structure. *(Heathrow Visitors Centre)*

BOAC's first major maintenance base at Heathrow in 1954. *(Author's collection)*

The airport's runways were – and still are – surrounded by large areas of grass which require regular maintenance. This tractor is towing grass-cutting equipment near an Icelandic Viscount aircraft in 1958. *(Nicky Carter)*

In order to reduce aircraft noise on the ground, BOAC built a tall and thick 'baffle wall', made from bricks, behind which engines could be run-up and tested and noise levels reduced. *(Barry Dix collection)*

Airport reporter, Ray Berry, remembers that during the late 1940s and early 1950s it was often difficult for many airport staff to find somewhere to eat:

Members of the public travelling along the A30 were treated to close-up views of airport activities in the 1950s. *(Nicky Carter)*

> Just outside the Bath Road entrance was 'Ben's', a small café (the sort of place we call a greasy spoon these days – but I think someone must have stolen his) where you could get hot snacks. Alongside was his café extension: rows of cast iron tables and a variety of stools and chairs under a corrugated tin roof, which made conversation impossible and leaked constantly in the rain.
>
> On the other side of the road was the proudly named 'Heathrow Restaurant', a chintzy tea-room with a mock gentility which boasted a fixed 'lunchtime' for a never-varying menu of shepherd's pie and two veg, sausage and mash and so on. And on the Bath Road, of course, there were three pubs: the Bricklayers' Arms (later renamed the Air Hostess), the Three Magpies and the Old Magpies, both of which boasted highwayman Dick Turpin as a former regular.
>
> Within the airport, an early company called Airwork Ltd provided a staff snack bar adjoining the old terminal building and opened the first Green Dragon Café in a long, low, corrugated iron Nissen hut. Later this same Nissen hut became a conference room hosting press events for a host of VIPs, including a venue for Laurence Olivier and Vivien Leigh to see off Marilyn Monroe and Arthur Miller on completion of her film *The Prince and the Showgirl* in 1957.
>
> I'm not aware that continuing official wartime rationing (as opposed to general food shortages) affected public catering to any great extent, any more than it had from 1939 to 1945, though I may have been fooled by the abilities and efficiency of professional caterers. Or perhaps the wartime black market was still active – and equally efficient.

June Pike (née Bibby) and Roger Haines from Staines, pretend to arrive from somewhere glamorous on a mock-up of a BOAC aircraft in the public enclosure at London Airport, during the 1950s. *(June Pike)*

Keith Hayward remembers:

> Airport conditions during the late 1940s and early 1950s were often bleak, but the famous Ben's Café was heaven-sent. It took the form of an old lean-to with a tent extension and it sustained us all. But Ben's was just superb and it continued until they demolished it to make way for the tunnel leading to the central area. Ben's had been there long before the airport. It started life as a place for lorry drivers travelling along the Bath Road. It always seemed to be open at any time of the day

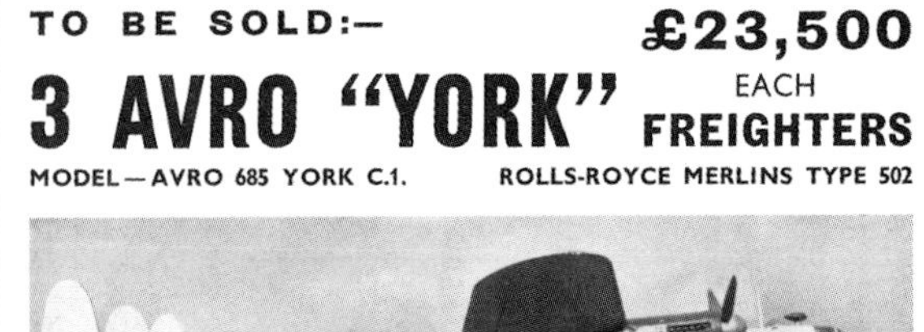

By 1953 many airlines were selling their old wartime Avro Lancastrians and Yorks and replacing them with more modern aircraft. *(Author's collection)*

or night. It was also one of the few places for miles around where you could buy cakes. Goodness knows how they got around the problem of sugar rationing. They served up a superb breakfast, but it was so full of smoke you couldn't see across the place – but the grub was excellent and at that time the only place that staff could get anything hot to eat. There was another little place along the Bath Road inside a converted house that sold cooked food and run by a lady from what would have been her front room.

A little later a place called the Green Dragon took over and a company called Airwork undertook the passenger catering. It was located just inside the airport boundary and had once been a freight shed. I'm not sure how it got its name; perhaps the doors had been painted green.

Business consultant Tony Hesketh-Gardener recalls Nissen huts alongside the Bath Road that 'provided the best afternoon teas for miles. Tablecloths, monogrammed china, silver-plated cutlery and waitress service. Furthermore, it was a place where many of us congregated for breakfast after hunt balls or the three annual Sandhurst balls. Tails, uniforms, dinner jackets, evening dresses abounded on those early mornings – usually between 3.30 and 4.30 a.m. The place never seemed to close and there was a full waitress service, tablecloths, china. My, how times have changed!'

London Airport became a magnet for people looking for jobs in the exciting world of air transport. In addition to employment as airline ground staff to work on check-in desks and escort passengers to waiting aircraft, there were vacancies for skilled aircraft engineers (and thanks to the RAF they were in good supply), cargo loaders, plus office administration staff. For every job vacancy at London Airport there was at least fifteen applicants and many were snapped up on the same day as advertised.

Between 1950 and 1955, Gwen Humphries from Hounslow, Middlesex, worked in the airport's personnel office – a Nissan hut known as Hut 29 and located on the Bath Road at Harlington Corner – for a weekly wage of £2 5s. Gwen recalls:

> Our job was to recruit staff for the airlines, including BOAC and Qantas, and scores of people came in every day looking for work. I remember that on one particular day 108 people came through our door wanting jobs at London Airport – and we found employment for them all as aircraft engineers, aircraft cleaners, clerical and catering staff. They came on their bikes, on the bus and some even walked. They also came for interviews with their parents in chauffeur driven Rolls-Royce cars, the sons and daughters of Lords and Ladies.

Above: The BEA engineering base at London Airport, on completion in 1954 and surrounded by new aircraft recently delivered to the airline's fleet. *(Heathrow Visitors Centre) Below, right:* An early advertisement promoting the advantages of air cargo! *(Author's collection)*

People used to fill in their job application forms resting on the walls of the Nissen hut as there were only a few tables and chairs and no room to spare. Lots of young men and women wanted jobs as cabin staff because they travelled to places where they could buy lady's nylons, which were virtually unobtainable in England at that time.

Our hut was about 100 yards from a runway used by York freighter aircraft bringing exotic animals into the country. We liked to watch people's faces when they travelled along the Bath Road in open-top buses and suddenly saw a giraffe appear above the trees, followed by elephants.

A notice was attached to a small gate warning airport staff to make sure they looked both ways before crossing the runway.

Frequent flyers – the royal family have been regular travellers from the airport ever since it was opened. Pictured here, on their way from the airport's VIP suite to a waiting aircraft ready to take them to Balmoral in 1954, is HRH the Queen Mother and HM the Queen with Princess Anne and Prince Charles. *(Heathrow Visitors Centre)*

The Alcock and Brown statue was first unveiled in 1954. *(Alan Gallop)*

In later years our office moved to a more modern building with a spiral glass staircase and we couldn't understand why seats directly beneath the stairs were so popular with men filling in their application forms. We later realised that as we came down the stairs the men could look up our skirts!

There was a wonderful spirit among everyone in those early days. You felt you were really working at the start of something wonderful – and, of course, we were. They were happy days.

In December 1953, passenger traffic at London Airport hit the 1 million passenger mark for the first time. By the end of the year, 1.2 million passengers had flown in and out of London's premier air gateway on over 62,000 flights. Some 23,000 tons of cargo had also passed through the airport and 527,000 members of the public had paid 6*d* to pass through the turnstiles at the public enclosure to thrill to the sight of giant silver aeroplanes from all over the world appear in the sky and land in London.

TEN

A Wonderful Beginning to the Elizabethan Age

WRITER PAUL TOWNEND observed in 1951 that air travel 'has made the world shrink like a walnut in its shell. Already liners like the Stratocruiser and Constellation take fifty to seventy passengers and soon the Bristol Brabazon will carry even more; the de Havilland Comet heralds the age of the jet airliners – and before very long we shall probably travel to work by helicopter instead of the 8.47 to Waterloo. Aviation will one day be as safe as a rural bus service and London Airport, the aerodrome of the future, will lead the world.'

By the end of 1951 – the year in which the country celebrated the Festival of Britain – 796,092 passengers were travelling through the airport annually and its temporary prefabricated terminals were reaching the limit of their capacity. It was once again time to call in the builders to begin working on the next phase of the London Airport development plan: to create the largest and finest airport in the world.

In 1950, British architect, Frederick Gibberd, was appointed by the Ministry of Transport and Civil Aviation to create stunning new futuristic designs for the airport.

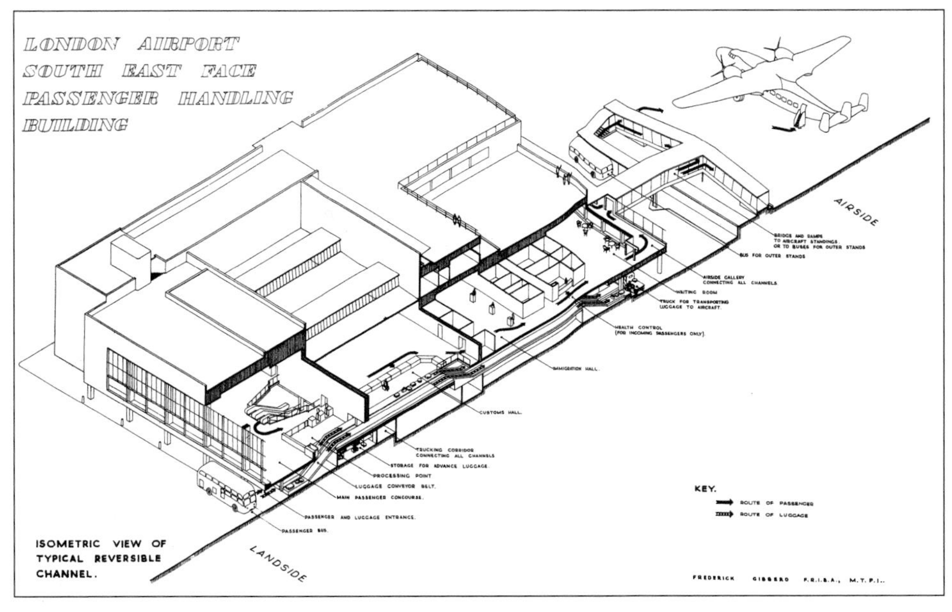

One of Frederick Gibberd's original plans for the new passenger terminal – now known as Terminal 2 – located on an island surrounded by runways and reached by a road traffic tunnel. *(Frederick Gibberd Archive)*

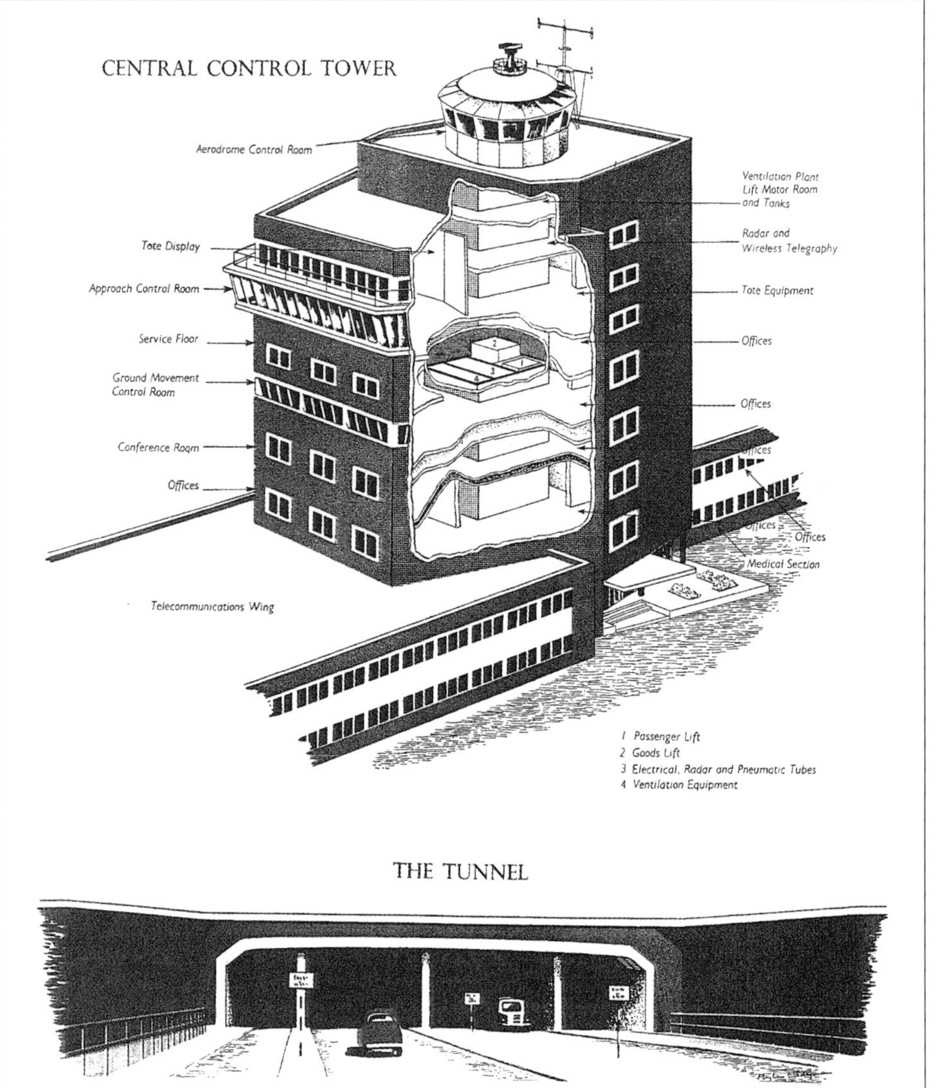

The focal point of Frederick Gibberd's 'airport city' was a 122ft-high control tower building providing uninterrupted views of the entire airfield. To reach the central area, travellers passed through a half-mile-long tunnel running underneath one of the main runways. *(Taylor Woodrow Construction Ltd)*

His work had been brought to the attention of the postwar Labour government's Minister for Town and County Planning, Lord Silkin, who commissioned Gibberd to draw up plans for a new town in Harlow, Essex. The project resulted in the creation of the country's first purpose-built peacetime town: an architectural model of its time. In later years, Gibberd was also principal architect of Liverpool's Roman Catholic Cathedral and a planning consultant to new towns in Swindon, Nuneaton and Leamington Spa, creating bright new shopping centres in the middle of old, worn-out and bomb-damaged communities. Where possible his schemes were integrated within existing designs and Gibberd's new shopping centres were often found behind original Victorian frontages.

London Airport was another matter. There were no Victorian frontages behind which Gibberd could conceal a large and modern public airline terminal, office buildings and a multi-storey control tower. The architect was given a blank canvas on which to create the first permanent buildings for his 'airport city', which would exist within a large 'island' inside the runway triangles. Ground space allocated was generous, covering a 158-acre triangular site.

The airport's central area was designed with a degree of foresight as well as over £21 million of taxpayers' money. Although the Ministry expected airport buildings to handle passenger traffic for many years to come, additional space was available within the site for at least two more terminals. Early planners, however, did not think beyond the end of the 1960s. The idea that the airport might eventually require more terminals towards the end of the twentieth century and another – possibly two – in the twenty-first century had not entered into its thinking.

Despite this lack of long-term foresight (and who in the 1950s could ever have imagined what the airport might be like sixty years later?), plans taking shape on Frederick Gibberd's drawing board were unlike anything ever seen before at an international airport. They were approved by the Royal Fine Art Commission and prior to building gangs moving in, Gibberd commented: 'The airport's design and construction embody the results of many years of study and experiment and no effort has been spared to ensure that the aesthetic appeal of the buildings matches the importance of their function. . . . There is room in the central area to accommodate enough buildings to handle all the passengers and freight that the runways can deliver to them.'

The focal point of Gibberd's 'airport city' was a new 122ft-high control tower building which would be at the centre of a highly complex system of radio and radar navigational aids, airfield lighting and ground movement control. Gibberd proudly

Frederick Gibberd's designs become a reality as work on the terminal and control tower near completion. *(BAA (Heathrow) Archive)*

At the top of the control tower, aerodrome control staff had good views of the entire airport – but still used binoculars for close-up views of the most distant areas. *(Author's collection)*

stated: 'It is expected that these technical facilities, when installed, will be the most advanced and comprehensive in the world.'

In the shadow of the control tower would be an advanced passenger terminal that would be a world of difference away from the temporary prefabricated buildings travellers were experiencing less than a mile away on the airport's north side. It would be super-modern, spacious, comfortable, containing everything sophisticated air travellers would soon come to accept as normal from a mid-twentieth-century air-conditioned airport passenger terminal, including shops, restaurants, cocktail bars, lounges, large panoramic windows, smart check-in desks and facilities allowing passengers to pass through controls and board aircraft quickly and efficiently.

Heathrow's control tower rises into the sky during the summer of 1953. *(Heathrow Visitors Centre)*

Adjacent to the terminal would be another building containing space for airport and airline offices, briefing rooms, a meteorological office and facilities for the airport's press corps. On its roof would be a special place for airport visitors, complete with viewing galleries offering the public grandstand vistas of aircraft arriving and departing to all four corners of the globe.

Gibberd designed his 'airport city' on a grid of 12ft with a steel-framed main structure on which would hang external walls of high-fired red bricks, stone and glass.

It was estimated that the new control tower would be ready for use in July 1955, the terminal in September 1955 and the office building with public viewing area in January 1956. Some of Britain's leading companies were hired to turn Gibberd's vision into reality. Sir William Halcrow & Partners were the principal consulting engineers with Taylor Woodrow Construction Ltd in charge of laying the foundations and the main building work, while Redpath, Brown & Company were responsible for the steel framework in each building.

Heathrow's famous landmark control tower will soon be replaced by a new one. The future of the old control tower has yet to be decided. *(Alan Gallop)*

The airport's new nerve centre, passenger and public buildings would be connected to the old airport area and the Bath Road by a 'vehicular subway' running underneath the original main runway and three parallel taxiways.

The airport's famous tunnel was constructed from a large and deep trench, known in the building trade as a 'cut and fill' job. Gibberd designed the trench, half a mile long, 200ft wide and 40ft deep, to house a rectangular reinforced concrete shell that would

The tunnel under construction. *(Taylor Woodrow Construction Ltd)*

be subdivided to provide two dual-lane carriageways each capable of handling 2,000 motor vehicles per hour, plus two separate cycle tracks and pedestrian pathways. Once the concrete shell was in place, the tunnel would measure 2,060ft long, 86ft wide and 23ft high.

A call went out for volunteers to ride through the finished tunnel in a London Transport double-decker bus. Although the tunnel was tall and wide enough to take a bus – with room to spare – doubts were raised that a large public vehicle full of passengers travelling at certain speeds through a restricted space could meet with disaster halfway through. Similar doubts were voiced when a train travelled through a railway tunnel for the first time.

There was no shortage of volunteers wanting to be among the first to travel through the airport's tunnel as bus number 81B made its way towards the entrance from the Bath Road. Large crowds of airport workers stood at either end as the bright red bus slowly made its way towards the inward entrance, followed by an ambulance and

A view of the airport tunnel shortly after its opening. Note the lack of traffic passing through. *(Author's collection)*

fire engine – just in case. The bus driver gradually increased speed as he travelled along the tunnel and shot out at the other end at a speed of 30mph – safe, unharmed and all in one piece. Millions of buses have passed safely through the tunnel since that day.

While construction was taking shape, London Airport's traffic figures were steadily increasing. By 1952, 860,760 passengers travelling with 23 airlines on over 52,000 flights were using the airport, which declared itself 'the busiest in Europe and one of the world's largest international air terminals'.

Elsewhere, more builders were at work, many of whom had been in steady employment at the airport for nearly seven years. Three aircraft maintenance areas had been completed. The largest, covering 240 acres east of the runway system, contained temporary hangars used by BOAC, while new hangars and a headquarters complex rose on the skyline for use in 1954. The headquarters building eventually found its way into the record books when its four 336ft span sections (known as pens) won it the accolade of being the world's largest reinforced concrete structure. It would be known affectionately to BOAC staff as the 'Kremlin'. Eight out of the ten new hangars planned for BEA were also opened on a site nearby and used to maintain Ambassador and Viscount aircraft. A 91-acre site was set aside for future development and would eventually become the site of the airport's dedicated cargo terminal.

While foundations were being poured for London Airport's buildings of the future, new British aircraft designed to cross the world's air lanes were ready to enter service. The jet age was about to arrive at London Airport.

An aerial shot of the control tower, new passenger terminal and (top right) building later known as the Queen's Building under construction. *(Barry Dix collection)*

The de Havilland Comet. This 1952 advertisement features the revolutionary plane's test pilot, Johnny 'Cat's Eyes' Cunningham. *(Author's collection)*

The de Havilland Comet I was a revolutionary new form of air transportation and the world's first pure jet passenger aircraft to enter commercial scheduled service. With flying speeds of over 500mph it was, in 1952, way ahead of its international rivals, designed to give BOAC a competitive advantage over foreign airlines.

It looked different from any other aircraft seen in the skies over London Airport; sleek, futuristic and with almost invisible engines contained within sweptback wings. It was designed to fly at altitudes of 40,000ft, previously unheard of, requiring effective cabin pressurisation. Flying at up to 500mph the Comet I was a world away, in terms of speed and comfort, from Avro Lancastrians and Yorks and entered service less than three years after its first test flight, during which it broke a handful of point-to-point speed records along the way.

The man in charge of putting the Comet through its testing paces was John Cunningham, OBE, DFC and bar and known across the country as Johnny 'Cat's Eyes' Cunningham following his RAF career commanding the famous Mosquito squadron. He had joined de Havilland at the age of 18 and following the war had worked on the Comet project since it was a plywood mock-up. As the airliner's chief test pilot, Cunningham flew hundreds of hours in the aircraft before it entered service with BOAC in 1952.

Various versions of the Comet were produced. Pictured here is a Comet 4, used successfully by both BOAC and BEA. *(de Havilland Archives)*

John Boulding, from Ashford, Middlesex, joined BOAC as an apprentice engineer at Whitchurch, south of Bristol, in October 1940. Whitchurch was BOAC's secret wartime headquarters and had been requisitioned by the Air Ministry for the duration of the war. After working for the airline in Egypt, he returned in October 1946 to work on Vikings, DC-3s, Lancastrians and Yorks at London Airport. In 1951 he was appointed an airframe inspector on BOAC's new aircraft – the Comet. John remembers:

John Boulding (second left) and colleagues in front of a BOAC Comet at London Airport in 1952. *(John Boulding)*

> I shall never forget my first sight of the Comet. It was amazing, sleek and beautiful with her engines hidden inside the wing. None of us had ever seen anything like it before. Mind you, we engineers all thought that the aluminium used to make the aircraft was too thin. It had been cut down to the absolute minimum in order to make the plane light. In fact, everything appeared to be rather on the thin side.
>
> After the Comet had been in service for a while, we all felt very confident in the aircraft and what it could do. Of course, we had no idea of the problems and tragedy that lay ahead for this wonderful plane.

Captain Cliff 'Alaby' Alabaster, by now flying BOAC Argonaut services to South America following BSAA's absorption into BOAC, became involved with the Comet during its development phase. He remembers his own first sight of the Comet I and recalled that 'she looked absolutely smashing' but learning to fly the new aircraft was different from piloting piston-engine equipment. After taking a Comet training course with other pilots at de Havilland's aircraft factory at Hatfield just before Christmas 1951, Alaby was one of the first pilots to fly the aircraft – G-ALYP – when it entered service on the 6,724-mile London–Johannesburg route on 2 May 1952. Hundreds of spectators and airport staff turned out to witness the departure of the world's first jet service. It was a great day for British civil aviation.

The Comet I travelled via Rome and Beirut with Captain Alistair Majende at the controls and Captain Trevor Marsden on the Beirut–Khartoum section. Alaby was at the controls for the final section between Khartoum and Johannesburg, carrying thirty-six passengers. At Livingstone, BOAC Chairman, Sir Miles Thomas, demonstrated just how smooth the Comet performed in flight by pulling down a seat-back table and standing a four-sided foreign coin on its end. Two hours later the coin was still standing in the same position.

Over 20,000 onlookers turned out to see the world's first jet aircraft passenger service land at Johannesburg after a flight lasting eighteen hours forty minutes – a new record for the route, which was previously covered by BOAC's piston-engine aircraft in thirty-two hours twenty-five minutes.

Captain Cliff Alabaster was a member of the crew flying part of the route followed by the first BOAC Comet from London to South Africa in 1952 and was also at the aircraft's controls for its final flight in 1965. *(Cliff Alabaster collection)*

A few days later the Comet was on its way back to London Airport at the end of its 12,000-mile round trip and arrived seven minutes early. At the airport, Sir Miles Thomas, predicated that from now on world travellers were going to demand jet-propelled aircraft and this would be good for British aircraft manufacturers. 'It is a complete vindication of BOAC's faith in the Comet when we ordered it straight off the drawing board and it makes a wonderful beginning to the Elizabethan age,' he said.

Everyone wanted to fly in the Comet 1. The Queen Mother and Princess Margaret became the airliner's first royal passengers and stars of stage, screen and sports arenas were happy to be photographed in front of the plane before and after flights. In September 1952 an extended version of the Comet 1, the Comet 3, was announced (the Comet 2 being an experimental test plane not built for commercial service). The new model would take up to seventy-six passengers and was designed for transatlantic crossings. Orders were received from BOAC and Air India, and Comet pilots, including Cliff Alabaster, were drafted in to help sell the aircraft to American airlines.

'I was detailed to show some Pan American pilots over the Comet at London Airport', Alaby recalls. 'They were very impressed because there was no equivalent American machine. They went back to their airline stating that they were going to recommend the Comet to their board.'

In October 1952, the President of Pan American Airways, Juan Trippe, announced that his company had placed an order for three Comet 3 airliners for delivery towards the end of 1956, with an option for an additional aircraft. The Comet 3s would be the first jet airliners used by an American carrier and their purchase was the first occasion that a US company had gone outside the United States to buy airliners for regular services. It was explained, by Sir Miles Thomas, that the delivery date of 1956 had been made possible because BOAC had agreed to release to Pan American Airways early deliveries of Comet 3s earmarked for the corporation.

At around the same time, Captain Eddie Rickenbacker, President of Eastern Airlines and the famous American fighter 'ace' of the First World War passed through London Airport on his way to discussions with de Havilland. He later flew in the Comet 2 prototype and expressed great satisfaction with its performance, saying he was prepared to spend about £35.7 million on Comet aircraft and spares. He added that on returning to the US he would investigate whether jet airliners projected by the Douglas, Boeing and Lockheed companies would be ready as late as 1960. If he found this was the case, he would be prepared to take delivery of Comet 3s in 1957. Captain Rickenbacker also said: 'There is nothing available like the Comet in the USA in any stage of conception, let alone the drawing board.'

Then, on 26 October 1952, less than six months after the inaugural Comet service had left London Airport, disaster struck. A Comet 1 service flying from Johannesburg to London crashed on take-off with thirty-three passengers onboard after a scheduled stop in Rome. It was a wet evening and the plane careered off the runway, hitting a large pile of soil which ripped out the undercarriage. There were no fatalities and pilot error was identified as the cause. The captain was later demoted to flying York freighters. In January 1953, a Comet 1 undershot the runway at Entebbe, killing an airport worker and in March a Comet crashed at Karachi while being delivered to an airline in Australia. The crew of five plus six technicians were all killed and the brand new plane was completely destroyed. Pilot error was again blamed, but the airline cancelled their order for a further two planes.

On 2 May 1953, on the first anniversary of the Comet's inaugural service, Comet 1 G-ALYV, flying from Singapore to London, exploded in flight during a tropical storm somewhere close to Calcutta. Forty-three passengers and crew were lost. Weeks later a Comet 1 operated by a French airline overshot the runway at Dakar and was destroyed – the fifth Comet accident in eighteen months. American airlines cancelled their orders, losing de Havilland £40 million. Suddenly the future of Britain's great passenger jet airliner looked bleak.

In January 1954, BOAC Comet G-ALYP, flying from Singapore to London, disintegrated at 27,000ft near the Mediterranean island of Elba. Twenty-nine

G-APMF
BEA
Lord Douglas, Chairman of B.E.A. says:
"Last year our passenger traffic rose 20 per cent —which is almost half as much again as the world average.
This most satisfactory expansion owed much to the further fare reductions which we were able to introduce and to the appearance on the routes of B.E.A.'s first pure-jet aircraft, the Comet 4B, which entered service in April".
It is the same everywhere—
low fares and Comet jet standards
mean traffic growth and profit
COMET
(Rolls-Royce Avon jet engines)
the incomparable medium-stage airliner
DE HAVILLAND MEMBER COMPANY OF THE HAWKER SIDDELEY GROUP

passengers, including ten children, plus six of the crew perished in the disaster. The airline issued an urgent statement to passengers through the media:

> As a measure of prudence, normal Comet passenger services are being temporarily suspended to enable minute and unhurried technical examination of every aircraft in the Comet fleet to be carried out at London Airport. Sir Miles Thomas has decided to devote himself almost exclusively to probing the Comet mishap, with Sir Geoffrey de Havilland and the highest authorities in Britain. His decision is based on a desire to retain the good name of the Comets.

Close inspection of the grounded aircraft produced no clues as to why there had been so many accidents. Modifications were carried out, including fitting special armour plating around the engines. The Ministry of Transport and Civil Aviation's Accident Investigation Branch continued their inquiries, using pieces of crashed aircraft brought back to the UK from various sites. Detailed investigations also took place following each crash. Meanwhile, BOAC was losing £50,000 for every week that it kept its Comets on the ground and ten weeks after the Elba tragedy reintroduced the aircraft into service.

John Boulding was part of the team assigned to examine every inch of the Comet for defects. He recalls:

> We spent three months examining the aircraft in great detail and couldn't find anything significantly wrong. By this time the engineers, who were sceptical about the Comet's abilities at the start, were now totally confident about what it could do. We had changed from having doubts and worries about the aeroplane to being totally confident in its abilities. We thought it was a great machine, even though it was now in trouble.
>
> The aircraft's designers gave us a long list of modifications to undertake. When it was allowed back into service we were sure that the Comet would once again prove itself. But disaster struck once again.

Despite sabotage theories appearing in the media, plenty of people still wanted to fly in the Comet and by April 1954 the aircraft was back in service. One of the BOAC aircraft was chartered to South African Airways for services from London to Johannesburg. On 7 April the aircraft had arrived in Rome for a scheduled refuelling stop when an Italian engineer discovered that thirty wing bolts had become loosened and the fault traced back to BOAC engineering at London Airport. After a long delay while the bolts were tightened, the aircraft continued on its journey with fourteen passengers and a crew of seven. Just minutes out of Rome, the aircraft disappeared from the radar screen killing all onboard. Comets were again removed from service.

Over 100 people in total had lost their lives flying in Comets and by 1954 the aircraft now had the worst safety record in civil aviation history. The aircraft's Certificate of Air Worthiness was officially removed and Comets were stranded on three continents. BOAC was forced to take some of its older, smaller and slower

Opposite: Aviation trade press advertisements for the Comet play up its commercial advantages. *(Author's collection)*

Hermes, Constellation and Stratocruiser aircraft out of mothballs and reintroduce them on long-haul routes. John Boulding says that the older planes kept BOAC in business until the Comet came back into the fleet and the Bristol Britannia was introduced: 'another plane which had more than its fair share of teething problems when it first arrived'.

Investigations continued and BOAC donated one of its Comets for destructive testing at the Royal Aircraft Establishment's investigation centre at Farnborough. Similarities from crash sites began to emerge. Sabotage theories were dismissed. Close internal examination of crash victims revealed similar types of injuries that could only have been caused through explosive decompression and that the Comet's fuselage was unable to withstand the pressure of flying. Minute investigations led accident investigators to believe that metal fatigue had affected the bodywork, causing the aircraft to blow apart while in flight. The fatigue could be specifically narrowed down to the corner of a window in the aircraft's cabin and two positions along the fuselage.

An official court of inquiry opened in October 1954 and sat for 22 days over a 5-week period under the direction of Lord Cohen. It published its report in February 1955, stating that exhaustive investigations had been carried out with a view to reconstructing the actual disasters. These investigations were described by Sir Lionel Heald, representing the Crown, as 'one of the most remarkable pieces of scientific detective work ever done'. It had included a novel method of testing a whole Comet immersed in a huge water tank and subjected to heavy pressures. In his report, Lord Cohen stated that he had 'unhesitatingly' reached the decision that the Elba disaster had been caused by the structural failure of the pressure cabin brought about by metal fatigue. Although it had been impossible to recover any appreciable wreckage from the second disaster, and thereby give a positive verdict on its cause in view of the similarity of circumstances, it was 'at least possible' that the cause of the Naples disaster had been the same.

In addition to water-tank pressure tests, another Comet, manned by more than twenty scientists, had carried out experimental flights for more than 100 hours under conditions as near as possible to those known to exist at the time of the crash. 'The accidents were not due to the wrongful act or default or to the negligence of any party or any person in the employment of any party', said Lord Cohen.

John Boulding said that a small number of aircraft engineers knew about metal fatigue but it was almost unknown to the wider circle of aviation professionals.

The Comet 1 remained grounded and a new version, known as the Comet 4, was announced containing major structural modifications highlighted by the crash investigations. In March 1955 BOAC announced plans to order twenty of the new aircraft for delivery in 1958 – but in the meantime Britain had no commercial jet aircraft in use and lost time as the United States forged ahead with its own jet-age plans.

The Comet made a terrific comeback. Over 100 went into service before the de Havilland production line closed in 1962. Most provided BOAC, BEA and several foreign airlines, plus the RAF Transport Command, with many years of excellent service. Many were successfully sold on to other airlines including Gatwick-based Dan

Hundreds of spectators stand on top of Heathrow's famous tunnel to watch the start of the London–New Zealand Air Race in 1956. *(Barry Dix collection)*

Air, which was still using the aircraft well into the 1970s. But the Comet air accidents made many foreign airlines nervous of purchasing British aircraft. American carriers, who had originally shown interest in the Comet, switched their orders to new home-grown jet aircraft taking shape at Boeing's production line near Seattle and the Douglas aircraft factory near Long Beach, California. The 130-passenger Boeing 707 Stratoliner and 125-passenger Douglas DC-8 were both successfully sold to US-based airlines and scores of others across the world, triggering off another transatlantic race with London Airport as the starting post for BOAC.

In October 1959, BOAC and Pan American went head-to-head on whose jet airliner would be first across the Atlantic. BOAC's Comet 4 was scheduled to fly from London to New York while Pan American's shining new Boeing 707 would fly to Paris. Who would be the winner? Did it really matter? Publicity people working for both airlines thought so and BOAC won the day when their Comet 4 touched down in New York minutes ahead of Pan American's Boeing 707 landing in Paris.

So while BOAC won the day, British aircraft manufacturers lost the race to produce the first truly successful passenger jet airliner to remain in continuous service with commercial airlines. For every new British airliner, there would always be an American rival.

The Bristol Britannia's rival was the Douglas DC-6, while the Vickers Viscount was forced to square up against the Lockheed Electra. In later years the Vickers VC-10 and de Havilland Trident found favour at home with BOAC and BEA plus a few other carriers, but were rejected as unsuitable by American companies. The story would be similar a decade later when Britain and France came together to produce the world's first supersonic passenger jet, the Concorde.

Whatever the aircraft type – British, American, French, Anglo-French, Dutch, Swedish or Russian made – they have all became familiar sights at London Airport during its first six decades as airlines continue to operate planes that they consider to be best suited for their needs. In today's dynamic and competitive world of aircraft production, market leaders remain America's Boeing and Britain through its role in the Airbus consortium, shared with France, Italy, Germany and Spain.

The Cold War was at its height in the 1950s, a period when the world's two great superpowers – the United States and the USSR – waged a continuous war of words which occasionally resulted in dirty deeds. Britain was often caught in the middle and despite fears of sometimes discovering 'a red under the bed', trade agreements between the UK and USSR continued.

By 1956, Russian airline Aeroflot had been operating a limited operation between Moscow and London Airport using a noisy Li-2 propliner, which carried a small number of business travellers plus staff working at the Soviet Embassy in London (each of which was suspected of being a spy). No tourists travelled on the flight as entry visas were impossible to obtain and the only people wanting to visit the Russian capital were trade unionists and members of the British Communist Party.

In March 1956, Aeroflot announced that it would be bringing a different aircraft to London on the 22nd. The airline said that instead of flying its usual Li-2 from Moscow, a jet designed by the legendary Russian aircraft designer Alexei Tupolev would be landing in London. Onboard the plane – a TU-104 – would be Colonel Ivan Serov, the USSR's top security chief for military intelligence, arriving to make sure that arrangements were satisfactory for an official visit later in the month of Communist Party first secretary, Nikita Khrushchev and Soviet premier Nikolai Bulganin.

Because the Comet had been grounded and America's Boeing 707 had still to be introduced into service, the arrival of Aeroflot's new aircraft in UK airspace marked the return of a commercial jet aircraft to London Airport – and no one quite knew what to expect. They were in for a shock.

Instead of the ancient and clapped-out Li-2 boneshaker, a slim and sleek silver-painted jetliner with a red flag decorated with a hammer and sickle on the tailplane was approaching the runway. A glass nosecone gave the game away that it had originally been designed for military use.

The Russians were eager for their new aircraft to be seen and the press had been invited to record its arrival and interview the sinister Colonel Serov. There was just one problem. Once it had landed, the TU-104 stood higher off the ground than any other aircraft using London Airport – including the Comet – and there were no passenger steps tall enough to reach the Russian aircraft's doorway. While the

For many years, Croydon was London's main airport and the main operating base of Imperial Airways. *(Author's collection)*

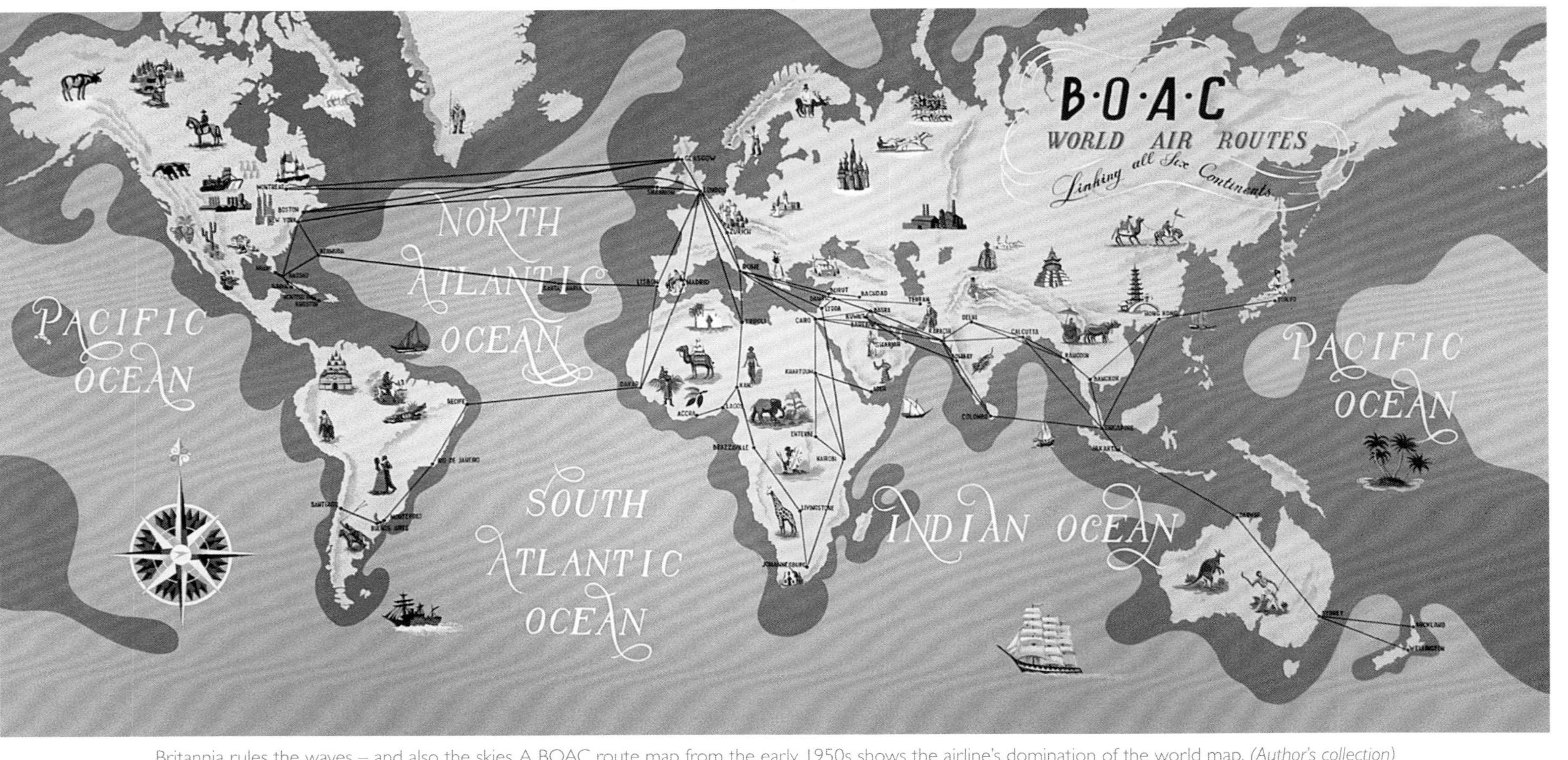

Britannia rules the waves – and also the skies. A BOAC route map from the early 1950s shows the airline's domination of the world map. *(Author's collection)*

Heathrow's famous landmark control tower, built in the 1950s and soon to close, after over half a century of service, to be replaced with a new one. *(Author's collection)*

Heathrow's new passenger terminal opened its doors for the first time in 1955 and allowed many airlines to move from the cramped and temporary accommodation they had used since 1946. *(Author's collection)*

'Welcome aboard.' A stewardess prepares to welcome passengers onboard a Caravelle jet aircraft at London Airport in the late 1950s. *(Author's collection)*

The day that the British Airports Authority began to run Heathrow and other airports was 1 April 1966. At that time 12.2 million travellers were passing through Heathrow. *(BAA (Heathrow) Archive)*

St George's Chapel is located underground and in the shadow of the Control Tower. *(BAA (Heathrow) Archive)*

Below: Pan American was the first airline to take delivery of a Boeing 747 Jumbo Jet. The airline brought the massive plane into Heathrow Airport for the first time in January 1970. The aircraft is pictured taking off for New York after operating the first service. *(Flo Kingdon collection)*

Heathrow Airport as seen from the air in the mid-1990s before the great debate about Terminal 5 had begun. *(BAA (Heathrow) Archive)*

Heathrow Terminal 3 – originally known as the Oceanic Terminal – has been modified, expanded and refurbished over the years to cope with the growing number of passengers travelling on long-haul flights. *(BAA (Heathrow) Archive)*

For over half a century a major sewage works – known as Perry Oaks – ran alongside the airport's western perimeter. The photograph shows the close proximity of the sewage plant to aircraft parking stands. Perry Oaks is now the site for Terminal 5. *(BAA (Heathrow) Archive)*

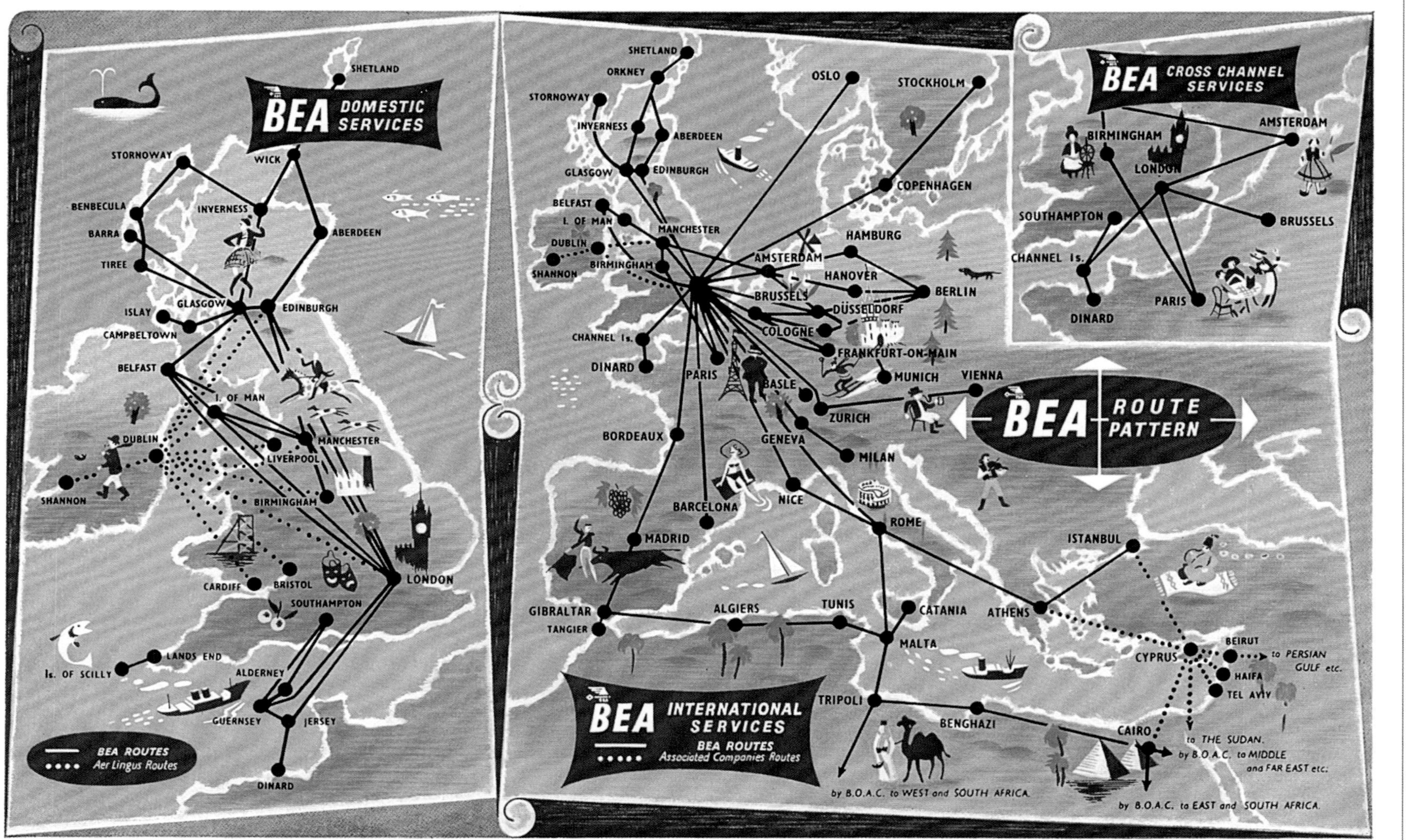

Areas of the world not served from Britain by BOAC were connected by BEA across the UK and Europe. *(Author's collection)*

Enjoy the luxurious lower-deck lounge on *The President:* double-decked "Strato" Clippers. Or choose *The Rainbow,* popular tourist service with giant "Super-6" Clippers. More flights, more often, direct to more cities in Europe by Pan Am!

You're on the most popular airline to EUROPE when you choose Pan American

10 times every day giant Pan American Clippers span the Atlantic

They've carried more passengers, 650,000 —and made more crossings, 44,500— than any other airline

You get the feeling the moment you board your Clipper* that Pan Am knows how to run an airline.

It's not alone the snap and precision of ground personnel, the superb airmanship of U.S. crews, the luxurious Clippers themselves, the frequency and convenience of flights—it's also the sure, understanding way in which you are treated, with hospitality, with friendliness, and with attentive consideration.

Attention to each passenger's needs, plus an unmatched record of air pioneering and leadership—that's what makes Pan Am the choice of experienced travelers.

Call your Travel Agent or Pan American.

*Trade-Mark, Reg. U. S. Pat. Off.

No change of plane to EUROPE from

New York, Boston, Philadelphia . . . and from Chicago and Detroit, starting April 30

Typical one-way fares from New York	RAINBOW	PRESIDENT
SHANNON	$261	$371
LONDON	290	400
PARIS	310	420
ROME	360	487
STOCKHOLM	356	466
LISBON	310	406

Fares, shown to nearest dollar and subject to government approval, are slightly less from Boston, slightly more from Phila., Chicago and Detroit (Chicago and Detroit, *RAINBOW* only)

More people fly to Europe by 

World's Most Experienced Airline

During the 1950s, airlines, including Pan American, traded on a luxury image to attract passengers on transatlantic services to London Airport. *(Author's collection)*

PAN AMERICAN STARTS FIRST JET

The No. 1 airline across the Atlantic welcomes you to a magic world of travel! Fares as low as 453^{60} round trip to London, 489^{60} to Paris . . . daily from New York.

Pan American carries more people across the Atlantic than any other two airlines combined

LONDON 6½ HOURS

PARIS 7 hrs.

No increase in minimum fares

ST IN LATIN AMERICA . . . FIRST 'ROUND THE WORLD

The first Jet Clippers that you will ride in are Boeing 707s, the most thoroughly flight-tested airliners ever to enter commercial service.

VICE TO EUROPE THIS FALL!

Pan Am's Jet Clippers* are the first transatlantic jet airliners. They are *pure* jets, a major advance over turbo-props. Four massive jet engines give you beautifully quiet, vibration-free comfort at 600 mph. Jet Clippers will offer the finest, fastest transatlantic service including new *economy* class at no increase in fares.

Coming: Jet Clipper service to Latin America, across the Pacific and 'round the world. For fall reservations, call your Travel Agent or one of the 53 offices of Pan Am in the U.S. and Canada. For a free, colorful, fact-filled Jet brochure, write: Pan American, Dept. 707, Box 1790, New York 17, N. Y. In Canada, P. O. Box 811, Toronto.

*Trade-Mark, Reg. U.S. Pat. Off.

PAN AMERICAN

WORLD'S MOST EXPERIENCED AIRLINE

Pan American was at the forefront of introducing new aircraft on transatlantic routes. In October 1958 the airline introduced sightseers at London Airport to their first glimpse of its new jet, the Boeing 707, which could fly from New York to London in six and a half hours. *(Author's collection)*

Pan American used Lockheed Constellation aircraft on New York–London routes until Boeing 707s were introduced in the late 1950s. *(Author's collection)*

Independent airline British Eagle was an early forerunner of today's low-cost airlines. Bankers withdrew their backing for the company in November 1968. *(Author's collection)*

After sixty years of continuous operation, the sun has yet to set on Heathrow Airport. *(BAA (Heathrow) Archive)*

March 1956 and the first Russian jet aircraft, a TU-104, touches down at London Airport. It took everyone by surprise. *(Author's collection)*

Comrade Colonel and his delegation remained in their seats looking down on a hoard of pressmen on the tarmac below, airport officials were dashing around trying to find something – a ladder perhaps – that could be used to get the Russian VIPs onto the apron.

Fortunately, a set of flexible steps used by BOAC aircraft engineers was found to be tall enough – just – to reach the aircraft doorway. They were shaky and only one passenger at a time could stand on them but they served their purpose.

When the door finally opened, Colonel Serov was first in the doorway. Wearing a huge greatcoat and fur hat, he stood at the top of the makeshift steps smiling broadly and proudly showing off a set of stainless steel false teeth.

'This beautiful plane is friendship plane', he told reporters. 'I come here in friendship. UK, USSR, let's be friends.'

After the Colonel's motorcade had whisked him away to Claridges, where Khrushchev and Bulganin would also be staying after arriving in Britain onboard a Soviet naval cruiser, the press were allowed to enter the new Russian jet to see if it looked just as good on the inside as it did on the outside.

Instead of discovering a luxuriously fitted aircraft interior, the press walked into something which one described as 'more like the inside of a second class Victorian railway carriage'. Draped over the seat backs and armrests were lace antimacassars – ornate covers that would have been more at home in Mr Khrushchev's Kremlin apartment. Ornate brass lamps with heavy shades were fitted to the walls making the plane look more like the corridor of a dubious hotel.

The reporters were delighted to discover a pair of double doors at either end of the passenger cabin. On opening them, a small ante-room was discovered containing a two-seater, red velvet upholstered settee where passengers could wait before entering yet another small room – the aircraft toilet; just two loos in the entire aircraft for fifty passengers and five crew.

Aeroflot officials who had remained onboard the aircraft were delighted with the media response, reading their excitement and popping flashbulbs as British approval of their beautiful new plane, which the Russians were hoping to sell to British airlines, who were in desperate need of a reliable jet aircraft.

The following day's newspapers were full of TU-104 pictures and stories asking readers if they could believe that inside this modern jet exterior was concealed a time capsule containing interior design dating back to the days of the Tsars.

However, the Russians had the last laugh. Although none of the aircraft were ever sold to Western nations, they served Aeroflot well for the next thirty years. Although the antimacassars and ornate lights eventually made way for more modern interiors, the settees remained in the toilet ante-room – usually surrounded by rattling crates of a drink Aeroflot claimed was lemonade but which passengers said tasted more like gunpowder.

There was to be one other major aircraft disaster at London Airport before the end of the 1950s. On 1 October 1956 a large group of special guests gathered in the VIP lounge to welcome the arrival back in Britain of the Avro Vulcan bomber, which the RAF had taken on a worldwide selling tour. The giant delta-wing bomber would not normally land at a commercial airport, but facilities for guests and the media at London Airport were deemed superior to those available elsewhere and the airport was chosen for its publicity value.

While VIPs enjoyed hospitality in their suite, a severe rainstorm lashed the tarmac. As the Vulcan began its approach to London Airport the crew was told about local weather conditions and reduced visibility. They were invited to divert elsewhere if they were unhappy about conditions at London Airport and it was confirmed that the Vulcan carried sufficient fuel to fly elsewhere.

An Avro Vulcan bomber crashed at London Airport in October 1956 during a heavy rainstorm. *(Author's collection)*

Onboard was Air Marshal Sir Harry Broadhurst, air officer commander-in-chief of RAF Bomber Command as co-pilot, a crew of three other RAF officers plus a representative of the aircraft manufacturer A.V. Roe.

Shortly after 10:00 a.m. and at a height of 1,500ft and 5 nautical miles from touch-down, the aircraft began its descent, talked down by a London Airport air traffic controller. It was agreed that once the Vulcan's altimeter reached 300ft it would still be possible to overshoot the runway and begin climbing again if weather conditions remained unsuitable.

While the weather was at its worst the Vulcan struck the tarmac, removing both undercarriage units and throwing the bomber's controls into confusion. The aircraft then rose up sharply to a height of between 200 and 300ft, totally out of control. An order was given to abandon the Vulcan and the Captain triggered his ejector seat. After repeating the order, the co-pilot also ejected. Both pilot and co-pilot must have realised when the order was given that owing to the low altitude neither they nor the other Vulcan occupants had little chance of escape and their own chances of survival were negligible. Seconds later the nose and starboard wing dropped and the Vulcan crashed into a field on the airport's edge. The crew that remained onboard plus the passenger all perished. Both the pilot and co-pilot who had ejected survived.

A court of inquiry found nothing to suggest any technical failure in the aircraft but concluded that the Captain made an error of judgement flying below the agreed 300ft altitude and that the air traffic controller should have warned the pilot of his proximity to the ground. There was later speculation that Air Vice-Marshal Broadhurst had ignored advice about diverting to another airport so as not to disappoint VIPs waiting to welcome the Vulcan home. It was rumoured that instead of travelling in the co-pilot's seat, Broadhurst was actually at the Vulcan's controls as it approached London Airport. This was never proven.

ELEVEN

This is the Show that *Must* Go On

THE NEW BRICK AND GLASS airport city in the centre of the runway triangle was nearing completion in April 1955 – and the Queen had promised to open it officially once finishing touches had been completed and the site cleared of builders and construction vehicles.

Taylor Woodrow, the main contractor, produced a special brochure for the occasion. It is worth quoting some of the sections here, if only to share some of the copywriter's enthusiasm for London Airport's new central area – known to staff as Skyport City.

> The tunnel at London Airport is the smooth, mysterious link between an old world and a new one. Beyond the tunnel, like a diamond set in a paste of emeralds, lies the streamlined capital of Britain's airways – precise, brilliant, compact. Here, inside a pattern of eight miles of runways, the administration, air traffic control and passenger handling buildings are fitted like a perfect jigsaw. Here, design and planning have been concerned even with the smallest details. This is London – London Airport Central. One of the major visible tokens of the resilience of twentieth century Elizabethan Britain.
>
> To the non-stop drama of the airport, the tunnel is the curtain raiser . . . ingeniously ventilated and subtly lit, the tunnel is itself a monument to British engineering.
>
> But the tunnel is only the beginning. The first thing that opens the motorist's eyes as he cruises up out of the tunnel into a new world, is an arresting two-storey, T-shaped building crowned by a nine-storey tower. This is the air traffic control building; and the control room with the sloping blue glass windows surmounts the tower – the electronic brain of the diamond city. From this tower every movement of every aircraft on the ground or in the London air is charted and controlled. . . . The fascinated visitor might be tempted to think of all this as the most magnificent clockwork toy in the world. But there is more to this than clockwork. And this is no toy.
>
> The air traffic control building was built to last – and also built to please. So it was constructed in steel framework encased in concrete, and the finishing touches were put to its outside walls with a pleasing combination of brick, stone and tiles. Like the other new London Airport buildings, it gives an enduring impression of elegance married to strength. And it introduces our visitors to the charm of English brick. . . .

> In the lower part of the tower: the management offices. In the left of the T, on the south side: the staff restaurants and kitchens. The design and decoration of the staff restaurants are enough, in themselves, to make appetite easy. A lavishness of height in the rooms, a generosity of space between tables, a superb acreage of window glass, an unashamed gaiety of colour – all of these the stuff of which relaxation is made. And they are the essential condiments of eating. Here, for a change, you eat surrounded by the twentieth century. And, however old fashioned you may think you are, you like it.

The control tower was something of a marvel. It contained under-floor heating, something unheard of in Britain during the early 1950s. Its offices were straight out of

HM the Queen arrives to open London Airport's new buildings in December 1955. *(Author's collection)*

an American movie – bright, spacious and modern. It was also said that, from the top, air traffic controllers could see Windsor Castle in one direction and the chimneys of Battersea Power Station in the other. The brochure continued:

> If the control tower is the electronic brain of the diamond city, the heart is the passenger handling building. To the passenger arriving in London by air for the first time in recent years, the elegant glass and stone gallery which runs the whole length of the building looks like a sudden piece of magic. This is London? This *is* London! This symphony of glass-walled footbridges, this gay and debonair pattern of blue and yellow is London's new front door.
>
> Walk into the central entrance hall, then walk up to the first floor. There you find yourself in something which could be the foyer of the grandest and most civilised of Grand Hotels. This is the main concourse, complete with shops, post office, buffet, car hire agencies, children's nursery and two hairdressing saloons.
>
> And so, outside again, where passengers in the lounges and waiting rooms look out through the long glass gallery and down upon a world of birds of passage. And where, from the terraced roof-garden 'waving base' friends and relatives wave their 'hullos' and 'goodbyes' to the passengers of the airlines of fourteen nations.
>
> The non-stop drama of London Airport is one of the most magnetic spectacles of the world of 1955. Played on a stage of 2,820 acres, with a cast of some 1,724,000 passengers – it is something which no conceivable Hollywood epic could contrive to emulate, either for scale or for the feeling of actuality. This is the show that *must* go on.
>
> The eastern apex building, which continues the airport's distinctive theme of brick, stone and glass, is designed to meet the needs of two distinct groups of people: those who help to make this spectacular show and those who come to watch it. That is to say, the aircraft crews and the operational staffs of the international airlines on one hand, and the spectators on the other.
>
> A staircase leads from the entrance hall up to the exhibition hall on the first floor; and this hall opens out into a large roof garden overlooking the airfield and aprons . . . wherever the spectator goes within the eastern apex building he has a seat in the stalls.
>
> So there it is – London Airport Central, one of the wonders of twentieth century Britain. Not all of it is completed yet. Some of it may not be completed until 1960. In the traditional British manner, London's airport was a quiet starter. Highly polished new built airports in Holland and Germany and France and elsewhere were glinting their welcome to air passengers for some years before London Airport was opened for operations. But when it is finally completed this airport may well prove to be the principal monument by which – for fulfilment of purpose, for distinction of design and for excellence of construction – British architecture and constructional engineering would choose to be judged by future generations. In fact, the whole face of London Airport is set fair towards the jet age future.
>
> Well might the visitor, who had been privileged to see the whole machinery of the airport, remark: 'The new London Airport is the proudest thing that has been built in Britain since the war.'

The Queen, with the Duke of Edinburgh, inaugurated the buildings in London Airport's shining new diamond city on 16 December 1955 and revealed that the Eastern Apex Building would be renamed the Queen's Building.

Her Majesty told invited guests: 'The inauguration of this great terminal today marks an important stage in the story of London Airport. In the ten years which have passed since the earliest development of the site, the airport has grown in size and in international fame. . . . We may say with pride that it ranks among the foremost in the world. Whatever form air travel may take in future, and we may be certain that striking changes lie ahead, London Airport will, I am sure, continue to grow in importance as one of the world centres of air traffic.'

The airport's new terminal enjoyed a traffic-free existence in 1955. *(Author's collection)*

The main passenger terminal, christened the Europa Building, would handle passengers and aircraft travelling to all parts of Europe. A special section at the western end would be used for domestic traffic and named the Britannic Building. Today the building is known as Terminal 2 and its concrete taxiways and aprons are located on the same spot where Richard Fairey had built his Great West Aerodrome two decades before.

Thanks to new aircraft and an ever-growing demand for air travel, airlines began to develop interesting new ways of flying to London from different parts of the world during the closing years of the 1950s.

In 1957, a new direct service from Los Angeles to London Airport was introduced by American airline TWA, flying over the North Pole in a Lockheed Constellation. This became the world's first non-stop flight from California to London, covering 5,500 miles in eighteen hours and thirty-two minutes and it created a new world endurance record for distance and time in the air for a civil airliner. Previously the journey had taken twenty-four hours, travelling via New York. TWA proudly boasted that the new route followed the 'great circle' flying 150 miles south of the magnetic Pole, crossing northern Canada and the Hudson Bay, passing the southern tip of Greenland, across Ireland and on to London Airport. Today's transatlantic airlines, flying to California in modern Boeing aircraft, still follow the same polar route, covering the journey in ten hours or less.

The first American jet aircraft to enter commercial service made its passenger debut in August 1958. Originally named the Stratoliner and later renamed the Boeing 707, the aircraft was to become a legendary American icon. The first airline to use the plane, Pan American, planned to use it on its prestigious New York–London routes from the beginning and in September 1958, just one month after it had entered commercial flying, the Boeing 707 touched down at London Airport on a training mission for the company's air crews – and without passengers. The aircraft would also be measured for noise as it arrived and departed from the airport, following serious concerns about the din the new jet might create once it entered regular service.

Boeing also hoped that the 707's London visit would help persuade BOAC that the American-built jet would fit perfectly into the airline's fleet. It had the opposite effect. Days before the 707 touched down in London, BOAC announced that its own newly delivered British-built Comet 4 aircraft would be used on transatlantic routes from October – three weeks before Pan American received certification to fly passengers over the Atlantic in 707s, on routes from New York to Paris. BOAC claimed the distinction of operating the first jet transatlantic service by flying two Comet 4s simultaneously from London to New York and New York to London days ahead of their American rivals.

BOAC's ability to quickly exploit this opportunity stole some of Pan American's thunder by using a jet aircraft on the route. It would be another five weeks before Pan American had sufficient 707s in its fleet to offer a daily service between New York and London, by which time BOAC had established itself as the premier transatlantic jet operator. However, once passengers had the choice of flying with either jet operator,

Pan American won the day. The 707 flew faster than the Comet 4, it carried more passengers and the service was sold through an aggressive advertising campaign that emphasised speed, comfort – and low air fares.

The advertising campaign worked. By 1958, the British public were in love with everything American, thanks to the glamour created by its movies, television shows, rock 'n' roll music, people, casual clothing, wide open spaces, thrilling cities, laid-back lifestyle – and fabulously designed jet aircraft. Over 19,000 passengers flew across the Atlantic to London and Paris with Pan American during the Boeing 707's first six weeks of operation, compared with nearly 4,000 on BOAC's Comet services.

BOAC realised that while its Comet 4 and Bristol Britannia aircraft were excellent pieces of equipment, they were no match for the Boeing 707. Dozens of airlines had placed orders for the aircraft and the media began to declare that unless BOAC also signed up with Boeing, the state airline would be left behind. In response, the airline

Introducing the Bristol Britannia – the 'Whispering Giant' – which BOAC used successfully on long-haul routes for many years. *(Author's collection)*

declared that it was 'satisfied that our fleet requirements for well into the 1960s are already met by the [British-built] aircraft on order'.

A year later BOAC had changed its mind and obtained permission from the government to place an order for fifteen Boeing 707s, costing £2.9 million each. There was some consolation for Britain's aviation industry – the engines would be provided by Rolls-Royce. BOAC's first Boeing 707 entered service on London Airport–New York routes on 28 April 1960.

The arrival of American aircraft was similar to the cavalry riding over the hill to rescue the wagon train. BOAC desperately needed a new prestige route service and in April 1959 inaugurated a round-the-world operation. Introduction of the 707s and new Comet 4s freed up some of its gas-turbine-powered Bristol Britannia turboprops to perform the task. The global operation was, in fact, the joining up of two different services travelling around the world in different directions and meeting up in Tokyo, where passengers swapped aircraft for the rest of their chosen route. Eastbound services travelled from London Airport via Frankfurt, Beirut, Karachi, Delhi, Calcutta, Bangkok and Hong Kong before landing in Tokyo; while the westbound service travelled via New York, San Francisco and Honolulu to Tokyo.

The round-the-world service was offered twice weekly in both directions – and was truly a long haul, taking three and a half days to fly eastbound routes and four and a half days to fly the route westbound. Not only were there stops every few hours in either direction, there was also a twelve-hour layover in San Francisco and a twenty-four-hour stopover in Hong Kong.

Only certain parts of the route were a success for BOAC and as the airline moved towards the 1960s financial problems experienced by the airline and London Airport began to rear their heads in a very public way.

TWELVE

Time for a Great Day Out at the Queen's Building

NEW TERMINAL BUILDINGS at the airport's centre relieved the old temporary prefabs on the north side of 60 per cent of its passengers. Now that the old terminal was less congested, airlines were able to build their own private lounges for increasing numbers of travellers prepared to pay higher fares to fly first class to long-haul destinations in North America, Africa and Asia. It would be another six years before passengers using the terminal would be given a shining new glass and chrome terminal of their own within the diamond city.

BOAC engineer Don Parry recalls the relaxed style of working at the old terminal:

> In the mid-1950s I was posted to BOAC's Britannia fleet. At that time crews reported for duty an hour and a half before departure. Most of us arrived early in order to grab a pre-flight meal at the adjacent aircrew mess, where Brown Windsor Soup was a staple. It was a gentle start to a trip that allowed everyone to meet and get to know each other. There was no designated crew car park and those fortunate enough to have a vehicle parked it on the side of the road or on a patch of spare ground. There was never any difficulty on securing a spot.
>
> As the flight engineer, I would then walk over to the engineering office (a hut, actually) to check on the state of the aircraft and then you strolled over to your plane, which nestled neatly among the Stratocruisers, Constellations and DC-6s bearing the great names of aviation, like Pan American, TWA and the exotically named Panair do Brazil.
>
> In retrospect it all seemed so relaxed. The refuelling bowser was always available and not in a rush to go somewhere else. No problems with air traffic control take-off slots. We just called the control tower when we were ready to start. Departure was simple; we just taxied out and took off. There was rarely more than one aircraft ahead of us and we had all the convenience of a swift, rolling start out on the runway.
>
> Sometimes my wife would accompany me to see me off. I never recall her not having a seat in the north-side terminal coffee shop. I would then leave to go to the engineering office and she would pass through the restaurant to the small enclosed viewing areas at the rear. As the Britannia taxied out, we could offer mutual waves. Innocent days, gone forever. No wonder I have a degree of sympathy for today's crews. Commercial aviation's romantic phase is long past.

The Queen's Building and its public roof gardens became Britain's top visitor attraction following its opening in 1955. *(Author's collection)*

By the spring of 1956, visitors watching the non-stop procession of the world's airliners had turned the roof garden above the Queen's Building into London's most visited attraction. The admission price of 1s for adults and 6*d* for children generated thousands of pounds in revenue for the airport and roof gardens admission soon outrivalled Windsor Castle, Madam Tussauds and the Tower of London.

Everybody wanted to watch aircraft take off and land from the roof of the Queen's Building, which in its first year of opening attracted around 1 million visitors. It offered all the ingredients of a great family day out in the second half of the 1950s and throughout the 1960s. First, there was the experience of travelling through the famous tunnel (well worth the 2*d* bus fare alone) and climbing off at the entrance to the Queen's Building. Then came the pleasure of climbing the staircase and passing fantastic, ultra-modern aircraft pictures and Festival of Britain-inspired drawings on the walls. And then out onto the spacious roof gardens, built to handle 10,000 people –

often attracting that many spectators in the space of a single day. From here visitors enjoyed a vast panorama of the airport with wonderful views of aircraft taking off, landing and taxiing, passengers walking to and from Viscounts and Vanguards, Caravelles, Elizabethans, Dakotas, Comets and all kinds of strange-looking aircraft flying to London from the Soviet Union, Hungary, Czechoslovakia and Poland.

The friendly invasion of the Queen's Building represented a special day out for visitors happy to dress up for the occasion. Men put on suits and ties, wives dressed in their best frocks and hats while children wore school uniforms. It was as if each and every visitor wanted to be mistaken for a passenger instead of a day-tripper, despite

A trip to the Queen's Building roof gardens represented a special day out for visitors who were prepared to dress up for the occasion. Men put on suits and ties, wives dressed in their best frocks while children wore school uniforms. It was as if each and every visitor wanted to be mistaken for a rich airline passenger. *(Author's collection)*

The chic 1950s-style bar and café area in the new passenger terminal. *(BAA (Heathrow) Archives)*

Passenger escalators and baggage conveyors were a key feature of the new passenger terminal. *(BAA (Heathrow) Archives)*

packed lunches and picnic hampers brought along in case the Queen's Building cafés and restaurants proved too costly.

Day-trippers came to London Airport from across the country, prepared to sit in a stuffy charabanc for four or five hours in order to spend just a short time on the Queen's Building, or climb onto another coach for a guided airport tour, before driving home again to Wales, Yorkshire or Devon. They also came from towns and villages surrounding the airport. Vincent Vere from Richmond upon Thames, Surrey spent two years as a BOAC visitor guide. He remembers:

> I was escorting a coach full of visitors around the airport's perimeter road and proudly announced to passengers that if they looked to their right they could see a runway which was made in the late 1940s and a lady at the back of the bus said, 'Yes I know, it used to be part of my back yard.'

Staff working for BOAC were encouraged to bring families and friends to the airport on Sundays for free guided tours. Former employee, Don Parry, remembers: 'The visits allowed us to show our nearest and dearest the airport in action. They always ended with an excellent afternoon tea back in the airline's headquarters known as the "Kremlin" – a utilitarian designed building which a newspaper once claimed had been named because it reflected the number of communist trade unionists who worked inside.'

The Ministry of Transport and Civil Aviation claimed in 1956 that the 'Queen's Building expresses the recognition by London Airport of the new role international airports must accept. For today, in addition to organising the dispatch and reception of passengers and freight by air to and from the most distant parts of the earth, a great airport must be prepared to be treated as, in itself, a place of interest.'

Former Flying Officer Flo Kingdon, who had served with the WRAF in the 1950s, including a spell as a broadcaster with the British Forces Network in Egypt and Cyprus, was one of two commentators on the roof of the Queen's Building. Like hundreds of others returning to Civvy Street after serving in the forces, Flo needed a job.

> Just after coming out of the WRAF, I attended a course designed to help officers re-settle into civilian life. I was there alongside Group Captains, Wing Commanders, Flight Officers and other ranks. One morning, during a tea break, we took it in turns to look through a copy of *The Times* lying on a table. We were searching through the appointments section for our first jobs in Civvy Street. Someone saw a position advertised at London Airport for a public enclosure commentator on the Queen's Building and said: 'You can do that, that's just the job for you', so I applied. I'd been turned down for other jobs and was surprised to be invited to an interview with the Ministry for Civil Aviation in Berkeley Square. They asked me how familiar I was with civil aircraft. I'd been used to RAF military aircraft for the past few years, so told

The new airport terminal was spacious and well lit – and totally different in style to the old temporary terminal just one mile away. *(BAA (Heathrow) Archives)*

them I didn't see any problem recognising civil aircraft. But they turned me down. And then a couple of days later they contacted me to say that the successful applicant had backed out and was I still interested? A week later I was in the glass-walled commentary box on the roof garden viewing area on top of the Queen's Building telling crowds of visitors about aircraft taking off and landing.

Former Flying Officer Flo Kingdon became one of the first public commentators on the Queen's Building roof gardens. *(Author's collection)*

My colleague was a man called Stan Little, a natural entertainer who always appeared in pantomimes at Christmas time. He was the airport's first public enclosure commentator and we took it in turns to do the job, often doubling up on busy weekends. It wasn't unusual to work ten-hour long days.

Those were great days. We used to get information about aircraft movements from a daily schedule which told us what flights would be arriving and departing, times they would be moving in and out, and the type of aircraft used. We also spoke regularly on the phone with the control tower who would alert us when aircraft were approaching ready to land or preparing for take-off. A typical commentary might go like this: 'And if you look over to your left, you will see a BOAC Bristol Britannia arriving on runway number five from Montreal. This British-built airliner has four turbo-prop engines and can carry up to 149 passengers, depending on its series. It can fly for up to 5,000 miles at a cruising speed of 325mph.'

The public lapped it up and our commentaries probably created a desire to travel by air with more people than many advertising campaigns. People looked down from the Queen's Building and saw the first members of the jetset boarding aircraft. Naturally, they wanted to be down there on the tarmac with them, too – and 10 years later, many were doing exactly that.

We were also responsible for telling the public about any celebrities who might be onboard aircraft. I'd tell the public that on the BEA Viscount directly in front is the film star Diana Dors, and hundreds of people would drop their telescopes and sandwiches and rush to the railings to wave and try to get a glimpse of her. Most celebrities were very good and would usually look up and give the spectators a nice big wave. Some might even blow them a kiss.

I recall an occasion when an Air India Boeing 707 jet was unable to lower its nose wheel and attempted to land on runway 28-right. I was aware of the problem, but didn't immediately tell the spectators in case it managed to land normally. I held my breath as it got closer and sure enough, sparks and smoke flew in all directions as it scraped along the runway and out of my field of vision. I then told the public: 'Probably some of you might have noticed that the aircraft just landed has experienced a few nose wheel problems and our airport emergency services have the problem under control. Now the next plane arriving in front of you will be….'

I worked as a commentator for nine years and had a wonderful time. People were very polite and well behaved, although plane spotters often used to come and knock on the window and ask dozens of questions about what planes might be landing in the next six hours.

If anyone got bored watching the aircraft and listening to the commentaries, there was a small children's playground, a paddling pool, a souvenir shop, a sunken garden and there were easy chairs and coin-in-the-slot telescopes. If it rained, there was plenty of cover. If it was hot, it was a safe place for schoolchildren to be on a warm school summer holiday day out, armed with a duffle bag containing a sandwich box, bottle of pop, pair of binoculars and a pencil and notebook to write down aircraft numbers. This breed became known as 'aircraft spotters' and hundreds – mostly boys aged between 12 and 16 – would pour out of double-decker buses and invade the Queen's Building for eight hours at a time before going home for tea. They would be back again the following day, out of their mothers' way, out of trouble, out of harm and hungry to see aircraft dropping in from all over the globe, dreaming of the day when they, too, would become passengers or – better still – sit behind the controls of a Comet, Britannia or Super Constellation. The Queen's Building is probably responsible for inspiring many young people to apply for jobs with airlines or aspire to travel to far-flung places. The roof gardens and spectator balconies were places where dreams were made, careers planned and excitement about aircraft and travel generated.

The Queen's Building allowed visitors to get up close to aircraft from all over the world. Pictured are a BEA DC-3 Dakota and the building behind – with the BOAC poster – which is the airport's oldest building, Fairey Aviation's original Great West Aerodrome hangar, later used by the airport's fire service. It has now been demolished. *(Heathrow Visitors Centre)*

By 1959, 1 million annual visitors were paying to visit the roof gardens. By the late 1980s this had dwindled to just a few thousand plane spotters. When the Queen's Building finally closed its doors to visitors in the early '80s, after the airport authorities (quite correctly) considered it to be the perfect place from which to launch a terrorist attack on aircraft, the roof gardens had become a tatty version of their former selves. Watching aeroplanes was no longer a novelty. In an age where the public uses planes in the same way as the London Underground, the airport was no longer a place for a great day out. New passenger piers and building extensions had also begun to obscure many of the perfect views once enjoyed by visitors. Now, die-hard aircraft spotters preferred to watch planes from the rooftops of public car parks or from positions beneath the flight path.

The completed central area showing the new passenger terminal (right) and the Queen's Building and roof gardens. *(Barry Dix collection)*

'Wish you were here at London Airport?' A typical postcard from the airport in the late 1950s. *(Author's collection)*

But for millions of visitors during the heady days of the late '50s and '60s, the Queen's Building was a magical and wonderful place, remembered with affectionate nostalgia for great days gone by at London Airport. . . .

THIRTEEN

THE SWINGING '60s

Flying Finances and Britain's New Front Door, Yeah, Yeah, Yeah!

IN AUGUST 1961, Anthony Thornycroft, the latest politician to stand in shoes owned by the Ministry of Aviation, told Parliament that the Conservative government 'is determined that British airports should pay their way'. He added: 'We have been seeking to put our airports on a commercial basis; we don't regard them as part of the welfare state.' For years the airports had been running at a loss trying to keep up with the level of money invested in them. The worst offender was London Airport. The cost of creating the airport in the first place followed by massive investments, building the new central area, meant that it would be years before it would ever recover its costs and go into profit.

Former Chairman of the British Airports Authority (BAA), Sir Peter Masefield – who began his professional career working for Richard Fairey's aircraft-building company – recalls: 'The [history of] British airports had been an appalling catalogue of costly and time-consuming public inquiries, decisions deferred, decisions overturned, decisions that were obviously mistaken – and seen to be so at the time – and golden opportunities missed. We British have a history of dragging our decisions for as long as possible, as if time and money were unimportant.'

In 1959 the government considered handing airports serving the capital over to an independent body and published a white paper two years later in June 1961. The Airports Authority Bill was presented to Parliament on 6 November 1964 and the first BAA meeting took place just a year after that. The day that BAA actually began to run the airports was 1 April 1966 – 'on April Fool's Day, of course', remembers Sir Peter. At that time, 12.2 million travellers annually were passing through Heathrow.

BAA inherited a bureaucratic and loss-making airport system and, in addition to Heathrow, it took over the management of Gatwick, Stansted and Prestwick Airport in Scotland. Sir Peter claims the airports had suffered under poor management for years 'and the only directive handed down by the government was that we should run the airport properly, consulting with local residents but not interfering with navigation services'. In reality, the Masefield team had to become familiar with the airports and their problems, introduce new operating procedures 'appropriate to a harsh new commercial environment', find and equip offices, recruit staff and decide endless details of future policy.

An army of opponents tried to block every move and Sir Peter remembers the outrage when it was announced that he would be BAA's first Chairman who was perceived as 'pro-aviation', which was considered a bad thing. 'Back in the 1830s a vociferous minority tried to stop the railways', he notes in his memoirs, *Flight Path*.

It was not only airports that were in serious financial trouble. In 1963 a government white paper, called *The Financial Problems of BOAC*, set out plans for turning the airline's fortunes around and extend government powers to make further loans to finance deficits on revenue accounts.

BOAC defended its poor performance by stating that 'the corporation could not be purely commercial'. It said that, where possible, it had tried to buy British aircraft and help the industry build new airliners. The corporation claimed 'it was completely wrong that it should be expected to do something which was not commercial and yet get nothing for it and bloody crazy that when the airline had lost money it should be expected to go on paying interest on that money until kingdom come'.

The truth was that while BOAC was a prestige international airline, it was in debt up to it tail fins. Between 1946 and 1951, the airline enjoyed a monopoly on routes from London Airport to 'the colonies' and created favourable partnerships on routes linking Commonwealth nations. But the corporation's costs were abnormally high – mainly the result of flying wartime aircraft adapted for civil use during the late 1940s – and had received £32 million in grants from the exchequer during these years.

Despite the Comet disasters in 1952/3 and subsequent purchase of Boeing 707s, the corporation showed a profit between 1952 and 1956 but made a loss of over £80 million in subsequent years. The airline attributed this to the independence of many colonies that had started their own airlines, the cost of introducing new aircraft into the fleet, investments in associate companies, and internal organisation and management costs.

There was talk of a merger between BOAC and BEA. The two airlines could combine common functions in engineering, catering and some short-haul routes. One airline could also act as a 'feeder' for the other. BOAC admitted that this would not solve its immediate problems and BEA 'felt that any merger would destroy our singleness of purpose and *esprit de corps*'. Staff from both airlines breathed a huge collective sigh of relief for the next decade.

In 1959/60, BOAC employed 191,131 staff. The following year this had risen to 20,787 and by 1962/3 21,686 people were employed by the airline. In order to claw money back, BOAC sold its 15 per cent equity in the Hong Kong airline Cathay Pacific, 40 per cent holding in Ghana Airways, 16 per cent share in Nigeria Airways and 48 per cent share in the Lebanese airline MEA. It released its 90 per cent shareholding in the Caribbean airline BWIA (British West Indies Airways) for just £520,000 while at the same time losing a managerial contract to run Kuwait Airways.

It would take BOAC over a decade before it returned to profit, by which time it had finally merged with BEA, axed hundreds of jobs and non-profit-making routes, and launched itself on the London Stock Exchange.

The old and 'temporary' prefabricated terminal buildings on the north side of London Airport were an embarrassment to the thirteen airlines using them at the end of 1961. But it didn't matter. In November of that year they would finally start to close the old buildings down for good – although they would remain standing for several more years, used as a base for the airport's cargo operations. Most of the terminal's furniture, fixtures and fittings also went into the skips. They had been installed at the end of the 1940s and now looked shabby, faded and as out of date as Avro Lancastrians, as Britain entered the exciting new decade of promise dubbed 'the swinging '60s'.

On 13 November 1961, BOAC and some of its associated airlines set up shop in their gleaming new home – a building again designed by Frederick Gibberd – but instead of using red brick for his terminal, the architect used steel, glass and marble. Dubbed 'Britain's new front door', it was known to the rest of the world as the Oceanic terminal. Other long-haul airlines would follow BOAC through the tunnel over the next few months at the rate of one new airline every few weeks, until the move was complete in March 1962.

The last remaining airlines moved out of the temporary north-side passenger building to a new terminal – called Oceanic – in 1961. The new building, built from glass and marble, housed all long-haul airlines operating through the airport. *(Barry Dix collection; Flo Kingdon collection)*

Like the Control Tower, Europa terminal and Queen's Building, the new building was located on the inside of the runway triangle at its south-west corner and on the exact spot where a small settlement called Heath Row had stood just fifteen years before. The Oceanic terminal was built for international jetsetters: passengers who turned up at the airport in their best clothes, carrying expensive luggage and passing over large tips to airport porters. It was rectangular in shape, 430ft by 55ft and designed to handle several thousand passengers each hour of the day.

Built at a cost of £3 million, the terminal was a modern, fashionable and brightly lit building with marble floors, open-plan staircases, buffet-style restaurants, cocktail bars – including a famous one known as the Tavern in the Sky – shops selling duty-free goods, newspapers and London souvenirs.

Before opening its doors to passengers, its exterior was used in a film called *The VIPs*, starring Richard Burton, Elizabeth Taylor, Orson Welles and Margaret Rutherford plus a host of other international performers. The plot involved a mixed bag of travellers passing through the new terminal but stranded by fog. The interior of the new building was accurately re-created on a sound stage at nearby Pinewood Studios where the sound of jets taking off and landing would not get in the way of filming. Playing the part of a young Brenard airport reporter attempting to interview the Orson Welles character was a young man who would later become one of television's best-known faces. His name was David Frost.

The new terminal was uncomfortably hot in summer and freezing cold in winter and no amount of maintenance could solve the problem. And then, in the 1980s, when the terminal had been open for over twenty years, a refurbishment programme began which revealed a 1960s tile-cutting machine had been left deep inside the building's labyrinth of utility ducts and was blocking the heating and air-conditioning vent. Suddenly, temperatures inside the building began to improve for the first time since 1961.

One of the terminal's most famous landmarks was a group of twelve chandeliers that graced the ceiling above the check-in area. Each light fitting hung from a steel cable attached to a large winding mechanism which was located in the ceiling cavity. Engineers would unwind and gently lower chandeliers to the ground for cleaning and maintenance. On one occasion, maintenance men were attempting to lower one of the chandeliers and could not understand why it refused to descend. On further investigation it was discovered that the wheel mechanism controlling the light fitting had become partially jammed. Engineers, however, failed to notice the steel cable gently unwinding in great coils. Suddenly the chandelier dropped at great speed towards engineers on the ground below. They scattered in all directions, being chased by forty bouncing 100-watt lamp bulbs. Fortunately, the chandelier reached the end of its travels about 2ft above the terminal floor. The engineers spent the rest of their shift sweeping up thousands of tiny fragments of glass. They all lived to tell the tale.

The floor of the terminal's dedicated car park was originally laid with an unusual coating – peanut shells. Partly as a low-cost experiment and partly as a political gesture towards an East African country, someone in a high place had the bright idea that the shells would make an ideal surface if held in place with ex-railway sleepers. The idea proved to be a disaster and motorists using the car park hated the idea – especially ladies wearing high-heel or open-toe shoes. The English weather eventually made the porous surface wet and soggy and before long the entire surface was ruined and substituted with concrete.

The Oceanic terminal was always busy, and the number of passengers passing through was swelled by meeters and greeters plus hundreds of local people to whom the airport was a prime source of evening entertainment. As night fell, entire families would pile into their cars and drive through the tunnel from nearby towns, park for free and go into the terminal to 'people watch'. Here was a rare chance to see real Arabs wearing traditional dishdasha robes, dainty Japanese ladies in kimonos, Africans and Asians wearing a variety of strange-looking hats and turbans and tall Texans who appeared even taller in their 'good old boy' cowboy boots and Stetsons.

The visitors also came to the terminal to enjoy 'frothy coffee' and American-style muffins at the snack bar. They, too, wanted to be mistaken for international jetsetters and by mingling with different nationalities in the terminal that is exactly what they became for an hour or two every evening. And you never knew who you might also catch sight of in the Oceanic terminal – a famous film star, a millionaire, Miss World . . . or your next-door neighbour.

After the airlines had moved out of the north-side shanty town, all that was left of the original airport complex were the offices and warehouses forming the airport's cargo terminal, a maintenance department and a scattering of two-storey offices used by airlines and other commercial companies.

Years before, Bill Brenard had moved his newsroom and photographic darkroom from one of the primitive ex-military caravans to one of the former residential houses along the Bath Road – known as Fern Villas – and turned it into editorial offices. A former fish and chip shop next door was converted into a darkroom, and its manager, Geoff Matthews, swore that he could still smell cod frying well into the 1960s.

A new airport telephone centre, called the Skyport Exchange, was also opened along the Bath Road and every airport company was assigned a number with the prefix SKY. Brenard's news agency somehow acquired the unique number of SKY 1234, while the airport switchboard ended up with SKY 4321. There was further confusion when Harrods, the famous Knightsbridge store, was assigned the telephone number of SLO (as in SLOane) 1234. Every day, scores of elderly and short-sighted ladies would mistakenly misdial the number and instead of talking to Harrods ended up speaking to newsdesk staff working for Brenard's. On slow news days, young news staff would take advantage of this by answering the phone and pretending to be the store's lady's foundation underwear department or a non-English-speaking person in the food hall. Neither Brenard's nor Harrods would give up their prestige telephone numbers, creating hours of endless fun for the young reporters and endless confusion for lady telephone users in Middle England.

Two large and specially designed American-style airport hotels had also been opened along the airport's perimeter on the Bath Road. Largest was the 160-room Skyways Hotel which was so popular that within a year of opening a further 100 rooms were added. The hotel boasted that it offered a swimming pool, was

The Skyways Hotel was one of the airport's first American-style hotels to be built along the Bath Road. It became world famous after movie star Sophia Loren's jewels were stolen from her room. *(Author's collection)*

The Ariel Hotel takes shape, along the Bath Road at Harlington Corner, rising above the Coach and Horses pub, now long gone. *(Barry Dix collection)*

soundproof and that every room was equipped with a television and a telephone – something almost unheard of in a British hotel in the early 1960s. The Skyways Hotel also offered guests 'the longest upholstered bar in the country'. This, however, was not its main claim to fame. One of the first VIP guests to stay at the hotel was the Italian film star Sophia Loren whose jewellery was stolen from her room while she took dinner in the restaurant. None of Sophia's jewels, necklaces, tiaras and earrings was ever recovered. 'I shall never stay at this hotel again', Sophia told a Brenard's reporter. 'Miss Loren should have placed her valuables in the hotel safe,' said the manager.

The second hotel was a circular building close to the telephone exchange and called the Ariel. A joke circulating around the airport was that when everyone was asleep in the hotel's bedrooms, their feet all met in the middle.

The Ariel Hotel was the second major airport hotel – famous for its circular construction which some said had been influenced by the design of London's Royal Albert Hall. *(Author's collection)*

By the end of 1962, London Airport was handling 6.1 million annual passengers. Since its opening sixteen years before, 41.6 million passengers had flown in and out of the airport. By the end of 1963, 1 million passengers would be passing through the airport every month. In 1966 Heathrow had established its position as fourth in the world in terms of passengers and seventh in terms of aircraft movements. This was a boom time for mass passenger travel as more people around the world travelled farther afield for holidays and to conduct business.

Unless they were scared of flying, anyone who was anyone in the world of show business, sport or current affairs eventually found themselves at London Airport. The same applies today. But in the 1960s the passengers everyone wanted to see were four young Liverpudlians who had taken the music world by storm – the Beatles. John, Paul, George and Ringo had already passed through the airport several times prior to their return to England following a sensational visit to America in February 1964. In the US the group had appeared on Ed Sullivan's television show. A few months before, Sullivan and his wife were checking in at the Oceanic building for a flight home to New York and heard the sound of screaming coming from the other end of the terminal. They saw dozens of hysterical teenage girls running through the building, chased by police. When the poker-faced American TV presenter asked an airline check-in girl what the problem might be, he was told that the Beatles were travelling from the airport that day. 'Who are the Beatles?' asked Sullivan. Four months later, the Beatles flew from the same terminal to appear on his show.

Cartoonist David Langdon's comment on aircraft noise at London Airport and the recent return to the UK of the Beatles – and personally signed by each member of the 'Fab Four'. *(Flo Kingdon collection)*

The pop group's return to London has become part of the airport's history. It was deemed so important that it was transmitted 'live' on television. Nearly 4,000 female fans descended on the airport to catch a glimpse of their idols. Queen's Building commentator Flo Kingdon, who later went on to be an airport public relations officer and part of the Queen's Building management team, remembers the day:

> Fans began to arrive at the airport early in the morning and immediately caused problems when they began to gather inside the terminal building. The police decided to divert them all towards the Queen's Building where they could be better contained. Many of them didn't want to leave the terminal, where they thought they would have a chance to reach out and touch one of the Beatles and several became rather hysterical and had to be taken to the airport's medical room.
>
> Once the kids arrived on the roof gardens, I began to assure them over the loudspeakers that this was by far the best place to see the 'Fab Four'. Pan American planned to taxi the aircraft – a Boeing 707 – around to the tarmac directly in front of the Queen's Building instead of Terminal 3.
>
> The pandemonium began all over again as soon as the aircraft approached the runway. Girls were fainting, weeping, climbing on top of walls and seats and I began to be concerned that there might be an accident. But once the aircraft taxied around the corner and came to a standstill, the kids were given a fantastic grandstand view of all four Beatles as they appeared in the aircraft doorway. The trouble was that as soon as the aircraft door opened and the Beatles appeared,

everyone surged forward to get a better look and part of a wall collapsed. It could have been a disaster, but fortunately no one was seriously hurt. The Beatles waved to everyone from the aircraft steps and never stopped waving, even when they reached the tarmac. This was at the height of what was known as 'Beatlemania' and the screaming was deafening. I don't think anybody could hear my commentary that day. Today, whenever you see TV documentary programmes about the Beatles, they always show this famous airport arrival.

Nine cars were damaged by hysterical Beatles fans at London Airport that day and the Beatles' management generously settled all insurance claims. Such was the power of publicity for the group – and also for Pan American – that television and newspaper stories about the London Airport arrival reached all four corners of the world.

When the Beatles flew out of the airport with TWA the following year, each member of the group was presented with a special red airline bag containing their names and the airline's logo. One of the bags was recently sold at auction in the United States for $25,000.

There would be many other pop star welcomes at London Airport throughout the 1960s and '70s – the Beach Boys, the Osmonds, David Cassidy – when the Queen's Building would again be pressed into service as the best possible viewing point for fans to see their idols. Teenage fan worship still exists, but nothing like it did in the swinging '60s when all you needed was love, love, love and anyone could fly with Lucy in the sky – with diamonds.

London Airport entered the 1960s by handling over 5 million travellers. By the end of the decade this had risen to around 15 million. British airlines using the airport used the biggest, fastest – and often the noisiest – aircraft to transport record numbers of passengers in and out of 'swinging London'.

In November 1963, BOAC introduced the British-made VC-10 into its fleet and began phasing out Comets and Britannias on its eastern and African routes. The aircraft, as much a child of the '60s as Carnaby Street and the Cavern, was built at Vickers' manu-facturing base in Weybridge. It was designed to compete with American jets which, by now, had set the standards for international air travel.

The VC-10 was described by BOAC as 'an exciting new shape in the sky and the most advanced airliner BOAC has ever brought into service. . . . It is a quiet, smooth and comfortable plane. With its clean sweptback wings and smooth engine nacelles snuggling close to the fuselage beneath a high tailplane, the sleek lines of the VC-10 convey an impression of purposeful energy. . . . The engines are positioned at the rear so that the broad sweep of the wings may be kept free for high-lift devices, which give the aircraft its modest appetite for concrete compared to the vociferous demands of earlier jetliners of similar weight and size.'

BOAC ordered twelve standard VC-10s and thirty larger, long-range 150-passenger 'Super VC-10s', together costing over £150 million. They gave the airline years of excellent service, but they were noisy. As the VC-10 came thundering down the runway and almost stood on its tail as soon as the front nose wheel left the ground, it emitted a deafening roar from its Rolls-Royce Conway turbojets, breaking all previous aircraft noise levels. Complaints about aircraft noise from local residents and people living under the flight path reached all-time records once the VC-10 came into regular passenger service.

BOAC's VC-10s became as familiar a sight at Heathrow as BEA's Tridents, a short- to medium-range aircraft powered by rear-mounted turbojets and built to accommodate 100 passengers. By March 1965, fifteen Tridents had been delivered to BEA and were flying all over Europe, and a further eight joined the fleet the following year. The Trident became the backbone of BEA's fleet and a very popular plane with passengers and the airline's Heathrow-based engineering staff. Larger versions of the Trident followed in later years and, unlike the VC-10, were also bought by a variety of other commercial airlines including Cyprus Airways and thirty-three were sold to the Central Aviation Administration of China.

Another popular British aircraft from this time was the BAC One-Eleven, a jet designed to carry around eighty passengers on short-haul routes. Unlike the VC-10 and Tridents, the One-Eleven was successfully exported to a number of other countries in Europe, Africa, and the Far East – and to at least one American operator.

The international aircraft manufacturing market remained competitive, but few airlines on the European side of the Atlantic truly appreciated that a new type of aircraft was taking shape on designer drawing boards at Boeing's Seattle plant. The prototype design was known as the 'Jumbo Jet' simply because it was designed to carry up to four times more passengers than anything else available in commercial aviation. To handle the new big jets, airports receiving them would need to invest in enlarged passenger piers to cope with expanded numbers of people using the new aircraft and extend the length of runways on which they would land and take off.

The commercial introduction of the VC10 was heralded by an extensive advertising campaign, including a supplement in *The Times*. *(Author's collection)*

But in the mid-1960s, few European airlines were paying attention to what was soon to take shape in an American aircraft manufacturing plant. Britain and France were too busy concentrating on another project. In December 1962 it was announced that a joint UK–French agreement had been signed to develop the world's first supersonic jet. Nobody was sure what it might look like and some newspapers even attempted to create their own designs, which looked like a cross between something out of a Dan Dare story in the boy's comic *The Eagle* and a low-budget Hollywood science fiction 'B' movie. But the joint project did have a name – Concorde.

FOURTEEN

The Rise and Fall of British Eagle

ONE OF BAA'S FIRST TASKS, when it took over management of London Airport in 1966, was to change the airport's name back to Heathrow or, to be correct, Heathrow Airport (London). For the last twenty years the airport's name had been abbreviated to LAP, now it would be known as LHR: London Heathrow. It would take years for the name to catch on and many former airport staff now retired still refer to it by its old name.

In 1968, BAA opened its latest terminal – the third Frederick Gibberd-designed building at Heathrow and a return to the architect's original red-brick decorative design. This would be known as Terminal 1 and the home of all BEA's pan-European

Terminal 1 under construction in 1968. *(BAA (Heathrow) Archive)*

Terminal 1 opened its doors in April 1969 – the same day that British Eagle went into liquidation. *(BAA (Heathrow) Archive)*

services. The original Europa terminal would now be renamed Terminal 2 and be used by continental European airlines while the Oceanic Building would now be renamed Terminal 3.

When Terminal 1 was opened, by the Queen in April 1969, it became the largest airline terminal in Europe in terms of space, terminal capacity and the number of aircraft boarding gates available. It was also the third terminal designed by Gibberd, who now had three different architectural styles on view at the airport. Each was efficient and functional – yet each looked different, reflecting the architect's own vision at the time of design. Many considered that the three different terminals looked odd. Gibberd countered that each was built with different requirements in mind and that air transport had grown so rapidly since his first terminal opened, thirteen years previously, that new buildings based on old designs would not solve the airport's problem of how to deal with rising demand.

Whereas BEA and BOAC were the airport's principal UK airlines, there was also a small squadron of other British carriers that provided airline passengers with alternatives on many domestic and short-haul European routes from Terminals 1 and 2. Many of the airlines had been created following the formation of the Air Transport

HM the Queen officially opens the airport's new Terminal 1.
(BAA (Heathrow) Archive)

Licensing Board in 1960, which led to the formation of long-forgotten airlines such as BKS Air Transport, Northeast Airlines, Cambrian Airways and Derby Airways (which eventually became British Midland).

Prior to 1960 several other airlines had also arrived and departed, merged or gone bankrupt – Hunting Clan, Skyways, Olley Air Services, Euravia Ltd (which later became part of Britannia Airways) and Westpoint Aviation. And then there was British Eagle, a successful and popular airline that was prepared to take on the big boys and then allowed to die a swift and very public death.

BRITISH EAGLE

British Eagle was one of London Airport's most innovative airlines – but intense competition and a loss of major contracts forced it out of business in 1969. *(Author's collection)*

British Eagle began life as Eagle Aviation in 1948 during the Berlin Airlift. It was founded by a pilot called Harold Bamberg who had plenty of enthusiasm, technical ability and a pair of aeroplanes – former RAF Halifax bombers – that he used to fly 7,300 tons of food and coal to the beleaguered German city on over 1,000 flights over a ten-month period.

Following the end of the airlift in 1949, Bamberg set himself up as a charter carrier and purchased an Avro York. His reputation, plus the flair that was to characterise him in later years, resulted in the introduction of scheduled services between Blackbushe Airport in Surrey and Belgrade; the first postwar British air link to the Yugoslav capital. Services to Denmark and Sweden followed. By 1955 Eagle Aviation was operating ten Vickers Vikings and two DC-3s and Bamberg was directing his considerable energy into building a truly British independent airline.

Bamberg moved into a plush office at Marble Arch, ordered a fleet of Douglas DC-6s and began campaigning to become Britain's first low-cost airline. He called his plan the 'VLF' – Very Low Fares – challenge: an idea to offer fares much lower than those available through BEA and other domestic airlines. The scheme met with resistance from the government who finally decided what airlines could charge.

In 1959, Eagle flew over 170,000 passengers and had acquired a valuable contract to transport British troops from and to Blackbushe on behalf of the government. The airline's fleet continued to grow and Bamberg now offered competitive services to Italy, Austria, France, Luxembourg, Belgium, Majorca and the Channel Islands.

Until this time, under the Air Corporations Act of 1946, private airlines were excluded from scheduled routes except – under exceptional circumstances – as 'associates' of the major corporations. Government liberalisation at last removed the monopoly held by BOAC and BEA allowing British Eagle to expand both its fleet and routes. Bamberg responded quickly by introducing scheduled services to Bermuda and the Bahamas, and entered into an equity partnership agreement with the Cunard Steam-Ship Company to operate competitive fares across the North Atlantic.

Bamberg dreamed of becoming the second British long-haul airline alongside BOAC transatlantic routes and Cunard provided British Eagle with the capital support it needed to purchase modern jets 'plus the prestige of Britain's great history of trading on the North Atlantic and the experience of our seventeen sales offices on the North American continent'. Cunard was the operation's majority shareholder.

In 1960, British Eagle transferred operations from Blackbushe to London Airport in readiness to become a major player on the European and transatlantic airline scene. In December 1960, the newly renamed Cunard Eagle Airways ordered a pair of Boeing 707s at a cost of £2.6 million each for delivery in 1962. In May 1961, the airline was granted a licence to operate daily services between London and New York in direct competition to BOAC, Pan American and TWA – but with just three months to go before the new American-built jets were due for delivery, BOAC appealed against the decision and Cunard Eagle's licence was revoked by the Minister of Aviation who cited 'excess capacity' on the route.

With his customary energy, Bamberg set about renegotiating his North Atlantic licences by applying for routes over the 'mid-Atlantic' between London and Miami and new transatlantic jet services were launched in May 1962. A second route between London and Jamaica followed and the airline's engineering base tooled up in readiness to begin working on Boeing 707 equipment.

Harold Bamberg, Chairman of British Eagle International Airlines Ltd. *(Dennis Martin)*

However, dirty work was taking place behind the scenes. BOAC wanted Bamberg's airline crushed and entered into secret negotiations with Cunard to form a new airline to be called BOAC Cunard. This new £30 million company then snatched Bamberg's Atlantic licences, its two Boeing 707s and some crew. Cunard Eagle was left with only a few scheduled services and a top-heavy engineering organisation geared to the operation of big jets.

Bamberg had been 'sold down the river' by Cunard. He had two options available: close down his airline or sell his interest to another company. He chose the latter route and arranged for a management buyout of Cunard's 60 per cent holding in the Eagle group.

Eagle was reborn on 1 March 1963 as British Eagle International Airlines and the name Cunard was unceremoniously dropped. Once again, Bamberg was in charge of the airline he had founded fifteen years earlier – a company he stated was 'a forward-thinking and industrious British independent airline'. In 1963 the airline carried 153,436 passengers, employed 850 staff and made a loss of £80,000. By 1966 Bamberg's airline carried over 1 million passengers, had created jobs for 2,500 staff, made a profit of £600,000 and operated a fleet of seventeen Bristol Britannias, six Vickers Viscounts, five BAC One-Elevens and a pair of Boeing 707s. A rosy future lay ahead.

And then in November 1968 Bamberg's airline came crashing down around him. None of the 2,500 staff were expecting it, although regular articles by Bamberg in the airline's staff newspaper warned them that Harold Wilson's Labour-controlled government was not giving independent airlines an easy time. The airline's Heathrow passengers were confronted with notices on check-in desks telling them that flights were cancelled and British Eagle had ceased trading. The last British Eagle flight to operate was a BAC One-Eleven service from Liverpool to Heathrow. When it had taken off, the airline had been a going concern. When it landed in London, less than an hour later, the crew were told that they no longer had jobs.

What went wrong?

The government of the day had done its best to slap down the country's independent airlines, taking away their scheduled services and preventing them from growing, thereby depriving them of the power to generate income and depriving them of the opportunity to obtain long-term, low-cost financing. BOAC was still claiming that Eagle's weekly service to the Bahamas was hurting its own operations to the destination and pleaded to the government for help. The government saw fit to revoke Eagle's licence just as the airline was about to sign new financial agreements for the next stage of its expansion. In the eyes of BOAC, British Eagle had the effrontery to offer opposition to a state-owned carrier who screamed blue murder every time a new route was given to an independent airline, with the result that it was usually revoked. According to BOAC, every new route awarded to an independent airline threatened to put it out of business. As a result, backers, bankers and investors got cold feet, saw that the government was not prepared to help independent airlines – and pulled the plug on their support.

The government was also winding down the number of military bases it operated overseas and had drastically reduced the number of troop flights British Eagle operated on its behalf.

The final straw came at the end of October 1968 when British Eagle was faced with heavy bills for fuel, landing charges and wages that rendered the company insolvent. Hambros, the airline's bankers, had been prepared to assist other ailing companies, but regarded British Eagle as a lost cause. The *Sunday Telegraph* accused Bamberg of 'being brim full of bright ideas but he lacks the capacity for detailed administration and Hambros was unconvinced that the airline was sufficiently well run to be worth bailing out. Even so, Mr Bamberg emerges with credit. He offered to throw in his entire personal fortune.'

Why didn't the government step in?

The government's attitude towards privately run airlines was equivocal, regarding them as something to be suffered rather than nourished. The Board of Trade thought that if commercial bankers were not prepared to support a private airline it did not see why public funds should be used. There were also serious doubts about the quality of British Eagle's management. The government knew that the public at large would not suffer because BEA and BOAC would mop up British Eagle's passenger and cargo traffic.

A dramatic advertisement in *The Times* on 13 November 1968, written and paid for by Lawrence W. Levine, a Wall Street banker representing several American airlines, addressed to 'the political leaders in England – especially the Prime Minister', stated that 'if the government wants to help the country move forward, if it wants England to have a major role in civil aviation without hurting BOAC, if it wants those 2,500 Eagle jobs back with a possibility of making that 5,000 jobs later on – then I suggest that it cuts the 'double talk' and stops sitting around trying to figure out how to liquidate the empire that took thousands of years to build – and give Eagle's liquidators a couple of routes and give them quickly – instead of waiting around for a report by a distinguished commission whose conclusions anyone in the industry, in my opinion, could have given two years ago.'

Two British Eagle aircraft, named Justice and Good Fortune, at London Airport on the day the airline ceased operations in 1969. *(Barry Dix collection)*

Former British Eagle staff member, Dennis Martin from Woking, Surrey, remembers:

> It is ironic that the same day that Terminal 1 opened for business coincided with the announcement that British Eagle was to go into liquidation. Our first flights to Edinburgh, Glasgow and Belfast all left on schedule, and then at about 2.00 p.m. the news came through that our backers [Hambros Bank] had withdrawn their support on the basis of future plans [or lack of them] in the aviation industry by the government. Everyone was stunned. The airline had been part of our lives – and suddenly it was no longer there. We were powerless to do anything.

Jim Russell from Staines, Middlesex, remembers that British Eagle staff were summoned to the airline's main hangar at Heathrow 'to be told the airline had run out of money and that operations would cease'.

He adds: 'The wind down of British bases overseas and the withdrawal of Cunard's interest all seemed to come too near together. We worked damned hard to keep our airline going, but it was not to be.

'I remember well that evening, walking around Heathrow wondering how I was going to support my family – my wife Liz (who didn't yet know the situation), my two boys, Iain and Colin whose birthday party was that evening, a mortgage and two dogs.'

Shortly after leaving British Eagle Jim opened a DIY shop in Staines and was later joined by Dennis Martin who introduced a gardening, plumbing and electrical department at the shop known as the Handyman.

And so British Eagle was allowed to die, quickly and in pain, Heathrow lost one of its major airlines and hundreds of airport-based staffs were thrown out of work. Harold Bamberg later re-emerged as a private businessman in charge of Bamberg Enterprises, which specialised in commercial building schemes, including the creation of polo playing arenas. He also became the UK representative for the American executive jet manufacturing company Beechcraft.

Bamberg's name is now almost forgotten by the UK's airline industry, but his legacy has resulted in the creation of a new breed of airline entrepreneur prepared to take on the government and competing airlines in order to break their monopoly and offer lower fares to popular destinations. Others who followed in Bamberg's wake include buccaneering Sir Freddie Laker, Virgin Atlantic's Sir Richard Branson, BMI's Sir Michael Bishop and founders of the late twentieth century's low-cost 'no frills' airlines, EasyJet's Stelios Haji-Ioannou and Ryanair's Chief Executive, Michael O'Leary. It is to Harold Bamberg that they owe a debt of gratitude – although many may not be prepared to admit it.

FIFTEEN

St George and the Airport

THE BUILDERS WERE BACK at work at Heathrow in 1967 digging a large hole in a plot of land beneath one side of the control tower. Some said that a nuclear bunker was taking shape beneath the airport in the event of a Russian attack. Others said that the airport authority was conducting an experimental building project creating underground offices and that, if the idea was successful, the airport would be riddled with subterranean workplaces.

When the cranes and mechanical diggers moved in, only a handful of people were aware that the gaping hole would eventually house a multi-faith chapel which would be open to airport staff and passengers alike and named after England's very own patron saint, St George.

Many found it difficult to accept that in the middle of one of the world's busiest, most crowded and congested airports, a chapel offering peace, quiet and tranquillity for prayer and reflection would succeed. And to begin with, they were correct.

When completed, in October 1968, the chapel took the form of an underground cave. All that can be seen of St George's from ground level is a tall cross marking the spot beneath which faiths of all kinds, from Anglicans to Muslims, Roman Catholics to Salvationists, Presbyterians to Buddhists and Methodists to Sikhs, congregate to worship in a single place. A rabbi also visits the airport regularly, although does not use the chapel believing that in Judaism if someone wishes to pray, they can pray anywhere because God is everywhere.

To reach the chapel, worshippers climb down a wide spiral staircase leading to a sensitively lit domed area containing three altars. Chaplains from different faiths conduct services at various times of the day and are on hand to befriend and support airport staff and passengers. The chaplains also walk the terminals each day talking to airline personnel and travellers. They are easily recognised by their identity badges.

The Revd Ben Lewers was appointed St George's first Anglican airport chaplain. He came to the airport as a 36-year-old former Army second lieutenant who had attended Lincoln Theological College and worked as a curate in Northampton and as Priest-in-Charge of the Church of the Good Shepherd in Hounslow West. He was asked to take on the Heathrow job by the Bishop of Kensington, the Rt Revd Ronnie Goodchild. Ben remembers:

The Revd Ben Lewers, first Anglican chaplain at Heathrow's St George's Chapel. *(Ben Lewers)*

Work on completing the chapel was in an advanced stage when I first saw the site. My first job was to get a grip on the layout and geography of the airport. At the same time I managed to establish some excellent contacts and relationships with airport people. I remember arriving on 1 May 1968, said matins and then looked at all that expanse of grass and runways – and rang the police. The idea was to get to know them as they, like me, had a relationship with the entire area and its people. We got on very well together and the relationship grew and blossomed.

Heathrow's underground St George's Chapel in the shadow of the Control Tower. *(Alan Gallop)*

The chapel was dedicated by Michael Ramsay, Archbishop of Canterbury, Cardinal Heenan, the Cardinal Archbishop of Westminster and the Moderator of the Free Church Federal Council. The Queen, with the Duke of Edinburgh, paid a special visit to the chapel when she officially opened Terminal 1.

The challenge was to get the chapel up and running in company with my colleagues, Father Peter Knott and the Revd Ewart Wilson, a Methodist minister. We always got on well together. Then I established a visiting programme, which took me all over the airport. Most Monday afternoons, for example, found me in BEA's general workshop. It was important to get permission from both management and unions to be a visitor in such places, and this I always did.

It was important to establish a routine. I had to do my homework to find out who was who and the people in a position to give me permission to enter restricted areas. I was able to negotiate for passes, which allowed me to go wherever I wanted. I made a number of friendships over the years, some of which still exist to this day. Other tasks and opportunities were dealt with as they arrived – and not always successfully.

I had a congregation of between twenty to thirty for the opening Anglican service and then for the next six months, practically nobody came. I used to light candles, put on my vestments, wait, then take them off again and go home. The Roman Catholics were in a much better state; indeed it was once said that it was a wonder that Aer Lingus [the Irish national airline] flew at all on a Sunday morning. Things did improve, but there were never a great many people at our 9.00 a.m. Sunday services. I also held services at 1.00 p.m. on Wednesdays. My wife and three sons, who had previously sung in a local choir, used to come. Once, on my way home, my wife asked, 'Darling, could you sometimes preach a sermon when there were not three, but two or four people in the congregation?' A 7-year-old voice then remarked sepulchrally from the back of the car, 'Or no people at all.'

I worked with a wide variety of people and special groups at the airport. I helped set up an organisation called Travellers' Help, which assisted passengers passing through Heathrow who had problems which fell outside of the remit of airport staff. For instance, there was once a passenger who was being deported and who landed in London on a January day aboard an Aeroflot flight wearing shorts and badly in need of a warm pair of trousers. These were provided. Much of my work was, of course, of a confidential nature as is the way with much ministry.

My own Bishop used to visit once a year and during the time I was at Heathrow the Archbishop of Canterbury travelled through many times. As his 'branch manager' I made it my business to see him off and greet him as often as I could. It was always a pleasant task.

I thoroughly enjoyed my seven years at St George's Chapel. It was a great opportunity and a tremendous privilege. All ministry is, of course, but to exercise it at a place like Heathrow Airport was quite exciting.

To sum up, many people asked me what I did at Heathrow. To answer that I have developed a mnemonic based on the word WITNESS. It runs like this:

W – Worship, chapel, etc.
I – Industrial mission, visiting, etc.
T – Travellers' Help
N – Needs of the Third World. We did what we could to promote these needs.
E – Ecumenical relationships
S – Services to those in need. We set up a small counselling service for staff.
S – Service to the church, i.e. this useful world and its parts.

Ben Lewers retired in 1997 after nearly seventeen years as Provost of Derby Cathedral. He remains an active member of the Bridport, Dorset, community where he is a parish councillor, school governor and, with his wife Sally, an avid gardener.

Another much-missed figure at St George's Chapel is Roman Catholic priest Father Brian Laycock. Born in Adelaide, Australia, in 1932, Father Brian started his working life as a dentist with the Royal Australian Flying Dental Corps before training for the priesthood. He arrived on the Heathrow scene in 1974, rising each day at 4.45 a.m. to pray in the chapel for some hours before starting his busy schedule of visits and twice-daily masses (four on Sundays) plus Novena and Benediction in the afternoon.

Father Brian also held all-night prayer vigils every month, and his congregation turned up from all over the world. He is described by a member of his congregation as a man who 'poured out his life for the Gospel and was truly a man of God'. Poor health forced Father Brian to retire in February 2000. He died in 2004 and is much missed by his large congregation of airport staff, passengers and visitors.

St George's Chapel today offers a multi-faith prayer room near the entrance to the chapel. Inside, the space is kept plain in order to respect individual beliefs. Faith texts and prayer mats are available.

The chaplains and their volunteers exist to help everyone, regardless of their faith, and offer help in many practical ways. Some conduct services at the nearby Harmondsworth Immigrant Detention Centre and at British Airways' headquarters located close to the airport's main entrance. The chaplains may represent different beliefs, but they are united in their work at Heathrow, promoting the message that they are there to help anyone in need, whatever their religion, nationality, situation or final destination.

SIXTEEN

Star Girls, Galley Slaves and Trolley Dollies

ALTHOUGH BRITISH SOUTH AFRICAN AIRWAYS and the London press hailed Mary Guthrie as Britain's first air hostess in 1946, the claim was not strictly true. Ten years before, a young lady called Daphne Kearley was paid £12 per week to work for an airline called Air Dispatch to fly on the company's Avro 642 airliners, travelling on short journeys between Croydon and Le Bourget, near Paris. Daphne's job was to show passengers to their seats and, once airborne, serve pre-packed meals of smoked salmon and caviar. When not flying with Air Dispatch, Daphne was also expected to take dictation and type letters for her airline bosses. She provided a similar service for passengers in the Croydon Airport terminal.

Mary Guthrie – Britain's first postwar air hostess, proudly wears her ATA wings on her uniform as she prepares to board an Avro York in 1947. *(Mary Cunningham collection)*

Six years before Daphne took to the skies above southern Britain, Ellen Church, a 26-year-old registered nurse from Iowa, with a pilot's licence, approached Boeing Air Transport in the United States with a proposal to offer passengers a nurse-stewardess service on long flights. Boeing agreed to a three-month-long experiment and Ellen recruited seven other nurses to serve as the original team of Sky Girls. Their maiden flight took place on 15 May 1930 on a twenty-four-seat plane flying between San Francisco and Chicago. The journey took twenty hours and included stops at thirteen other airfields.

Passengers liked the Sky Girls and the airline decided to keep them and hire more. Other airlines followed suit and, although she only worked at the job for eighteen months, Ellen became one of the first women to work in the airline industry and the first to serve as a manager. She became a decorated nurse during the Second World War, after serving in Africa, Italy, France and England, and later worked as a hospital administrator before being killed in a horse-riding accident in 1965.

Air Vice-Marshal Donald Bennett had seen American air hostesses in action during business visits to North America. He was impressed with their efficiency and style – two ingredients he wanted for his own airline when it commenced flying to Latin America in 1946.

Mary Guthrie and her fellow crew members. *(Mary Cunningham collection)*

Mary Guthrie was picked from 100 applicants and shortly before the departure of the first flight, the *Daily Mail* reported that BSAA had been looking for a girl who was 'intelligent, level headed and charming, who knew something about planes and nursing and had command of at least one foreign language. Miss Guthrie fulfilled all of these qualifications. She is tall, slim and blue eyed and has a mass of wavy light brown hair. All the food that will be taken onboard is frozen and Miss Guthrie will have the job of unfreezing and heating it in a small kitchenette. In South America she will do the shopping for the return trip. Miss Guthrie does not like her present uniform and I understand that she will soon get a more feminine type of dress.'

Sixty years after that historic first flight from London and from the comfort of her home in Somerset, Mrs Mary Cunningham (née Guthrie) recalls those early days of flying as one of BSAA's Star Girls:

> I was born in Thornton Heath, Surrey, in 1921 and had a private education before entering Montrose Ladies College in Kent. When war broke out in 1939, I was studying at RADA. When my older brother James, an RAF Spitfire pilot, was shot down over Malta, a great friend and I decided we would join the VAD – Voluntary Aid Detachment [which trained staff in first aid, nursing and supplied ambulance drivers, civil defence workers and welfare officers]. I gained experience as a nurse and one evening in 1943, while working on night duty, I learned from a patient

that women could win their wings and become pilots. I thought 'what a good idea, why not', so I joined the ATA – Air Transport Auxiliary – and they taught me to fly. It took about three months to learn and then another three months to master navigation and engines. As third officer Guthrie, I flew a Fairchild and then some early Spitfires, ferrying them from one RAF maintenance base to another. It was very enjoyable. They were good days, very exciting and I remember them with affection.

I decided to carry on flying after the war and was working towards gaining a commercial licence, which meant learning more about navigation – and that's when I met Cliff Alabaster – Alaby – when I went to BSAA's Grafton Street offices in December 1945. He mentioned that the airline needed something called an 'air hostess' and introduced me to a Mr Huff, the personnel manager, who asked me if I had any nursing experience. I told him I was RAF nursing trained and spoke French – and he offered me the job. I didn't know what an air hostess was – and I didn't know that 100 other applicants were hoping to land the job. I was sent for two days' training at Joe Lyons in Marble Arch and learned how to heat up food in an aircraft galley, one plate at a time. The first time I saw the aircraft galley itself was when we took off on the first flight out of Heathrow in January 1946.

A BEA stewardess, 1947 style (left), and one of the airline's in-flight cabin staff in 1971. *(Brenard Press)*

I was told to write down any snags I came across on the flight and I noted down over 100 different items – and as far as I know, the airline tore the list up!

Like everyone else at that time, I was wearing a military-style serge uniform and my ATA wings when I arrived at the airport for the first time. There appeared to be a lot of activity going on and people rushing about all over the place, but the airport looked more like a building site. I could see only one plane and that was the Avro Lancastrian I would be travelling on. It looked a bit lonely sitting there all by itself.

We all stood around in the cold next to the aircraft and under the wing while Lord Winster declared the airport open. Air Vice-Marshal Bennett also said a few words. Even though he was Captain of the flight he wore a civilian suit underneath an RAF greatcoat. And then we climbed up the steps into the aircraft – my first opportunity to view the galley that I would be working in. And then off we went.

The galley was tiny. We only had cold water and no detergent to wash up in – and to wash the crockery and glasses, I had to sit down because there wasn't room to stand. All the pots and pans were stowed away on floor level so there was a lot of stooping and crouching involved preparing meals and clearing up.

BSAA Star Girls in front of one of the airline's Avro Yorks at London Airport. *(Keith Hayward collection)*

On the outward journey, the airport's first passengers ate chicken-à-la-king [diced chicken cooked in mushrooms, butter and peppers – although the last two items were still rationed and difficult to come by, so they were probably substituted with something else]. The food was brought in frozen from Lyons, thawed out, reheated and served. It didn't look very pretty or appetising on the plate. And it had a funny smell, too – nothing like chicken as we now know it. But everyone ate it. We took on other supplies whenever we stopped to refuel and they were much nicer than the frozen variety – known as 'frood' – from London.

To pass from the galley into the cabin I had to negotiate a metal spar coming across at an angle from the floor to the ceiling. It was part of the aeroplane's design and like a rib – good job I was wearing trousers. It didn't happen to me, but one of my colleagues was serving soup or something and tripped over the spar, tipping the meal all over a passenger.

I felt airsick a couple of times on that flight and so did some passengers. Remember, we were flying in a non-pressurised aircraft, cruising at an altitude of only 10,000ft. Although I wasn't actually sick on the flight, I was on some later ones.

One of the passengers kindly helped me wash up and another wanted to give me a tip at the end of the journey. Did I accept? Of course! We only earned £5 a week and were allowed to draw another £5 each time we landed – so if you landed more than five times you ended up owing the company money. I always seemed to owe more than I earned. I had been earning £9 a week with the ATA and here I was in Civvy Street earning £4 less. But it didn't matter because life was so exciting then. We had been living six years with blackouts and food rationing and air raids – and now here I was on my way to a sunny paradise called South America.

The flight was a long one and I thought it might go on forever. The only time we stopped was for refuelling, otherwise we went on without any sleep. We were all dog tired when we arrived – but very excited to be in South America, a place that was all bright and shiny, colourful and sunny. Not like the cold and gloomy postwar England we had left behind. And don't forget, we were young and had plenty of energy. I loved the glamour of it all.

I had no idea that we were making history with that first flight. I knew it was special because of all the fuss that was going on and the media attention, but I had no inkling that it was an historic day. There is some dispute about which flight was the first official departure from Heathrow – ours or a BOAC service, which went to Australia a few months later. Of course, it was ours. Otherwise, what was all that fuss going on on 1 January 1946? The newspapers and cinema newsreels were full of stories about us, but I don't recall there being much about the BOAC service leaving weeks later. A few years ago I wrote to BOAC pointing this out and they didn't believe me, so I sent them a pile of cuttings about our flight and they wrote back telling me how lucky I had been to be an air hostess at that time. They were right, too.

I went down to South America three times with BSAA – and then was given the sack. We were coming back from South America and stopping over in Lisbon, where all my crew were going off to Estoril for the night to have a super time. When we arrived at the airport, a chap in white gloves came onto the aircraft and ordered me to look after the passengers in Lisbon for the night. I told him that was the job of the ground staff and he asked me if I was refusing to cooperate. I said 'that's right – I'm off to Estoril with my crew'. So when I got back to London I was sacked – not because of what I had said, but the way in which I had said it. In the end they allowed me to resign. I wasn't at all upset because I went on to get my commercial flying licence.

After leaving BSAA I worked as an air hostess with a charter company called Skyways and my money rose to £13 per week – big money in those days. We were flying all over the Middle East and Europe. I also ferried aircraft for them – Spitfires and Hurricanes when they won a contract to deliver aircraft from Dunsfold to the Portuguese Air Force. I did that for three months.

I started to get frightened after a Skyways DC-3 I was travelling in as a stewardess developed engine trouble and landed in a field somewhere in the Alps near Geneva. When we evacuated the aircraft, I should have removed all the cutlery, but forgot – and the airline sent me a bill for it all. I didn't pay because I was so incensed.

After I was married and started having children, I stopped flying. Although I had been Britain's first peacetime air hostess, I had no desire to be the country's first female commercial airline pilot.

A few years ago I was sitting on a plane on the tarmac at Gatwick and the Captain announced over the tannoy that the plane needed a new wheel. I wanted to get off, so I got off – and the Captain stormed after me demanding to know what I thought I was doing. I told him that I wanted to see which wheel he was changing. He took me back onboard and after another hour he said that the wheel had been fixed – but it was the wrong wheel. So we stayed on the plane for what seemed like an age and the Captain came back on the tannoy to say that his flying hours had run out and he was off. All the cabin crew were complaining and I remember thinking: 'What would Don Bennett have made of all this?' He would never have tolerated it for a moment, let alone several hours. I wrote and complained to the company and they ignored my letters until my husband got on the phone and announced himself as Captain Cunningham – they must have thought he was an airline Captain, but he was actually a naval Captain.

When I fly on aircraft today and see cabin staff wheeling their trolleys up and down the passenger cabin, I thank God I don't have to do that job anymore. It was fun when I used to do it – but today it's just a job. In my day we all shared the same spirit – call it pioneering spirit if you like. We got on with the job, sometimes in difficult circumstances and tried to move forward all the time. I'm not sure if that is the case today. But today's cabin staff look wonderful. I did the job for two years and that was enough.

Today's cabin staff are more or less flying waitresses – and waiters. But like us, they work really hard and their body clocks must go haywire sometimes. I'm not sure if they get much time off these days. We were lucky and could often get out and see some of the countries we visited. I'm not sure if cabin staff today have much of a career ahead of them. It was like that in my day, too. We didn't have careers – we had jobs. You worked at it for a few years and then went on to do something else, got another job, started a family. It was never a job for life.

Back in 1946 a group of soldiers had seen Mary's photograph in a newspaper and wrote to ask if they could be founder members of her fan club. Mary roars with laughter at the memory and even louder when reminded that she has become something of a legend being the first air hostess to fly from London's new airport. When told that she looked quite a dish as a young girl back in 1946 – and still looks great sixty years on – she giggles girlishly but refuses to have her photograph taken. 'I would rather people remember me as I was, rather than how I look today.'

A group of air hostesses smile for the camera after completing their training at London Airport in 1951. *(Author's collection)*

A few days after returning to London, Britain's top writer on 'female matters', Joanna Chase of the *Daily Herald* was sent to interview Mary at her mother's house in London. Both the airline and national newspapers had been flooded with letters from girls wanting to know how they could land glamorous jobs as Star Girls, flying to places where there was no rationing, the sun always shone and nylons were in plentiful supply. The article paints a wonderful picture of what life was like for an air hostess sixty years ago:

> Judging by the number of girls who have called in the last few days at the offices of BSAA, a job of an air hostess seems to be the ambition of a great many women. But few of the young women who have dreams of spending their lives in the air seem to have their feet on the ground. Being an air hostess is a tough job for the young, the brave and the free. It is not an easy way of leading a pleasant life, and out of every dozen girls who want such a job, only two are in any way suitable, according to the Star Light authorities.
>
> What does it take to be a Star Girl? First of all, a tough physique. Personality, brains, charm, looks count for nothing at all unless you can pass a stiff medical examination and come through A1. Miss Guthrie, first of the postwar British air hostesses, had no sleep at all during the Lancastrian flight to South America. She cannot relax for a moment as she has fourteen passengers and five crew to cook for, wash up for, tuck in with pillows and blankets and watch for sleeplessness and air sickness. Hers is the hand which provides and serves the meals, checks tickets, passports, luggage. An air hostess has to be a nurse, a hotelier, a cook, a linguist, a general information bureau – and a very charming woman.
>
> Her first duty is to check in passports, tickets and luggage. She has to see that passengers understand the various currency and regulations of the country to which they are travelling. Once onboard they are in her care. If there is an accident and the plane comes down in the sea and everyone has to take to dinghies, then she has to provide comfort and cheer for all the practical purposes of fourteen people still in her charge, including, as far as feeding is concerned, the crew. You need to be brave and have a good deal of nursing or the mothering instinct to be a success at this job.
>
> And the second thing you need – and this is rare in a woman – is no desire to put down roots. An air hostess has no home life at all. She gets two days off, perhaps at home, but more often on the station at one of the ports of call, where she will live in quarters near the airfield or in the wing of a hotel specially taken over for the purpose. It is in many ways a lonely life for a woman, although one may find plenty of amusing acquaintances – and sometimes even a husband. Pan American Airways say that the average length of time their air hostesses remain in their jobs is from 8–10 months for the girls so often marry among the passengers they meet, or else they find it too lonely and just give it up.
>
> For this, as well as for the other reasons, the ideal age for the job is between 20–25 when a woman feels she would like to see something of the world before settling down, and when she has no commitments or responsibilities to tie her.
>
> Any girl applying for the job has to take a month's course, during which she is paid to learn first aid, cooking, the details of foreign currency, international law and

something of the habits of geography of the country to which passengers are carried. In addition to the wide general knowledge necessary for the job, languages are of great importance and BSAA expect all of their girls to take a 3-month course in Spanish or Portuguese. If they pass these exams, they get a bonus of £25 and an increase in salary.

Salaries start at a basic rate of £350 but work out in practice at something over £400 once additional allowances have been paid. So far, no plans have been made to increase salaries, but air hostesses come under the general pensions and insurance scheme of BSAA staff. The job is most suitable for ex-service WRAFs, three of whom have been taken on in the last week – but there are not a lot of these jobs going.

Thanks to Mary Guthrie and generations of ladies who followed her into the skies, every little girl growing up in Britain during the 1950s and 1960s wanted to become an air hostess. Articles, films and advertising glamorised a job that gave girls a chance to travel the world and wear uniforms which became increasingly smart, sophisticated and – by the time the 1960s had arrived – made female cabin staff look every bit as chic and sexy as anything worn by Twiggy or Jean Shrimpton.

And let's not forget the men. Stewards had been travelling on the world's airlines ever since Imperial Airways' services criss-crossed the globe ferrying passengers to all parts of the British Empire. Many were former head waiters from hotels and fashionable restaurants, charged with the task of replicating the same sophisticated atmosphere found at the Ritz and the Astor in small, rattling dining areas adjacent to noisy propeller engines transporting passengers over oceans, mountains, deserts, jungles and plains.

The U.S. ambassador would like to meet you.

Her mission: take you to America on a TWA jet. We fly from most everywhere in Europe to more U.S. cities than any other transatlantic airline (one airline all the way). But no matter. The main thing is that smile, and that feeling you've got a friend the second you're on board. It's what starts a good thing going—with us, with our country.

Call your travel agent or TWA and see what we mean.

*Service mark owned exclusively by Trans World Airlines, Inc.

American airline TWA traded on the charm of their in-flight staff to sell the airline's services. *(Author's collection)*

But flying also had its downside and on occasions airline cabin staff – stewards and stewardesses – have sacrificed their lives in the line of duty. Over the years scores of airline personnel have been killed in accidents both on the ground and in the air. Many have become heroes, and recognised for their unstinting courage and bravery to save lives while sacrificing their own.

Barbara Jane Harrison, age 22 – known to her family as Jane – was one such person. Yorkshire-born Jane worked as a BOAC stewardess. She acquired a passion to travel after working as a nanny looking after the two young children of an American family in

The late Jane Harrison, George Cross recipient. *(Sue Buck)*

San Francisco. In 1968 she was living in London. Her sister, Susan Buck, remembered her as 'an adventurer, an outdoor girl who enjoyed life'. Her aunt, Rita Shaw, said: 'Nothing seemed to bother her. She was always calm in the time of crisis. She was happy and full of life.'

On 8 April 1968, Jane was working on Boeing 707 G-ARWE – *Whiskey Echo* – and shortly after taking off from Heathrow, number two engine caught fire and subsequently fell from the aircraft leaving a fierce fire burning on the port wing. The aircraft made an emergency landing and on touchdown the fire intensified.

Jane knew what do. Her training had prepared her for just such an incident and, as soon as the plane came to a halt on the runway, she rushed to the back of the aircraft to help the steward open the rear door, inflate the emergency chute and assist passengers to leave in an orderly manner. As it inflated, the chute twisted and the steward climbed out of the aircraft and onto the runway to straighten it out. Once out of the aircraft he was unable to return, leaving Jane alone to shepherd passengers towards the rear door and the chute to safety.

By now flames were starting to break out all over *Whiskey Echo*. Jane remained cool. She managed to get some passengers down the chute. Others were afraid and Jane gave them a helpful push to safety. When the flames had spread to the tailplane section of the aircraft, Jane realised that the rear door was becoming unsafe and she directed her passengers towards another exit while she remained at her post.

An elderly disabled passenger was seated in one of the last rows of seats and Jane went to his aid. Both she and the passenger were overcome by smoke, intense heat and flames. They died together as brave firefighters battled to save passengers still inside *Whiskey Echo*.

Jane is buried in Fulford Cemetery, York. On 8 August 1968, she was posthumously awarded the George Cross, the youngest recipient of the award. Neville Davis-Gordon, the chief steward travelling on the aircraft that day, received the British Empire Medal for Gallantry (Civil Division) for his part in the incident.

BOAC's Managing Director, Keith Granville, said later: 'We in BOAC will always remember the heroism and bravery of Miss Harrison and Mr Davis-Gordon.'

A plaque hangs on the wall inside St George's Chapel at Heathrow. It states:

> To commemorate the memory of BOAC stewardess Barbara Jane Harrison, age 22 years, who was posthumously awarded the George Cross for courage and selfless devotion to duty in the evacuation of passengers from a blazing Boeing 707 at Heathrow Airport on April 8, 1968. Passengers praised Miss Harrison's calmness and courage throughout the evacuation. At the last, although she could have saved herself, she gave her life attempting to help a crippled passenger to leave the aircraft.

Sixty years after Mary Guthrie slaved away in her tiny aircraft galley defrosting 'frood' for a handful of passengers, cabin crew jobs are still much sought after. It is hard work, as anyone who has ever sat in a seat onboard a crowded charter flight to the Mediterranean will testify. Cabin staff have been called 'trolley dollies', implying that they are stupid and nothing more than waiters and waitresses. Stupid? Far from it. Next to the flight deck crew, cabin staff perform the most important job on an aircraft – keeping passengers contented, comfortable and safe.

British Airways says that becoming a member of its cabin crew 'is a unique experience'. The airline adds: 'Our customers have their own unique needs and requirements. You'll find that every day holds a different challenge from the moment you welcome our customers aboard the aircraft, their safety and comfort are your responsibility. Your role includes all aspects of customer care from communication to serving refreshments. You will hold the key to our customers having a fantastic flight and most importantly, wanting to fly with us again.'

Today's cabin staff must be aged 19–54 at the time of their job application and be a minimum of 5ft 2in tall, 'with weight in such proportion . . . that the ability to perform all job functions is not hindered. The ability to, whilst facing forward, walk and fit comfortably down the aisle, fit quickly through the overwing window exit, and to fit into a jump seat harness without modification including closure without a seatbelt extension.'

Cabin staff must be educated to GCSE or equivalent standard, with passes in Maths and English, be fluent in English, both written and spoken, and enjoy a high standard of physical fitness. A GNVQ or equivalent qualification in nursing, hospitality, travel and tourism or care services plus twelve months' customer service experience is also required.

British Airways cabin staff today – professional yet relaxed after arriving at Heathrow from a long transatlantic flight. *(Alan Gallop)*

They must possess friendly and caring personalities, be competent in handling difficult situations, be confident communicators – and great listeners. As team players they must be able to remain calm and efficient under pressure, willing to treat everyone as an individual and take pride in personal grooming (meaning that visible body tattoos and piercings are definitely out!). They must be able to swim well and with confidence – and be prepared to work unsociable hours any day of the year, at any time, including weekends and public holidays.

In return, today's cabin staff can expect a basic starting salary of £10,000 per annum plus flying allowances which vary each month depending on trip allocation. Typical new-entrant cabin crew members can expect to earn in the region of £500 per month in addition to flying allowances. There are lots of 'perks' including the airline's profit-share scheme, regular bonus payments, and opportunities for reduced air fare travel and travel discounts.

It is all very different from Mary Guthrie's day – yet the job of flying cabin crew is more or less identical; only time has flown.

SEVENTEEN

Flying News: Time to Hold the Front Page

FOR THE LAST SIX DECADES, Heathrow has been one of the country's single most productive news-gathering centres. The press was there on its first day and, sixty years later, the airport still provides a steady flow of news copy and picture stories for the international media.

Bill Brenard's airport news-gathering operation finally closed its doors in the 1980s, by which time it had spawned the airport newspaper *Skyport* and a profitable printing business. Today, the Heathrow news beat is trodden by a former Brenard's reporter, Steve Meller, who arrived as a trainee copy boy fresh out of school in the 1970s and is retained by newspapers to cover the antics of showbiz celebrities, fashionable soccer players, flavour of the month pop stars and pompous politicians. He is also there to

An airport Nissen hut – once used as a staff canteen – became a press conference room when Laurence Olivier (left) and his wife Vivien Leigh (wearing hat) travelled to London Airport to say goodbye to Marilyn Monroe and Arthur Miller after the filming of *The Prince and the Showgirl* in 1957. *(Author's collection)*

report what the airport authority and airlines are up to and tell the world about ordinary folks who, for one reason or another, find themselves 'in the news'.

Steve works with a team of skilled news photographers, including former Brenard's colleagues Russell Clisby and David Dyson. In recent years their behind-the-scenes work, as anonymous airport media men, has become known to an international audience, thanks to the long-running 'fly-on-the-wall' documentary TV series *Airport* which follows a select number of staff around the unique workplace as they face 'a typical day'. The programme has turned Steve and his colleagues into celebrities who are often as well known as the people they try to interview and photograph.

Airport reporter Ray Watts (right) interviews pop star Elton John at Heathrow in the early 1980s. *(Brenard Press)*

Steve Meller admits that his new-found fame as a regular TV face sometimes has its downside and has been known to have his reporter's cover blown while discreetly waiting to interview someone newsworthy, by being 'outed' by passengers recognising him from TV and wanting his autograph.

Some might call Steve's photographer colleagues 'paparazzi' – but they would disagree. Most of the celebrities, as they emerge from aircraft and trip down airport corridors, are delighted to see them waiting. Chances are that their picture will be in an evening newspaper that same night or in a daily newspaper on the following morning's breakfast table. Agents, PR people and promoters go out of their way to let the airport press corps know that their clients will be passing through Heathrow and the great and the good, the bad and the ugly always take care to disappear into aircraft loos to wash, brush up and put on fresh make-up as their aircraft approaches London air space.

The press team are classed as airport 'trustworthies' and carry passes allowing them to move freely – more or less – throughout airport terminals and right up to the door of arriving and departing aircraft. The airlines love them – especially when they can snap Mr and Mrs Beckham and their children with one of their aircraft in the background. The airport authority loves them because they keep Heathrow in the news day after day. And airline staff love them, too, because they enjoy watching photographers rushing around taking the photographs that help fill their favourite newspapers.

Reporting techniques used by Steve Meller and his band of camera-wielding brothers are similar to those used by Ray Berry, who 'landed' at Heathrow on

Heathrow is the beat of airport pressmen Russell Clisby (left), Steve Meller (centre) and David Dyson.

2 December 1946. Born in north London in 1930, the second youngest of five children, Ray left school in 1945 after taking the school certificate just before his 16th birthday. He spent the entire first day of the summer holidays knocking on every door in Fleet Street asking for a job on a newspaper, 'an act of defiance against a careers-advice teacher who had contemptuously dismissed my request for information on journalism'. He took up the only offer of a copy boy at the London office of the *Manchester Evening News* and then spotted an advertisement the following year for an editorial assistant with a 'west London news agency' and was accepted by Brenard Air News Services at a London Airport interview.

Recalling the airport in those early days, Ray remembers:

> There was very much a service atmosphere about all airports in those early days. Many management posts with the airlines and civil service were filled with ex-RAF officers, from the Commandants at London Airport and Northolt Airport alike. Sir John D'Albiac, the airport's first Commandant, was a very good friend of the press and a popular man on the airport.
>
> I suppose the biggest difference between the way the airport's press corps worked at the airport in the 1940s and today was the contact and relations with staff in almost all areas. It was possible to see the same people every day and to make friendships that extended way beyond the airport environs. Usually this meant that you became a part of the airport in your own right, with the added advantage of crossing the rivalry barriers – if that is the word – between competing companies

and interests. It also took reporters into a side of the airport the public and the passengers rarely experienced, and gave airport reporters access to privileged information and the unique advantage of 'inside knowledge'. Occasionally this could be a disadvantage. To maintain longer-term friendships it was sometimes necessary to walk away from situations when your instincts told you that in news terms they might be significant.

There was considerable camaraderie at the airport in those years – and that helped make them the good old days. Reporters and photographers were themselves airport staff and usually treated as such. They were almost always on the scene for the unexpected event rather than trying to catch up – like being in the cinema for the start of the film rather than having to stay to see it round again.

After thirty years as an airport reporter, Ray 'crossed over' to the other side in the 1970s to head BAA's PR team. Today, he lives in happy retirement in Northampton, where his local airports are Luton and Birmingham. He rarely visits Heathrow, but when he does he finds it difficult to navigate around its roads and terminals. 'And even as a BAA shareholder, I intensely dislike the emphasis on commercial advertising. This horrifies me as much as a set of giant bottles which were erected in front of Terminal 2 in the early 1960s to advertise White Horse whisky. They were huge and horrified most people back in those days – including me.'

EIGHTEEN

THE SUPERSONIC '70s

Flying Jumbos, Concordes, Terrorists – and Time to Call in the Army

THE 1970S MARKED THE DECADE when the world became a smaller place and far-flung cities could be reached faster and cheaper than ever before. It was the decade of mass transit air travel and Heathrow was at the epicentre of this activity. As the decade began it was handling 15.4 million passengers. At its end it was handling 27 million.

The airport's runways had to be extended from 9,000ft to 12,000ft, during the autumn and winter of 1969, in readiness for the arrival of the first Boeing 747 Jumbo Jet in January 1970. Many of the world's leading airlines had placed orders for the massive aircraft, built to carry 385 passengers in comfort on routes that criss-crossed the globe.

Heathrow invested £11 million in a major refurbishment programme to accommodate the new giant aeroplane and the large influx of passengers it would carry to and from London. The age of the wide-body Jumbo Jet began at the airport shortly after 2.00 p.m. on 22 January 1970 when Pan American ferried the first 324 fare-paying Boeing 747 passengers across the Atlantic, 7 hours late thanks to technical problems in New York.

Airport staff and hundreds of sightseers who turned out to see the new aircraft land could scarcely believe their eyes when the first of Pan American's 25 Boeing 747s roared its way into Heathrow's Terminal 3, formerly known as the Oceanic terminal. They had read about it in newspapers and seen television bulletins about the aircraft's trials – but now they were seeing it for themselves and they wondered how anything so massive could ever get off the ground, let alone carry over 300 passengers plus crew and a bellyful of freight over the Atlantic.

The huge plane was due to return to New York later that evening but problems with one of the 747's doors caused take-off to be delayed for over four hours. The 350-ton aircraft had encountered a multitude of difficulties during its development stage. There was concern over the kind of engines to be used to power the massive aeroplane, followed by others regarding the speed it might take to evacuate passengers if the plane experienced an emergency. The Heathrow delays were simply the latest problems to be overcome.

No one could believe their eyes when they saw the first Boeing 747 Jumbo Jet arrive at Heathrow Airport on 22 January 1970. They asked: 'How could anything so big ever get off the ground, let alone fly across the Atlantic?' *(Top: Barry Dix collection; bottom: Flo Kingdon collection)*

A collection of Boeing 747s, 707s and DC-10s on a typical day at Heathrow in the summer of 1970. *(Barry Dix collection)*

By the time the first aircraft had landed in London, BOAC had ordered eleven Boeing 747s, but a pay dispute by pilots threatened to delay its introduction.

Within six months of its first New York–London service, Pan American had carried over 1 million passengers on the Jumbo. A year later nearly 100 Jumbo Jets were in operation with seventeen airlines and the number of passengers travelling on the plane increased to 7 million. Since then, the aircraft's safety record has been good and, although it has been involved in several incidents and accidents, none have been directly attributable to a fault with the aircraft, making it one of the most successful ever built. The Boeing 747 has dominated the airline passenger and cargo world for over three decades and, for the time being, remains the largest commercial passenger aircraft in existence – although this will change when the new Airbus A380 (which can seat between 555 and 840 passengers) comes into commercial operation at Heathrow in 2006.

Concorde was designed to fly at twice the speed of sound, the result of equal partnership in design and technology, between England and France. The supersonic aircraft made its unofficial Heathrow debut dramatically and unexpectedly on a wet Sunday afternoon, on 13 September 1970 – five years and four months before it was due to enter full commercial service. By this time, Heathrow's former commentator on the Queen's Building, Flo Kingdon, had moved on to become a member of the airport public relations team and remembers:

Concorde made its Heathrow debut dramatically and unexpectedly in September 1970 when it was diverted to the airport after its base at Filton was closed owing to bad weather. *(Flo Kingdon collection)*

I was busy working with reporters and photographers who had come to the airport to report the arrival of British hostages who had been unfortunate enough to be on an aircraft hijacked by Palestinian terrorists. The passengers had been brought across the airport to hold a press conference in a building on the airport's north side and we were just finishing when suddenly there was a loud roar. I looked out of the window and through the mist – and suddenly Concorde zoomed past out on the runway.

All the press crowded around me immediately wanting to know what was going on. Concorde was towed to a stand close to where the press conference had been held and I rushed over and climbed the aircraft stairs and knocked on the door (which was open). I asked to speak to whoever was in charge. It was Brian Trubshaw, Concorde's chief test pilot. I could see that seats had been taken out of the cabin and replaced with all kinds of monitoring equipment and I edged my way to the front, where I told Mr Trubshaw that I had a large press group with me who were interested in Concorde's mysterious arrival. I asked him if he was prepared to give an impromptu press conference. He laughed and then agreed to meet everyone in the Queen's Building. He told me that Concorde had flown out of Farnborough to conduct some test flights and was heading for Filton, near Bristol. But Filton was fogged out and he needed somewhere else to land – and he was bursting for a chance to try out Heathrow's runways, which would eventually become its main operating base.

That was typical of Heathrow. You never knew what was going to happen next. The press were delighted. They had come to the airport for one story and went away with two.

Concorde's next Heathrow visit was on 21 January 1976, when the supersonic aircraft made its maiden flight from London to Bahrain in the colours of British Airways – the airline created by merging together BOAC and BEA in 1974. An Air France Concorde was scheduled to depart from Paris to Rio de Janeiro at the same time and a

A pair of Concordes at Heathrow's Terminal 3. This much-loved aircraft always made heads turn whenever it took off or landed.
(Flo Kingdon collection)

massive party was held in an airport restaurant for the media and VIPs, including government ministers, members of the opposition party, British and French plane-makers. Large TV split-screens showed the two airliners waiting to take off on their respective tarmacs in London and Paris at exactly 11.30 a.m. As the supersonic jets roared down their runways, the room was hushed and all eyes fixed on the front nose wheel of both aircraft. Never mind *entente cordiale*, everyone wanted to know which Concorde would be first into the skies. Would it be the one outside the window at Heathrow or the Air France version in Paris? Everyone held their breath – and then the nose-wheel of the British Airways service lifted a full two seconds before the French plane.

It was a small victory for Britain, but the politicians in the room were triumphant and a great cheer went up. The press corps were happy too, as some serious betting had taken place as to which aircraft would be first off the ground. One pressman was so delighted with the result that he stepped backwards – and onto the foot of an up-and-coming Conservative politician who had been a great champion of Concorde. Her name was Mrs Margaret Thatcher and thirty years later the reporter still remembers her icy glare in his direction as Britain's future first female Prime Minister hobbled away muttering under her breath something about clumsy reporters who had obviously consumed too much free food and drink on offer that day.*

* The author can testify to the accuracy of this incident – he is 'that clumsy reporter'!

Concorde was designed to fly at cruising speeds of 1,350mph, allowing it to cover the journey to Bahrain two hours faster than subsonic jets. In 1976, British Airways boasted that the one-way fare was 'only £45 more than the normal first-class fare'. While flying at supersonic speeds at an altitude that allowed passengers to see the curvature of the earth, passengers dined on gourmet meals – canapés, smoked salmon, breast of duck bigarade or fillet of steak with Café de Paris butter, fresh strawberries with double cream, English cheeses, a choice of three wines, champagne, cognac . . . the list just went on. British Airways spent £33 on food and wine for every Concorde passenger. Travellers flying in the economy-class section of the airline's other aircraft were served food and drink costing only £3.50.

Concorde's sleek and modern aircraft galley was built from new lightweight material, controlled by sophisticated electronics to ensure that all meals were simply perfect. It was a million miles away from what Mary Guthrie had to put up with in her primitive Avro Lancastrian galley thirty years before.

Most of Britain's population took Concorde to their hearts, seeing the aircraft as a strong symbol of European technical cooperation and a great achievement for aviation. Concorde was wonderful to look at but she was a noisy beast. Whenever she roared into the air, hundreds of businesses in the Heathrow area had to excuse themselves while talking on the telephone until she had passed overhead. Every day, Concorde triggered off hundreds of car alarms sensitive to the vibration it caused on the ground. The noise was murder for anyone living under her flight path. Everything stopped until Concorde had flown overhead, which was mercifully quick. But everyone loved to watch her shoot up into the sky like a beautiful dart, even those at Heathrow who saw her come and go every day. Anyone who ever saw Concorde felt a certain pride in their hearts for this unique aeroplane. Although only a small percentage of the British population ever flew in her, the majority felt ownership in her in some way. She is badly missed.

British Airways made its first appearance in 1935 as the country's second major airline after Imperial Airways. The brand name disappeared four years later when Britain's airline industry was nationalised and the name of Imperial Airways dominated the world's air lanes. It would be another forty-four years before the name returned, after the state-controlled airline sector was restructured and a single national carrier was created when BOAC and BEA merged into a single 'super' airline called British Airways.

Staff working for the two airlines hated the idea of a merger and attempts to bring the two companies together in previous decades had fallen at the first fence. BOAC, whose intercontinental routes flew the British flag in North and South America, Africa, Asia and Australasia, considered itself vastly superior to BEA, which carried the Union Jack on European routes closer to home.

Prior to this, both airlines were hidebound by their respective cultural legacies, lack of focus, rising debt and ineffective management. Many passengers actually hated flying with BOAC. The company's aircraft were safe, reliable and comfortable, but they complained that the staff was often snooty and superior in their attitude (as opposed to Pan American, whose in-flight staff was famous for being rude and uncaring). The

BEA Tridents and BAC One-Elevens on the tarmac at Terminal 1. *(Barry Dix collection)*

media said that once the merger had taken place, British Airways would be abbreviated to BA – standing for 'bloody awful'.

Thomas Marks from High Wycombe joined BOAC's engineering staff at London Airport in the mid-1950s and recalls:

> There is no doubt about it, everyone working for BOAC prior to the merger considered themselves superior to just about everyone else working at London Airport. Looking back, I now feel ashamed of this attitude. I put it down to the fact that everyone working for BOAC felt they were ambassadors for Britain. We thought we were better in everything we did. BOAC had the best planes and flew to the world's smartest destinations, carrying our great tradition with us wherever we went.
>
> What we didn't know, of course, was that the airline was losing money and deep in debt. We occasionally read newspaper stories about the company's financial performance, but didn't believe them because management made no public comment about the company's financial affairs. Every month staff members were given a magazine called *BOAC Review* which was full of articles about how fantastic BOAC was and how staff made this possible. And we believed it. We genuinely thought that everything we did turned to gold, so it came as a massive shock in later years to learn that BOAC had been trading almost insolvent for a long time. People who had worked at the airport for years were forced into early retirement and

others made redundant. Even the public turned against us. We used to think that we were 'the world's favourite airline' and came to realise that we were far from being favourite. We soon stopped feeling superior, I can tell you. At one stage I even avoided telling people who I worked for, such was the public's attitude towards BOAC.

The merger with BEA was a difficult one, but it made perfect sense. It was a chance for the airline to re-invent itself; something it tends to do over again every few years.

In addition to fleets of modern aircraft and route licences to prime destinations, BOAC and BEA also had other major assets – landing and take-off slots at Heathrow Airport, the world's most profitable airport and real estate where each had its own headquarters and engineering bases.

The purpose of the merger was to combine the strengths offered by the two carriers, eliminate their combined weaknesses and create a profitable and customer-focused carrier, which would eventually become privatised. Everyone was happy; or so it seemed, apart from the staff working for the airlines. There was talk of industrial unrest. The prospect of redundancies loomed large as there was bound to be job duplications when the two airlines became one. There were many questions, and few answers seemed to be coming from respective managements. As a result there was wild speculation and inaccurate predications about the outcome.

The merger went ahead, a new joint management was appointed, aircraft were repainted in a new livery and financial losses continued. One member of the airline's accounts team joked that when the time came to produce an annual report and accounts, Tipp-Ex was delivered to the airline in 100-gallon cans.

At the time of the merger, John Boulding had risen to become BOAC's chief investigator of accidents and air safety (a position that later won him an MBE). He recalls that one of the first things the newly merged airline did was to take air safety into its control, appointing John in charge of air safety on long-distance routes and another staff member on short-haul and regional routes. In 1977 John was named chief air safety investigator for the entire airline. 'And all the time the merger was going through, I thought that I would be out of a job. So did hundreds, thousands of others', he recalls.

In 1991 Margaret Thatcher appointed Sir John King to be the airline's new Chairman. British Airways was carrying an overdraft of £1 billion. The corporation was top-heavy with staff and operated many unprofitable routes. Thatcher charged King with the task of turning the loss-making airline around and prepare it for privatisation, but refused to pour any further state aid into its future. She kept telling King: 'Remember John, there is no money.'

King was forced to cut one-third of all jobs, withdraw aircraft from unprofitable routes and reduce capacity. He appointed a new Board, including several directors from outside the airline industry who – like himself – could offer plenty of experience and success in other commercial business areas. One such new Board member was Colin Marshall, a man with plenty of senior management experience and who became the airline's new Chief Executive. The challenge facing King, Marshall and the airline's Board was to turn British Airways from an appalling to an appealing airline.

A priority task was to make the airline's staff begin to believe in their company once again. An ambitious training programme called 'Putting People First' was introduced across the organisation and Marshall himself spent time mingling with staff and passengers. A new advertising campaign was created by Saatchi and Saatchi, while Landor Associates, a US-based design company, produced new visual identification for the airline's fleet incorporating elements from the British flag on aircraft tailplanes and fuselages.

In 1997 British Airways was successfully floated on the London Stock Exchange. Staffs were given a stake in this success and offered shares in their company. After many years of dissatisfaction, they began to believe in their airline once again. The flotation united the company which went on to become a profitable carrier. It did not put an end to the airline's woes and, over the next few years, British Airways would face many new challenges. More staff and unprofitable routes would be axed and the airline forced to rethink its role in the face of challenges from low-cost carriers. But, unlike many other national flag carriers unable to survive challenges facing airlines in the early years of the twenty-first century (such as Sabena, Swissair plus other European and American carriers teetering on the edge of bankruptcy), British Airways is a great survivor with an even greater future ahead.

Industrial relations in Britain reached a low ebb in the 1970s. It was the decade in which the country was plunged into economic chaos and a three-day working week and the 'winter of discontent' became potent symbols. A wave of strikes paralysed the country and Britain's European neighbours dubbed industrial unrest 'the British disease'. Disputes involved refuse collectors, deep-sea fishermen, car workers, coal miners, postmen, lorry drivers, shipbuilders, hospital workers, civil servants, social workers, printing trade unions – even Beefeaters at the Tower of London. They were all unhappy with pay, working conditions, or both; they had all tried to negotiate with their respective managements and talks had failed. There was only one avenue left open to them – to down tools and go on strike.

Heathrow had its own share of industrial unrest in the 1970s. In March 1970 the airport was shut down for the first time in twenty-four years when its firemen – employed by BAA – walked out over a dispute about shift allowances and working conditions. It is illegal for an airport to operate without a full complement of fire officers on hand to deal with an emergency, should it arise, and aircraft sat on the tarmac unable to move for two days. No incoming planes could land either, costing airlines thousands of pounds in lost revenue. Collectively, the airlines put BAA under strong pressure to resolve the dispute and the airport's owners were forced into reaching a compromise with firemen and Heathrow reopened again for business. It took days to clear the backlog of delayed passengers.

Fred Gore from Stanwell, Middlesex, was at the centre of much of the airport's trade union activity at the time. Born in London's East End, Fred moved to Hanworth shortly before the Second World War and volunteered for the Royal Navy in 1943, working as a torpedo man. He learned basic electrics in the Navy and when the war ended became a member of the Electricians' Trade Union (ETU). He joined BEA as an aircraft electrician in the early 1950s and recalls:

Fred Gore returns to Heathrow to visit the site of his earlier trade union activities. *(Alan Gallop)*

Heathrow was a wonderful place to work at that time, but industrial relations left a lot to be desired. Although a constitution had been set up by the Labour government of the day – which in many ways was ahead of its time – day-to-day problems at Heathrow were not answered and there were a number of short stoppages and disputes.

A big electricians' strike in 1961 disrupted the airline for about five weeks. Within a week we had the airline grounded. To get around the problem and to keep flying, the airline airlifted equipment and instruments for maintenance to other airports, which resulted in my getting in touch with these airports. Working closely with the World Federation of Trade Unions (an international trade union organisation which supports and encourages action by trade unions in every country) I flew to some of these countries asking for their support. For example, I would fly out to Czechoslovakia, meet with their unions, make lots of contacts and ask them to support our cause by not cooperating with the airline. I did the same in the Soviet Union and countries all around the Iron Curtain states. They were all marvellous and most cooperative. It made the employer realise that you couldn't just fly an airliner out to another airport for maintenance. Lord Douglas, the Chairman of BEA at the time, said that if the strike went on any longer we would all be out of a job – including himself.

Strangely enough, once the dust had settled the airline started to expand its operations and one of the political decisions was to set up a service to Moscow. There were problems about which route the airline would fly. So I contacted my friends in Russia to see if they could help BEA establish a scheduled route between Moscow and London. Lord Douglas was most helpful in supplying me with all kinds of gifts to take there. So it wasn't all antagonism. The unions were in a position to help management. There was cooperation.

When the airlines merged to create British Airways there were fears, which always exist in a merger, that there would be redundancies. If you merge two instrument shops together, you're going to have what management believes will be job duplication and surpluses. So the new BA Board decided to call a conference for all senior staff and we were asked to submit questions we might have about the future. Management asked for questions beforehand so they could consider their answers. So we submitted questions asking for guarantees that there would be no redundancies and asked if that question could be addressed as number one.

The question was asked and Roy Watts, BEA's Chairman, read it out and then told us that no employer in the country would give workers such a guarantee. I and all the other union representatives – there must have been 200 of us – walked out the conference and went back to the base to report what had been said. A week later I was sent for by Roy Watts' office and told that the airline was prepared to guarantee there would be no redundancies, on the understanding that trade unions would cooperate with the merger.

We set up various working parties to look at different aspects of the merger and I was elected Chairman. Our job was to look at ways of bringing all sections together. This was an opportunity for workers themselves to try and resolve issues brought about by the merger. As a result, not one dispute arose from the merger. There were disagreements about wages, but nothing arising from the merger.

From that day onwards, it was agreed that if unions didn't reach agreement, you went back to the drawing board. It was important to keep on talking and negotiating. Eventually all sections were merged including outstations. My job was to go to all these outstations and talk about the merger. As a result we reached an agreement in which no one was forcefully made redundant at British Airways. Nobody. As union representatives, our job was to negotiate for good pensions, wages and working conditions. And we achieved that.

A major Heathrow dispute which hit the headlines late in 1969 followed news that a Canadian company called General Aviation Services (GAS) had been contracted to provide a range of ground services and maintenance for Heathrow airlines. After correspondence had been passed to the unions indicating that GAS intended to grab contracts for anything, from cabin services to engineering, ground staff opposed the arrival of a competitive company and took industrial action. Other unions representing staffs working for 200 firms came to their support.

The dispute that followed has gone down in the annals of Heathrow trade union history. Many union veterans now compare the GAS dispute with the 1971 Upper Clyde shipbuilders' strike in protest about shipyard redundancies and mass action in July 1972 when the state was forced to release five shop stewards – known as the Pentonville Five – imprisoned under Edward Heath's anti-union laws. Fred takes up the story:

GAS generated terrific opposition from the unions, because the company threatened their jobs. GAS opened premises on the airport's north side and bought new equipment – but failed to sign up any airlines. The unions were ready to campaign in opposition to them because our members' jobs were sacrosanct. There was a gradual build-up to opposing this company, which finally secured a contract from Iberia. It claimed to have three others, but I think they were just paper contracts. A mass meeting was called at Brentford Football Ground where I had the job of moving the resolution that unless they withdrew from Heathrow we would 'black' any airline or company using the services of GAS.

It was a terrific mass meeting, probably one of the biggest ever seen in the Heathrow area. About 15,000 people walked out of the airport to attend and the stadium was full (the biggest gate ever?). It was a terrific effort. The vote was unanimous in favour of a strike. There was also a demonstration in the airport's

Central Area where the police used dogs to try and control the men. This resulted in questions being later asked in Parliament.

BAA, the custodians of Heathrow, decided they would have to take action against us and injunctions were served on individuals. Strangely enough, I didn't get one. My colleagues all received one, but I didn't and I don't know why. But it made no difference. We were adamant that we would 'black' any airlines using GAS.

It was just before Christmas and court cases were about to be heard when a statement was released by BAA stating that as a gesture of Christmas goodwill, the injunctions would be withdrawn. The National Joint Council [NJC] was meeting on this subject in London and was, perhaps, not on the same wavelength as us who worked at the airport. These were full-time paid officials who didn't see things in the same way as we did. They wanted us to compromise and let GAS have a little bit of business. But we didn't want a foreign company coming into Heathrow, taking revenue from our own country and jobs away from union members.

I had a hell of a job trying to persuade them to see our point of view. Edward Heath [Prime Minister 1970–4] sent one of his special envoys to see me. He was an elderly man, a farmer, and he said he didn't know why he'd been picked for the job. He said he knew nothing about aeroplanes. His job was to try and build a bridge between the unions and the government of the day and go back to Number 10 with some kind of solution.

At the end of the day the NJC came down in favour of us and GAS went back from whence they came. What we did, we did for the benefit of the country as a whole. We needed to protect the job security of our members. We believed we were doing the right thing.

There were other disputes at Heathrow and according to Fred 'people used to claim that we came out on strike when the daffodils came out'. But once the unions had obtained procedural agreement to resolve differences, strikes became a thing of the past and unions and management were in a position to work towards settlements.

A 1971 newspaper described Fred as follows: 'He's left-wing, there's no doubt about that. But he would probably prefer the term progressive to militant.' 'He's a not a member of the lunatic left', said a colleague. 'I knew I could always count on him. I would much sooner see a positive man like Fred. . . . He's ruthless, but a very astute politician.'

On retirement from British Airways, Fred managed an unemployment centre in Hounslow and became a Labour councillor in Spelthorne Borough. Although now fully retired, Fred is still actively involved in trade union activities. He still believes that Heathrow is a great place for a career, but would like to see more young apprentices coming to the airport and undergoing training schemes. 'I can remember a time when 600 engineering apprentices were going through the system at one time. Once they had received their final City & Guilds certification, they could get a job on the shop floor. You would see ordinary working-class lads get an apprenticeship, go to a technical college and be recommended to go on to university. Many of today's managers are people who went through that system. Far fewer apprentices go through it today.'

Security also became a great issue at Heathrow – and other leading airports around the world – in the 1970s. Increasing numbers of aircraft were being hijacked by terrorists and attacked both on the ground and in the air. Passengers were taken hostage and murdered.

Although aircraft hijacking was nothing new, it reached new heights on 6 September 1970 – later dubbed 'Skyjack Sunday' – when five passenger planes were hijacked by militant members of the People's Front for the Liberation of Palestine demanding release of Arab dissidents held in a Swiss jail. The incident involved a BOAC VC-10 bound for Heathrow from Bombay, a TWA 707 from Frankfurt, a Swissair DC-8 from Zurich, an El Al Boeing 707 from Amsterdam and a Pan American Boeing 747 from Amsterdam.

The BOAC, TWA and Swissair planes were flown to a former RAF airfield in Jordan – known as Dawson's Field – while the Pan American aircraft was ordered to fly to Cairo. On the El Al flight a passenger managed to pin down a female Arab hijacker holding hand grenades called Leila Khalid, while an airline steward managed to tackle another terrorist. Shots were fired killing an Arab militant and wounding a crew member, but the pilot was able to make a daring emergency landing at Heathrow. Leila Khalid was arrested by armed police at Heathrow and taken away to Ealing police station. After twenty-eight days she was released in exchange for over 400 hostages.

In Cairo, hostage passengers were taken to safety while the giant Boeing 747 was blown up. Captive passengers sitting in the desert heat in Jordan were released and the three jets wired with dynamite and detonated.

Security at Heathrow was stepped up following 'Skyjack Sunday'. Passenger searches and devices for scanning baggage and cargo were introduced. Occasionally there would be breeches of security and someone – usually a newspaper reporter (but not one of the airport's resident press corps) – would claim to have carried a potentially dangerous item onboard an aircraft without detection.

Threats to airport security also came from sources closer to home. Following the 'Bloody Sunday' killings in Belfast in 1972 when thirteen men were shot dead by British paratroopers in Londonderry, the IRA stepped up its nationalistic terror campaign. BEA flights from Heathrow to Belfast were boarded and disembarked in a special security monitored area and searches of passengers and airport staff going about their work increased dramatically.

And then, one Saturday in 1974, the Army 'invaded' Heathrow Airport. Few people expected to see troops driving around the airport's perimeter roads in armoured vehicles and wandering through passenger terminals carrying guns – including the soldiers themselves.

Following a strong tip-off to government officials that the airport could expect a terrorist attack, Prime Minister Edward Heath ordered soldiers from the Blues and Royals regiment, based in nearby Windsor barracks, to descend on Heathrow Airport. The first anyone – including airport officials and the police – knew about the troop invasion was when four armoured vehicles rolled through the airport tunnel and proceeded to drive around roads in the central area causing traffic chaos. Military vehicles were also seen on the airport's southern perimeter road.

A British Airways Lockheed TriStar crosses Heathrow's famous tunnel. *(Flo Kingdon collection)*

When airport reporters contacted the airport's management asking for an explanation, officials were forced to admit that they had no idea what was going on. It soon became clear that the Ministry of Defence had experienced a 'communications breakdown' in attempts to inform the British Airports Authority that the Army was on its way. A group of reporters and photographers jumped into cars and made their way around airport roads to speak to soldiers. They soon encountered an armed vehicle, from the top of which a soldier stood waving his hands at the pressmen indicating that he wanted them to stop. The media men thought they were about to be arrested when the soldier asked: 'Excuse me gents, have you any idea what's going on? Do you know why we're here? Because nobody has told us the reason.'

Airport police were furious that the Army had descended onto their 'patch' and confirmed that they, too, had not been informed about its arrival. Security staff became confused when several armed soldiers demanded to be allowed to pass through passenger controls into departure lounges only accessible to authorised passengers and airport staff holding the correct passes. The soldiers were eventually allowed to pass through airport controls, providing they were accompanied by reluctant police officers. It appears that they only wanted to enter the lounge in order to get a cup of tea from the departure lounge cafeteria.

Hours after the troops had descended on the airport and film of their confused activities had appeared on lunchtime television news bulletins, the Ministry of Defence issued a statement confirming that a terrorist threat had been received and the Army ordered to place 'a ring of steel' around the airport. The 'ring of steel' was lifted at 5.00 p.m. when troops went home to Windsor. They failed to appear the following morning (Sunday) but came back at 9.00 a.m. the following Monday, pulling out again at 5.00 p.m. By the end of the week, Prime Minister Heath must have felt that he had made his point to whatever terrorist group had made the threat (it was never made clear who it was, but was probably the IRA) because Britain's 9.00 a.m.–5.00 p.m. Army failed to return the following week and only returned to the airport on the odd occasion. It would be another thirty years before the Army returned to the airport following a terrorist alert, this time on the orders of Tony Blair.

On Sunday 19 May 1974 – the same date that Merlyn Rees, then Secretary of State for Northern Ireland, announced a State of Emergency in Ulster – the IRA planted a series of bombs in Heathrow's Terminal 1 car park. The explosion could be heard across the airport. Two people were injured and rushed to hospital. Over fifty vehicles were damaged in the bomb-blackened car park, some of them totally written off.

Jokes surrounding the comings and goings of the Army at Heathrow suddenly stopped. The IRA had been allowed to get as close to Heathrow, its passengers and staff as it was possible to get. Although the damage could have been worse, the terrorists from Ulster had made their presence felt. They had issued their warning signal and nobody complained any more about being searched as they passed through Heathrow's security system.

It was not the last Heathrow heard from the IRA. They would return with a series of bombing attacks two decades later.

Following events in New York on 11 September 2001, when aircraft were hijacked and flown into the World Trade Center and Pentagon buildings, security at the world's airports has never been tighter. Security procedures are a necessary pain. They have cost airports and airlines huge amounts of money and resulted in a 'security tax' being built into the cost of all airline tickets.

Because of security procedures, passengers now have to arrive at airport check-in desks hours before departure in order to pass through screening devices. Long queues form as passengers remove jackets and coats, put mobile phones, loose change and keys into special containers, which pass through X-ray machines, while they walk through devices designed to register other suspect objects concealed in passengers' pockets. Sometimes passengers are also body searched and required to remove shoes for closer examination.

A nuisance? Yes. A necessity? Definitely. Heathrow today is one of the safest and most secure airports in the world, although there will always be someone prepared to put this to the test and challenge the limits of security staff and equipment, resulting in longer queues and delays.

Back in 1943, when Professor Abercrombie had laid out his plans for London's new airport he had envisaged a rail connection to central London via an 'electric railway to Waterloo and Victoria by means of a short branch to Feltham. A 2-mile extension of the tube railway from Hounslow West would also give direct connection with the Underground system.' The Underground railway finally arrived at Heathrow thirty-four years later.

It took the form of a £71 million extension of the Piccadilly Line to Hatton Cross, on the airport's edge, and later diving down beneath the airport's runways and curving around to a new Underground station in the heart of the airport's terminal complex, called Heathrow Central.

The Queen formally unveiled the Underground link on 16 December 1977, when Heathrow became the first airport in the world to offer a rapid rail link to a capital city centre. Heathrow to Piccadilly could be achieved in around thirty-five minutes. Her Majesty travelled to the new station by tube from Hatton Cross – designated a 'royal train' for the three-minute journey – which broke a ceremonial tape as it came to a standstill on the westbound platform. It arrived four minutes late.

Work on London Transport's Piccadilly Line extension nears completion. *(BAA (Heathrow) Archive)*

PRIVATE: NOT FOR PUBLICATION.

ROYAL TRAINS NOTICE

PICCADILLY LINE

OPENING OF HEATHROW CENTRAL STATION BY HER MAJESTY QUEEN ELIZABETH II

FRIDAY, 16th DECEMBER, 1977

Section.	Subject.
A	General Programme.
B	Working of Royal and Associated Special Trains.
C	Working of Northfields Station.
D	Working of Hatton Cross Station.
E	Working of Heathrow Central Station.
F	Traction Current Arrangements.
G	Allocation of Responsibilities.
H	First Aid.
J	Location of Emergency Men.
K	Press Facilities.
L	Security Arrangements.

55 Broadway, London SW1H 0BD.
9th December, 1977.
(1000)
200/TAH/29/48
Waterlow London 02806

J. GRAEME BRUCE,
Chief Operating Manager (Railways)

London Transport personnel were issued with special details about the royal opening of the Heathrow Central station on 16 December 1977. *(Author's collection)*

The Queen, whose grandfather George V had pioneered the 'tuppenny tube' in 1890, was taken on a tour of the station and purchased a ticket from one of the new machines. A reporter covering the occasion noted that she did not reach into her royal purse for coins, but was handed 80p by the station's chief booking clerk. The Queen paid tribute to airport staff as she unveiled a commemorative plaque marking the opening of the new service, designed to carry 11 million passengers in its first year. The single-fare cost of 80p compared favourably with the £1 bus fare into central London and £5.50 taxi fare.

Since 1977, the Piccadilly Line to Heathrow had been expanded to include a branch line to Terminal 4 and – at the time of writing – a further extension is rapidly burrowing its way underground towards the new Terminal 5.

In 1999, Tony Blair officially opened the Heathrow Express which provides fast, efficient travel between Heathrow and London Paddington in fifteen minutes. The rapid rail link was introduced after BAA announced that their vision was to see half of all passengers using the airport arriving and departing by public transport.

Heathrow Express cost £450 million to build. Trains run at fifteen-minute intervals and services start at 5.00 a.m., finishing just before midnight. At Paddington visitors can connect to the rest of the London Underground network allowing them to continue their journey further into London if required. Passengers with return air tickets can check in and complete boarding formalities at Paddington, leaving them free to head straight for the departure gate on arrival at Heathrow.

The Piccadilly Line and Heathrow Express are both examples of late twentieth-century transport technology for the capital's premier airport, originally conceived in the dark days of the Second World War and finally taking between thirty-three and fifty-four years to realise. Time certainly flies, but the wheels that make airport–city transport links turn take a little longer.

At a few minutes past 5.00 p.m., on a quiet Sunday afternoon in June 1972, 112 passengers boarded BEA Trident G-ARPI – known as *Papa India* – at Heathrow bound for Brussels. Six regular crew members were also rostered to fly on the aircraft that day. A few minutes after taking off from runway 28R, the plane dropped out of the sky and 6,000ft later crashed into a field on the edge of Staines, Middlesex – a populous town 3 miles south-west of the airport. *Papa India* missed the town centre and several residential roads by a few hundred yards.

Eyewitness Adrian Bailey, age 15, said: 'I heard the plane circling overhead and there was a spluttering sound as though the engines were cutting out – then there was a thud like a clap of thunder.' The fuselage ploughed into trees and the tail section landed 50 yds away from the rest of the wreckage.

Father Peter Knott, Roman Catholic chaplain at the airport's St George's Chapel, was driving along the A30 when he saw the aircraft plummet into the field. He was one of the first on the scene. He climbed a low fence and rushed to the wreckage, which lay in three large pieces with the tailplane sitting at an angle of 45 degrees into the air. He later recalled that the only sound to be heard, that early summer's evening, was birdsong. Inside the main fuselage section he found a scene of total devastation, dead passengers still strapped into their seats. As he moved down the aisle he noticed movement coming from one passenger. Clearly the passenger was close to death and Father Knott administered the last rights.

Moments later the local police, fire service and other rescuers were on the scene just as a fire broke out in the crashed plane. Flames were quickly extinguished and a passenger, discovered by Father Knott and still alive – a businessman from Dublin – was removed and taken to a local hospital, where he died shortly afterwards. A young girl was also found alive, but died moments after being removed from the wreckage. There were no other survivors and the crash of *Papa India* marked the first time that more than 100 people had been killed in a British air accident.

Days later, BEA Chairman, Sir Henry Marking, said that there was 'no reason to suspect sabotage'. A later inquiry by the Air Accidents Investigation Branch concluded that a 'speed error had caused the plane to stall'. An autopsy on Captain Stanley Keys, who was in charge of the flight that day, revealed that he was suffering from a heart condition which may have been causing him pain during the fatal take-off. It was later learned that, prior to boarding the flight, Captain Keys had been involved in a disagreement with another pilot in BEA's Heathrow Crew Room regarding a labour issue, which may have raised his blood pressure that in turn impaired his judgement while at the controls.

Other issues arose from the crash, most notably a lack of training among BEA crew about what action to take when a fellow crew member became incapacitated at the controls. It was generally accepted that the plane could have been saved if flying crew had been more aware of danger signals.

The *Papa India* disaster plunged Heathrow into a state of deep gloom for many weeks. People living in and around Staines were in deep shock. After twenty-six years, the town had grown used to Heathrow; hundreds of its residents worked there. The Trident's wreckage remained in the field for days while accident investigators carried out their inquiries. Local people passed the crash site every day on their way to and from their airport jobs. They reflected on how close part of their town and scores of its residents had come to being wiped out or injured by an aircraft flying from the place many depended on for their livelihoods.

Thirty-four years after *Papa India* fell from the sky, the field where its wreckage came to a halt and 118 passengers and crew died, remained an empty space. In June 2004, the people of Staines remembered the disaster by opening a memorial garden on the spot and unveiling a specially commissioned stained-glass window in nearby St Mary's Church.

At a service of dedication, local councillor, John O'Hara, said: 'All of us associated with that dreadful event, have our own memories, but Staines has always lacked a memorial to the tragedy, so that those who wish to reflect, may do so in dignity.' The window and garden were the result of moves within the Staines community to remedy the situation. Financial support came from BAA, British Airways and the local council.

'The *Papa India* disaster was the worst aircraft accident in British history and, with the exception of the Lockerbie outrage, that remains so today', said Councillor O'Hara. 'Time heals wounds, but we will never forget.'

NINETEEN

THE 1980s

We Lived at the Right Time

AS THE 1970S DREW TO A CLOSE, 27 million passengers were using Heathrow annually. Terminals were congested and there was an urgent need for an additional one – although two would have been better. Space in the central area was a problem and there was no room for more buildings of any size next to Terminals 1, 2 and 3 – but there was space alongside Heathrow's south-east perimeter.

By 1978, when an empty plot of land for Terminal 4 had been allocated, Frederick Gibberd – the man responsible for designing most of Heathrow's key buildings – had retired and the job of drawing up plans for the new building went to the architectural practice of Scott, Brownrigg & Turner. Their design was influenced by the post-modernist styles of Richard Rogers' Pompidou Centre in Paris and the London headquarters of the Stock Exchange; although the new terminal's exterior could not have been more different.

The site lay within the airport's boundaries close to the A30 Great South West Road and £200 million was allocated for its construction once a public inquiry had taken place. Following pressure from local councils surrounding Heathrow, up to half of the inquiry was held within local communities, allowing residents, businesses and elected representatives to state their case on their own doorsteps. In order to give everyone with something to say a chance, local inquiries were held in town halls and civic centres during afternoons and evenings. The rest of the inquiry took place at London's County Hall, beginning in May 1978.

In a report designed to promote its case for the new building, BAA said that the terminal would create between 3,000 and 6,000 new jobs by 1987. The report said that impact on local housing would be 'slight' and that road traffic would increase by 'no more than 17 per cent' once the terminal was open. The report also stated that Terminal 4 would allow Heathrow to handle 38 million passengers and that 'the terminal is needed as soon as possible to ensure the UK remains at the forefront of the world civil air transport industry'.

The public inquiry resulted in the BAA receiving the green light to go ahead and build the terminal. Objections were widespread, mostly on the grounds of noise, use of green-belt land in construction of access roads and disruption to community services. Some groups stated that the multi-million-pound investment could be better spent elsewhere in the country.

Terminal 4 takes shape in June 1983. *(BAA (Heathrow) Archive)*

The spacious new terminal was designed to accommodate twenty of the world's largest aircraft at one time. Its design would allow arriving and departing passengers to be totally segregated from each other. The departures area was massive – but so was the distance that some passengers had to travel in order to board aircraft parked at the furthest aircraft stands from the passenger lounge.

The terminal's large departure hall was deliberately built in the style of a great bare hall in order to discourage, what BAA calls, 'weepers' – friends or relatives travelling to the airport to say goodbye to passengers – from staying too long.

Areas around the building were carefully landscaped with a small series of undulating hills designed to reduce noise levels created by aircraft and motor traffic using the terminal. The hills separated the terminal and its roadways from part of the small community of Bedfont which almost ran up to the side of the new building.

British Airways Chairman, Lord King, desperately wanted his airline to occupy the entire new terminal on an exclusive basis but, following a heated exchange with BAA Chairman, Sir Norman Payne, King was told that it was not possible for a single airline to monopolise the building.

Terminal 4 under construction.
(BAA (Heathrow) Archive)

The Prince and Princess of Wales at Heathrow following the opening of Terminal 4. *(BAA (Heathrow) Archive)*

British Airways, however, became the terminal's main user when it was finally opened by the Prince and Princess of Wales on 1 April 1986, sharing it with several other carriers.

During the 1970s and 1980s, Heathrow acquired the unfortunate nickname of 'thiefrow' following a number of robberies from airport cargo buildings and passenger baggage. Airport staff was often placed under suspicion. The majority of Heathrow's employees were – and remain – honest, hard-working folk, but occasionally one bad apple would spoil it for the rest of the barrel and be accused of theft.

Heat radiates out of the engines of a collection of jets operated by European airlines at Heathrow in 1980. *(BAA (Heathrow) Archive)*

In November 1983, an armed gang, wearing balaclavas and security uniforms, carried out Britain's largest ever robbery at Heathrow. Over £25 million worth of gold bullion, destined for the Far East, was stolen from a warehouse owned by the Brinks Mat Company early one morning.

Police estimated that around six people were involved. The men overcame warehouse guards, terrorised them into revealing secret alarm codes, handcuffed them and then disabled electronic security devices. They hit one of the security guards over the head with a pistol and poured petrol over two others.

Once inside the security vault, the robbers used the warehouse's own forklift truck to transport seventy-six boxes containing nearly 7,000 gold ingots to a waiting van. £100,000 worth of cut and uncut diamonds were also seized. Fifteen minutes after the thieves had left, one of the security guards managed to raise the alarm.

Only three members of the gang were convicted. Two were jailed for twenty-five years and a third served fourteen years for handling some of the stolen gold. Despite a huge police investigation, most of the gold has still to be recovered having 'vanished' into the criminal underworld. It is also said that anyone wearing gold jewellery purchased in the UK after 1983, is probably wearing Brinks Mat gold.

In January 1986, three people arrived at British Airways' Heathrow headquarters with invitations to a luncheon party in their pockets. They were no strangers to the airport, although it had been some years since the trio had been there in their capacity as flying crew or airline passengers.

At the door they gave their names to a girl checking invitations. First to arrive was a smartly dressed 75-year-old gentleman who declined the glass of wine offered on arrival. He gave out his name in a booming voice: 'Air Vice-Marshal Donald Bennett, CB, CBE, DSO'. The man who had flown the first international flight from Heathrow had returned to the place where the airport's history had begun four decades before.

Bennett was guest of honour at a special celebration for 200 guests marking both the airport's 40th anniversary and the founding of British South American Airways, the airline that had made civil aviation history on 1 January 1946.

Some said that Bennett had turned into a bitter old man, in the habit of telephoning Heathrow's switchboard demanding to speak to the airport director to protest about the claim that the first Heathrow flight was one which took off on 25 March 1946 and not his Lancastrian, Star Light. The airport director ungraciously refused to return Bennett's calls and he was usually diverted to the airport's public relations department. Former airport reporter Ray Berry fielded one of Bennett's calls in his later role as a Heathrow PR man and remembers how angry and insulted the old Air Vice-Marshal appeared to be as he insisted that his flight be recognised as the airport's first departure.

It would have done the airport authority no harm to have backed down and let Bennett retain the glory that was rightfully his. The airport could, in fact, have championed Bennett and used him as a valuable promotional tool. Instead, they ungraciously ignored the old RAF Pathfinder and his early achievements for the airport.

Next to arrive was a smartly dressed lady, aged 65. Former BSAA colleagues recognised her as Star Girl Mary Guthrie – for the last thirty-five years Mrs Mary Cunningham. Now living in retirement with her family in Somerset, Mary rarely visited the airport, but was delighted to be back at Heathrow in the company of colleagues she had not seen in years.

As the room began to fill with people, another familiar face from forty years ago arrived at the door: Captain Cliff 'Alaby' Alabaster, navigator on the first flight. Pride of place in Alaby's home in Surrey is a scale model of the famous Comet jet that he flew for BOAC for many years, including its first and last flights for the airline, carrying the inscription on a plinth (borrowed from St Matthew's Gospel): 'So the last shall be first, and the first last.' Alaby was now retired, aged 68, and enjoying his free time sailing boats around the Mediterranean.

Meanwhile, over at Terminal 1, another event had been planned for the veterans. Waiting to greet the historic Heathrow trio was another airport and BSAA veteran, Keith Hayward, who, as a 16-year-old school leaver, had travelled to the airport with Bennett and Alaby to witness the departure of the first flight. Now, just three years away from retirement and working as senior passenger officer with British Airways in Terminal 1, Keith was the prime mover of today's reunion party and further recognition of the airport's first international departure.

Once the guests had all arrived, they were taken to the airline's VIP lounge in Terminal 1, where Bennett, Mary and Alaby unveiled a framed photograph commemorating their thirty-six-hour flight to Buenos Aires four decades earlier. The Air Vice-Marshal must have been delighted that his achievement had at last been recognised, even if it was by British Airways instead of the airport authority.

When asked later by a television reporter what Heathrow was like in those days, Bennett reflected: 'We didn't have any buildings then. The airport looked like a runway under construction, and that's exactly what it was. We used a hut as headquarters for British South American Airways and there was one other building for flying control. The whole atmosphere wasn't exactly make-do, but we had to get on with it despite the lack of posh buildings and expensive places for passengers to be held up in. We had to ask the contractors if they would clear the runway so we could take-off. In those days it was almost exciting, certainly very interesting. Today it's mundane in the extreme. We lived at the right time.'

The Air Vice-Marshal also used the occasion to take a potshot at the way airports were run in the 1980s. 'Back in 1946 I was one of those who believed that we should have eight airports, not one – and I still think I'm right. If you look around Heathrow on a busy day, you'll see exactly what I mean.'

Seven months later Bennett was dead. He passed away on 14 September 1986 – his seventy-sixth birthday. At the time of writing, Mary Cunningham, Cliff Alabaster and Keith Hayward are still going strong, enjoying their retirement, keeping in touch with children and grandchildren and reflecting on fine careers up in the air and on the ground at Heathrow. At the age of seventy-six, Keith, who worked at the airport from leaving school to retirement, today freely gives his time as honorary consultant archivist at British Airways' marvellous treasure trove of an archive, located near the airline's Heathrow maintenance base (and where that famous commemorative photograph is now displayed). *Long may they thrive!*

Together again after 40 years – Heathrow pioneers Captain Cliff Alabaster (left), Star Girl Mary Guthrie (now Mrs Cunningham) and Air Vice-Marshal Donald Bennett. *(Brenard Press)*

In December 1988, an anonymous telephone message was received at the US Embassy in Helsinki warning that a sabotage attempt would shortly be made against a Pan American aircraft flying between Frankfurt and the United States. Details of the call were passed on by the American Federal Aviation Administration to embassies around Europe and to the airline's headquarters. But the information was never made available to the public because it would harm the now ailing airline and cause unnecessary panic among the travelling public. In many areas, the threat was dismissed as a hoax.

On 21 December, Pan American Boeing 747, Maid of the Seas, and carrying 259 passengers and crew took off from Heathrow to New York. Around forty minutes into the journey, the flight disappeared from the radar screen at Prestwick Air Traffic Control Centre. There were reports that an explosion had taken place on the ground 15 miles north of the Scottish border. The plane had crashed from a height of 31,000ft onto the town of Lockerbie, between Carlisle and Dumfries. Everyone onboard was killed. A further eleven people on the ground also lost their lives that day, as the wreckage plunged through twenty houses and numerous cars, ploughing a deep crater into a residential street. The plane then exploded into a ball of fire, propelling debris across a wide area. The impact reached 1.6 on the Richter scale. 'It was virtually raining fire, liquid fire,' said an eyewitness.

The crash had been caused by a massive explosion in a baggage container positioned on the left-hand side of the forward cargo hold, scattering passengers, baggage, cargo and wreckage over a wide area of Lockerbie.

The subsequent police investigation was the biggest ever mounted in Scotland and was turned into a full-scale murder inquiry once evidence of a bomb was found by Britain's Air Accidents Investigation Branch. The organisation later confirmed that the Pan American jet had been sabotaged and traces of Semtex high explosives were discovered in the wreckage. The bomb had been hidden away inside a portable radio cassette player concealed in a suitcase.

Two men, accused of being Libyan intelligence agents, were later charged with planting the bomb in a piece of baggage checked in at Frankfurt Airport and due to be transferred to the ill-fated Pan American jet at Heathrow. One of them was jailed for life following an eighty-four-day trial under Scottish law and held in Holland, while his alleged accomplice was found not guilty.

Once again, Heathrow was placed under alert and security screening stepped-up. Passenger baggage and cargo containers were placed in special 'decompression chambers', which scanned units for suspect devices. Passenger searches were intensified and travellers advised to arrive at airport check-in desks even earlier in order to undergo extra security checks.

Today, over one-third of BAA's UK employees work in security-related jobs. The organisation was the world's first to introduce 100 per cent total baggage screening, and new security techniques are constantly being pioneered at Heathrow.

At the same time as plans were being drawn up for Terminal 4 in the 1970s, secret talks were taking place at the British Airports Authority's London offices for a fifth terminal, a building much larger than the others and built on the only site still available on what was now an extremely congested airport.

One of the last tasks facing Sir Peter Masefield, before he retired as BAA's Chairman in 1972, was to oversee plans for Heathrow's fifth terminal, which the organisation expected to be fully built and ready for use in 1990 on the redeveloped site of the Perry Oaks sludge works on the airport's western side. Knowing that a large-scale public inquiry would have to take place before builders moved in, BAA quietly put the Terminal 5 plans to one side – for the time being. The organisation had one other major plan to oversee before it could do anything else.

The plan was to float its shares on the stock market in 1987. Market analysts were sceptical about the success of the flotation, but investors brave enough to buy shares saw excellent returns in a short time. Now, Heathrow – and other airports run by the newly renamed BAA plc – had to operate on a commercial basis. The world watched and quickly saw that privatising airports was a good idea. Within three years, BAA had created a template for airport managements to follow and today it operates a successful consultancy for management or retail contracts of airports in Australia, Italy, Oman and the United States.

TWENTY

THE 1990s

Dirty Tricks, the IRA and the Longest Public Inquiry

OVER 40 MILLION PASSENGERS were using Heathrow at the start of the 1990s and, behind the scenes, plans were being finalised for the largest and most controversial construction project in Europe – Terminal 5.

It was no secret that BAA wanted another terminal to be sited on land covering 251 hectares on the airport's western edge, an area once occupied by the small country settlement of Perry Oaks, now site of a sewage works owned and operated by Thames Water Utilities. It was the only place large enough to accommodate a massive new terminal and the surrounding infrastructure needed to successfully feed cars, coaches, lorries, underground trains plus the world's largest airliners – including the 555-seat A380 – to and from the building.

Naturally, a public inquiry would be mounted to examine evidence for and against construction of the new terminal and an inquiry secretariat was set up well in advance of BAA's application being received in order to have everything ready for the time when organisations and individuals could come forward and present points of view.

By February 1993, BAA was ready to submit forty separate formal applications, orders and appeals under the Planning, Highways, Civil Aviation and Transport and Works Acts. By the following month, the organisation had submitted a further twenty applications relating to Terminal 5, including schemes to relocate the sewage works, divert the two rivers running around the site, building a new road connecting the terminal to the M25 motorway (which would be widened to cope with massive amounts of extra traffic), improvements to the M4 and extensions to the Heathrow Express railway and Piccadilly Line.

BAA put forward a strong argument in favour of a terminal designed to handle 17 million passengers annually and boost the airport's annual throughput to 80 million travellers annually. Estimated cost was in the region of £3.7 billion. It stated that as the world's busiest airport, Heathrow's success was 'vital to the local economy and the country as a whole'. It predicted that the number of people wanting to fly 'is forecast to double in the next fifteen years. Heathrow's existing four terminals cannot cope with this demand and the airport needs to expand. Both Gatwick and Stansted airports are growing fast, but London needs Terminal 5 as well if it is to meet the needs of the twenty-first century.'

According to BAA, 'without Terminal 5, Heathrow's position as Europe's leading gateway could be lost to other airports. Airlines seeking to grow their business could take their investment and jobs to Paris, Frankfurt and Amsterdam instead of London.' The organisation promised that 'thanks to expected advances in aircraft technology, there will be no overall increase in noise levels . . . and BAA will accept a legally binding guarantee that this is so'.

The terminal would also generate employment for thousands of people 'and provide around 6,000 construction jobs'. BAA claimed that the project 'has the support of the travel industry, trade unions, business groups and many community representatives – and local polls show residents strongly in favour'.

BAA's early Terminal 5 publicity failed to mention that the terminal also had a large number of objectors, including thirteen local authorities. Out of fifty major parties participating in the inquiry – including environmental groups and residents living around Heathrow – over 95 per cent were opposed to the terminal. Around 5,000 individuals and organisations formerly registered to speak for or against the construction project – 3,000 giving oral evidence and 2,000 submitting written representations. So large was the demand to give evidence that a special library had to be created to contain it all.

While arrangements for the Terminal 5 public inquiry rolled on, Heathrow and British Airways were both under attack from different quarters.

In 1993, British Airways ended one of the most bitter and protracted libel actions in aviation history following a humiliating courtroom climbdown. In the High Court, Christopher Clarke QC publicly apologised 'unreservedly' for an alleged 'dirty tricks' campaign against rival airline Virgin Atlantic.

The airlines had competed with each other head-to-head on transatlantic routes ever since Virgin had transferred operations from Gatwick to Heathrow in July 1991. Virgin's boss, Richard Branson, claimed that he had evidence that the British Airways' staff was in the habit of 'poaching' Virgin's customers and tampering with confidential company files. Branson also claimed that British Airways' PR consultants had been undermining him and his company in the City and through the media.

In an open letter to British Airways executive directors, Branson accused the airline of 'sharp business practices'. They responded by accusing Branson of publicity-seeking and the accusation was repeated by British Airways Chairman, Lord King, in a staff newspaper. The statements formed the basis of Branson's libel case and both British Airways and Lord King countersued over Virgin's original allegations.

The High Court heard that British Airways agreed to pay damages of £500,000 to Branson and £110,000 to his airline, as well as picking up legal costs of around £3 million.

In June 1993 Lord King retired from British Airways six months earlier than expected, to be replaced by Colin Marshall (now Lord Marshall). That year the airline

5 MORT
BOMBS
FIRED AT
attack signa
new campaign
IRA launc
mortar attack
IRA shatters
peace hopes
with attack
on Heathrow
MORTAR BLIT
ON HEATHR
Heathrow attack
breaks new groun
mortars
IRA fires

made a pre-tax profit of £301 million while Virgin Atlantic declared an operating loss of £9.3 million. Virgin went back into profit, however, in later years and went on to rival British Airways on major airline routes to Africa, Asia and Australia.

Nobody working at Heathrow in March 1994 will ever forget the three days when the IRA launched a series of mortar attacks on the airport. *(BAA (Heathrow) Archive)*

No one working at Heathrow Airport in March 1994 will ever forget three terrifying days when the IRA launched a series of mortar attacks on the airport, partially paralysing the capital's main air route. The IRA's plan was to blow up runways, cause death and injury to airport staff and passengers – including the Queen – and damage to aircraft, including Concorde.

Attack number one happened on the evening of 9 March, when IRA terrorists carried out a mortar attack from a car park next to the airport's Hatton Cross underground station. The attack followed a coded telephone warning to the airport switchboard. Although five mortars fell inside the airport grounds, none exploded. Concorde had touched down at Heathrow from New York just a few moments before. Police and security services searched the area looking for other vehicles containing mortars but found none.

The second attack came thirty hours later when another coded warning alerted the airport to expect further assaults on Terminal 4. Passengers and staff were evacuated from the building and runways closed, causing congestion and confusion in other terminals. This time the IRA had positioned themselves in a wooded area on the western side of the airport, from where they launched four mortars over the perimeter fence. Once again, none exploded. A Royal Air Force plane carrying the Queen landed at Heathrow while security forces were conducting a search of the terminal. Police carried out minute searches but discovered no further mortars.

Attack number three came on 13 March, when four IRA bombs were fired from a heavily camouflaged launcher buried in scrubland along the airport's southern perimeter. The airport was closed for two hours following the mortar attack and none of the devices exploded.

Although the IRA attacks had failed to kill, maim or damage Heathrow's passengers and staff, they had brought business to a standstill on three consecutive occasions and demonstrated just how vulnerable the airport was to attack.

Early in 1995, Roy Vandermeer QC was appointed Chief Inspector of the Terminal 5 inquiry. In April and May he called a series of pre-inquiry meetings to identify thirty different parties who would go on to play an active part in the proceedings, examine the main issues and how they would be handled, agree day-to-day ground rules, and how formal evidence would be exchanged. It was stated that, once the inquiry was under way, it would operate on totally transparent lines with daily verbatim transcripts of proceedings made available in printed form and via a special website.

A major problem facing Mr Vandermeer and his team was where the inquiry itself should be held. There were few venues in the Heathrow area large enough to accommodate both an inquiry hall and the large amount of office space needed to support the proceedings. The venue also needed to be close to Heathrow and the surrounding community, and it was agreed that an airport hotel could offer neutral ground for what was expected to be a long and controversial inquiry. Three hotels along Heathrow's famous 'strip' – the nickname given to the section of the Bath Road running alongside the airport, which, for the past thirty years, had come to resemble the famous Las Vegas thoroughfare housing hotels, casinos and nightclubs. But none of the hotels were keen to hire out their ballrooms or conference centres for a long and indefinite period because they risked losing regular clientele.

And then the manager of the Ramada (now Renaissance) Hotel – adjacent to the site where the airport's first flight had taken off in 1946 – suggested that the hotel's under-used swimming pool be converted into a meeting hall. It would mean that he could keep his function rooms open and, for a capital outlay, rent out the former swimming pool for what was expected to be a long period, plus fifty ground-floor bedrooms to be used as offices by the major parties and secretariat; a nice business deal!

The government had previously agreed that, in view of the exceptional nature of the inquiry, the Department of the Environment, rather than a local planning authority, would cover the cost of the main inquiry accommodation.

After two years of preparation, the Terminal 5 inquiry finally opened on 16 May 1995. Over 400 people turned up for the first day. The major players were identified as BAA plc (the applicant), British Airways (the terminal's major supporter), the Highways Agency (promoting Highways Orders), the London Borough of Hillingdon (the local planning authority opposing Terminal 5), Spelthorne Borough Council (also opposing) plus LHRT5 (a consortium of ten local authorities also against the terminal development). The Environment Agency and Royal Parks Agency were also involved for part of the time. Over thirty barristers, solicitors and advocates, including twelve QCs, appeared for these and other parties during the course of the inquiry.

Around twenty small third parties and individuals played a regular part in the proceedings, including the environmental and noise action groups Friends of the Earth and HACAN Clearskies. The groups represented themselves, as the secretariat had no resources to assist with anyone's legal costs, although some bedrooms were made available for office use by the smaller groups.

Despite deep feelings aroused in many by Terminal 5, the inquiry was conducted in a cooperative and orderly atmosphere throughout.

Over half of the inquiry time was taken up for three topics – the economic/aviation case for the proposals, surface access to the new terminal and noise. These covered the main issues of concern to objectors although the effects of the terminal on land use/ecology, air quality and construction impact were also important to local people.

Thirty-five parties made closing submissions at the end of the inquiry, taking forty 'sitting days'; BAA's closing speech took fourteen of them.

The inquiry finally closed on 17 March 1999, when recommendations were submitted to the Department of Trade and Industry. It had sat for 525 days spanning three years and ten months and entered the *Guinness Book of Records* as Britain's longest-running planning inquiry (overtaking the Sizewell B Nuclear Power Station inquiry, which ran for 340 days). The inquiry had cost over £80 million, of which £64 million was borne by BAA and British Airways and £17 million by central and local government. Local authorities opposing Terminal 5 spent over £7 million on opposing the terminal plan. Evidence was given by 734 witnesses representing over 50 major parties. Over 600 pieces of evidence were submitted along with 22,500 written representations – most of them expressing opposition to Terminal 5. The inquiry had generated 5,000 documents covering 80,000 pages and 30 million words. Under the inquiry rules, everyone had a statutory right to be heard and challenge the views of others and time allocated to hear their views.

Now they held their collective breath while awaiting a decision. . . .

The final outcome of the inquiry came on 20 November 2001, when the government gave its blessing to allow the terminal to go ahead with the next stage of planning. It would be ready for business in 2008. Thousands who had spent time gathering and giving evidence to the inquiry were disappointed. Others said that the outcome had been a foregone conclusion and that the inquiry itself a cosmetic (yet highly expensive) exercise for what was an inevitable outcome.

As the twentieth century drew to a close at Heathrow, BAA announced that 61.9 million passengers had passed through the airport in 1999.

TWENTY-ONE

2000 – AND BEYOND

Time Flies Back and Forth

WHILE THE TERMINAL 5 INQUIRY trundled on, eighty of Britain's top archaeologists were making plans to excavate the 250-acre site, which they were confident would reveal some fantastic objects that had been buried beneath the airport for thousands of years. Excavation plans were formulated as soon as BAA announced its intention to build a terminal at Perry Oaks.

Before the army of builders moved onto the airport, archaeologists from Wessex Archaeology and the Oxford Archaeological Unit brought their teams together for the largest excavation in British history. They were given just over a year to complete their 'dig'.

Before long, the archaeologists were unearthing evidence of communally farmed land divided into individual and family owned plots dating from around 2,000 BC. They discovered evidence of wells and boreholes and 80,000 individual objects including a 3,500-year-old wooden bowl and one of only two wooden buckets ever found from the same period; 2,000-year-old pottery cups were also uncovered along with 18,000 other pieces of pottery and 40,000 pieces of worked flint.

One archaeologist described the Terminal 5 site as giving 'unprecedented insight into the way mankind had used the landscape over the past 8,000 years', with pieces found from the Mesolithic or Middle Stone Age period and earliest farmers of the Neolithic period or the New Stone Age. Items from the Bronze and Iron Ages, Roman, Saxon and Medieval periods were all brought to light.

John Lewis, one of several archaeologists in charge of the dig, said: 'It was fascinating to discover that within the boundaries of the world's biggest international airport lies a record of how people used the landscape for 8,000 years, from the time when people were hunter-gatherers to the earliest farmers and later'.

The archaeological finds are now on permanent show at the Museum of London and the Heathrow Visitors Centre.

Around 450 armed troops were back at Heathrow at dawn on 12 February 2003, after a suspected Islamic plot to fire a missile at an airliner prompted Tony Blair to again send in the Army.

Troops used armoured Scimitar and Spartan reconnaissance vehicles to patrol the airport's 17-mile perimeter road, tunnel entrance and multi-storey car parks. Soldiers carrying semi-automatic weapons patrolled terminals just as the first of the airport's 150,000-a-day passengers began checking in. A back-up force of 1,300 police officers stood ready to be called if needed. The soldiers came from the 1st Battalion Grenadier Guards and Household Cavalry.

There was a heavy police presence around the airport too, and also in areas where aircraft taking off and landing might be low enough in the sky to be hit by a rocket missile. Scotland Yard said the security was 'precautionary' and related in part to the possibility that 'the end of the Muslim festival of Eid may be used by al-Qa'eda and associated networks to mount attacks. The strengthened security, which is most likely to be visible to the public at Heathrow, relates to a potential threat to the capital.'

Some politicians accused the government of calling out the Army simply to send signals to potential terrorists that the airport could swiftly be protected in the event of any threat. But following the 11 September attacks on New York, no one was taking any chances. It was later learned that Home Secretary David Blunkett had seriously considered shutting the airport down, but he later admitted this would have signified a victory for terrorists and be 'catastrophic' for Britain's trade and economy. 'We decided we needed to act and put in place preventative measures to pre-empt any action that was threatening us,' said Mr Blunkett.

Passengers departing from Heathrow seemed reassured by the increase in security measures – but it came as a shock to arriving travellers who saw armoured vehicles sitting on the tarmac next to refuelling, baggage and catering vehicles.

Today, terrorism is never far from the minds of Heathrow's security forces. They are frequently reminded that the airport is a prime target. Sometimes the reminders come from the strangest sources. In July 2004 a motorist, who had stopped to buy petrol at a Heathrow fuel station, spotted a large, bound document blowing along in the wind. The motorist recovered it and discovered that it appeared to contain confidential information detailing how terrorist threats were planned on potential sites – including Heathrow.

Instead of turning the dossier over to the police, the motorist thought it better to hand it over to the *Sun* newspaper, which made a big splash of the story before surrendering the file to the police. The newspaper said the document had been written the previous month and set out ways in which an airport could be protected from terrorist attack.

It also claimed that the dossier had said that Heathrow 'affords an excellent site to attack departing aircraft. The firing point is just over the fence into the field. This is a very large site with little cover. The only way to patrol this area is on foot. Consider dogs and the air support unit.'

David Blunkett later commented: 'The plans were obviously very good. Someone disposing of them in a way that allowed that to happen is very bad.'

Friday 25 October 2003 was a sad day in Heathrow's long history. Nobody died, nobody was ill. Nobody had lost their jobs and no airport companies had gone to the wall that day. But millions of people were about to lose a friend and they turned out in their thousands to say goodbye . . . to Concorde.

Following Concorde's farewell flight in October 2003, an example of the Anglo-French supersonic jet now stands on show – but going nowhere – on a Heathrow taxiway. *(Alan Gallop)*

On that day, the legendary Anglo-French sky goddess in British Airways' colours dropped her long nose for the final time after twenty-seven years of supersonic history. Twenty Concordes had been manufactured, fourteen went into service in 1976, split equally between Air France and British Airways. The supersonic jets had completed 50,000 flights and flown for over 140,000 flying hours – 100,000 of them at supersonic speeds. During that time, 2.5 million passengers had flown for 140 million miles, drinking 1 million bottles of champagne along the way. Now Concorde was making its final arrival before being consigned to aviation museums and history.

Thousands of Concorde fans ignored BAA's pleas to stay away from the airport and took a day off work to say an emotional farewell to their favourite aeroplane. They lined airport access roads, stood on top floors of multi-storey car parks and buildings to pay their last respects to the aircraft they all loved, but only a few had flown in. And, as the last three passenger flights approached Heathrow, many had tears in their eyes.

The final trio of Concordes landed at Heathrow within minutes of each other, carrying a mixture of show business celebrities, business tycoons and ordinary people who had won a competition in which a ride in the world's best-known plane was first prize. One Concorde arrived from New York, another from Edinburgh and a third after completing a trip for invited guests around the Bay of Biscay. All three taxied to the British Airways' engineering base, their crews hanging out of cockpit windows waving Union Jacks to the crowds.

A single Concorde remains at Heathrow, parked in a place where passengers looking out of aircraft windows while they taxi out for take-off get a close-up of a plane now going nowhere. Others have found homes in aviation museums in Barbados, Seattle, Manchester, Edinburgh, Brooklands Aviation Museum in Surrey and Filton Airport near Bristol, where much of the plane's early development work was undertaken. Pieces of the famous plane, along with its distinctive crockery and glassware, have been sold at auction for sky-high prices. The nosecone of a French Concorde was sold for $500,000 in 2003.

British Airways Chief Executive, Rod Eddington, said that there was 'a mixture of sadness and celebration' about the final flights. 'Concorde is a wonderful plane, an icon, but its time has come. It's an old plane – it doesn't look it – but it was designed in the 1950s and built in the 1960s.'

Although Heathrow will always be one of the first airports in the world to welcome new-age aircraft, it will never see the likes of Concorde again. The day will come when people say: 'I remember Concorde flying in and out of Heathrow. She was beautiful.' And people of all ages who came to bid farewell to her in October 2003 will turn to Concorde pictures in books and proudly show them to children, grandchildren, nieces and nephews, who will ask why the world's first supersonic plane is no longer flying. And as an answer, they will hear that Concorde outlived her usefulness, that airlines could no longer get the spare parts needed to keep her in the air, that she was expensive, no longer profitable – and noisy. They might hear how Richard Branson made a last-minute bid to buy all of British Airways' remaining Concordes for his Virgin Atlantic fleet and how BA had rejected his offer.

Time certainly knew how to fly in Concorde, the beautiful bird in which British skill and technology played a major part in its creation.

News that Heathrow was to get a new control tower was a surprise to everyone – except air traffic control staff working in the old tower, opened in 1955. Back in those days, the old tower had allowed controllers visual contact with all runways. But by the end of the 1990s, terminal extensions and new car parks had interrupted their vision and it was time to design a taller, more modern structure able to cope with the demands of an airport expected to be handling 89 million passengers by 2030.

The new and elegant tower – which will go into service in 2006, Heathrow's sixtieth anniversary year – bears no resemblance to the old one. Located at the western end of the airport's existing central terminal area and standing 285ft tall, the tower takes on the appearance of a giant lighthouse. Dwarfing Nelson's Column, it will give controllers unrivalled views across the entire airport and west London. The glass cab at the top is itself more than five storeys tall, weighing over 840 tons.

The tower was built in pieces before being towed to its site on three massive flatbed transporter lorries – similar to ones used by NASA to carry the space shuttle. A 82ft-tall section was jacked up to a height of 39ft to allow a prefabricated mast section to be slotted in underneath and so on until the building was completed and settled into its foundations. The tower is designed by the Richard Rogers Partnership and is expected to become a symbol of Heathrow in much the same way as the old tower became a Heathrow icon half a century before.

By March 2005, two and a half years into construction, work on Terminal 5 was over 50 per cent complete and ahead of schedule. Over 4,000 workers were employed on the site, many engaged on raising the terminal's massive 'wave-style' roof structure into place. When completed and put into use in 2008, this spectacular single-span structure will provide a bright and airy environment, with spectacular views, for passengers and staff.

Work raising the roof began in April 2004 when the first of six 2,460-ton steel sections was lifted 128ft into the air. Each 384ft arch section was assembled at ground level and roofing components fitted before being jacked up 131ft to their final position. One year and five subsequent lifting operations later, the dramatic roof was fully in place. The internal superstructure is made up of 25,580 tons of steel, which was installed at the rate of 688 tons each week.

At the same time, the historic twin rivers, an essential landmark on the Heathrow site since the seventeenth century, were successfully diverted along a new course around the edge of the Terminal 5 site.

Heathrow's new control tower looks very different to its two predecessors. The new tower is seen under construction during the summer of 2004. *(Alan Gallop)*

The Longford River and Duke of Northumberland's River had originally run through the middle of the construction site. It was necessary to alter their course and a two-year project began in which engineers created three and a half miles of new concrete channels to carry the twin rivers along the airport's western boundary to meet up with their original courses at the southern edge of the terminal site.

A major part of the work had been to make sure that as well as being ecologically sound, the rivers continue to provide an enhanced habitat in which native fish, plants and other river life could thrive. More than 80,000 pre-grown plants of 37 different species were brought from Norfolk to live in new river channels. Over 4,500 fish were caught in the rivers, including bream, chub, sticklebacks and eels, and were released into the nearby River Colne, while 550 freshwater mussels were transferred by hand to the new channel.

When Terminal 5 finally opens its check-in counters to passengers in 2008, Heathrow Airport will be sixty-two years old. The world's largest commercial aircraft, the Airbus A380 'super jumbo' will have been in operation for two years.

According to a report published by British Airways in 2005, more passengers will travel by air in the future as air fares fall in price – the result of innovative fares offered by low-cost airlines – and introduction of bigger aircraft. The report says that in 1991, the cost of a return flight to Australia was equivalent to five weeks' average salary in the UK and in 2005 it accounts for just over two weeks' average earnings. In ten years' time, analysts suggest that the return air fare from London to Sydney will be just one week's average weekly earnings – and half that again ten years later.

Will Heathrow have room for millions of extra passengers and aircraft movements? Will Terminal 5 solve all of the airport's problems for the distant future? The answer to both questions is – no. BAA has stated (in its *Heathrow Airport Interim Master Plan* – June 2005) that with Terminal 5, Heathrow will be equipped to handle around 80 million passengers annually by 2010/11. This will rise to 87 million passengers by 2015/16 and between 90 to 95 million passengers in its eighty-fourth anniversary year of 2030.

Where will these extra passengers be processed and dispatched to and from airliners of the future? Is there sufficient runway capacity at Heathrow to handle this additional traffic?

An artist's impression of what Terminal 5 will look like following its opening in 2008. *(BAA plc)*

A government White Paper called *The Future of Air Transport* makes it clear that the government supports 'a short (2,000 metres [6,561ft] as opposed to 4,000 metres [13,123ft]) third runway at Heathrow – after a second runway at Stansted – subject to compliance with strict conditions on air quality, noise and public transport access'. The document claims (as such documents usually do) that there is a good case for further airport development. 'The airport is of vital importance to the UK economy, attracting business to London and the South East and supporting 100,000 jobs (direct and indirect). A short, third runway would yield net economic benefits of some £6 billion (net present value) – the largest of all the new runway options examined in the run up to the White Paper.'

If the new runway scheme gets the green light from the government, it will be built to handle narrow-body planes. The airport's current runway system involves using one runway for take-offs and the second for landings. The new runway would be 'mixed mode' catering for both take-offs *and* landings, which are currently alternated to provide relief for local residents.

The paper recognises that further expansion will have environmental consequences and states that any further development would be conditional on air-quality standards, creation of no additional noise and improvements to public transport (especially rail) access to the airport in order to relieve pressure on the surrounding road network.

Where might this new, short runway be located? In an interview with Heathrow's weekly newspaper, *Skyport*, BAA's Chief Executive Designate, Mike Clasper, said: 'A third runway would require passenger handling facilities north of the Bath Road if it's going to make sense. If you want to call that Terminal 6, fine.'

Ironically, the site Mr Clasper suggests is similar – yet smaller in area – to one originally identified as a possible site for future airport expansion back in 1946; an area approximately 3⅓ miles long and around half a mile wide north of the Bath Road and the airport's existing runways and immediately south of Junction 4 of the M4 motorway. The new runway would be linked to Heathrow's existing runway system by a half-mile-long narrow taxiway running parallel with the M4 spur road linking the motorway with a road heading towards the airport tunnel. Plans show that, at the end of the new taxiway, the area will open out to accommodate the new runway which will devastate the ancient communities of Harmondsworth and Sipson and 700 homes, schools, playing fields, parks, shops, an industrial estate and a large hotel within those communities. Compensation plans will be available to 'homes blighted by these plans'.

BAA's *Heathrow Airport Interim Master Plan* cleverly reproduced the airport's original plans for 1946 in the document, widely circulated to the general public, local authorities and other interested parties. Other maps show various options the airport operating company might follow if the new runway is given the green light – including another terminal, arrivals and departures gates and aircraft parking stands. It also revealed plans to spend a further £3 billion over the next ten years to 'rejuvenate and develop the rest of the airport'.

The London Borough of Hillingdon – one of the councils most vocally opposed to Terminal 5 – says that 'the villages of Sipson and Harmondsworth would essentially be demolished to make way for the new runway and terminal buildings'. The council claims that two historic sites would be lost or forced to relocate – Harmondsworth's Great Barn built in 1426 and the twelfth-century Parish Church of St Mary – and its churchyard – located next to the village green.

Hillingdon, Spelthorne, Ealing and Hounslow councils have already made it clear that they will fight vigorously to defeat the proposal for the third runway. Hillingdon has set aside a fighting fund of £100,000 to argue the case and has joined forces with various anti-noise and environmental groups to make its voice heard louder.

BAA says: 'We've found a way to retain both the Harmondsworth Tithe Barn and St Mary's Church and graveyard. We do not underestimate, however, the scale of other impacts.' Such impacts might include noise that might be magnified for those living directly under new flight paths. Local roads would be under considerable strain from the extra traffic a busier airport might generate, causing congestion and bringing roads to frequent gridlock. Hillingdon says that 'extra activity from planes, cars and buses will bring further serious consequences to the air we breathe. For example, it is expected that in 2015, even without a third runway, 14,000 people would be exposed to levels of nitrogen dioxide that exceeds EU limits. This figure will become 35,000 if a third runway were built.'

Mick Temple, managing director of BAA Heathrow says: 'Heathrow is one of the world's great airports, but we recognise that it needs modernising. Terminal 5 gives us an opportunity to transform Heathrow in the coming years and this interim master plan is an important step towards achieving that.

'The aviation industry is constantly changing to reflect the evolving needs of air passengers and as an airport operator we also have to respond to meet these needs. What is certain is that Heathrow cannot afford to stand still. We need to plan for the future and ensure we provide excellent customer service and facilities to both our passengers and airlines.'

If BAA wishes to pursue the plan – one of several schemes under consideration looking at future air options in the UK – there will be the inevitable public inquiry; a long, complex, labour-intensive, time-consuming and expensive business for all concerned. In all probability it will last as long – if not longer – than the record-breaking Terminal 5 inquiry. Its final outcome is anyone's guess.

Sixty years old is an age when most people are either newly retired or starting to think about putting their feet up after decades of hard work. Heathrow is not a person but a way of life for thousands of people, many of whom have been employed there for their entire working lives, and it has yet to reach its prime. Love it or hate it, Heathrow is likely to be there for at least another sixty years. Whether it will be allowed to grow outside its existing boundaries in that time remains to be seen.

And while politicians, councils and pressure groups argue, life at Heathrow goes on; the airport, in fact, teems with life morning, noon and often through the night. It currently provides employment for nearly 50,000 people and sustains about 200,000 other jobs across the country. The airport generates £2 billion in local wages, acts as a gateway for 63 million passengers per year, flying with over 90 airlines to or from around 170 destinations and handles nearly 1.2 million tons of air cargo, making it one of the world's leading trading gateways. This will rise to almost 1.5 million tons by 2009 and nearly 2 million tons in 2015. Thanks to its fabulous shops, the airport has become one of the country's leading retail centres. The airport is a key economic driver, generating around £5 billion every year for the country.

By the time Heathrow celebrates its sixtieth anniversary in 2006, it will have handled around 1.4 billion passengers flying on over 14 million flights. Not bad for a building site that handled just 5 passengers on its first day and 60,000 passengers, 2,400 tons of cargo and 9,000 movements in its first year, six long decades ago.

Goodness, how time flies....

BIBLIOGRAPHY

Balfour, Harold, *Wings Over Westminster*, Hutchinson & Co., London, 1973

Barton, N.J., *The Lost Rivers of London*, Phoenix House Ltd (London)/Leicester University Press, Leicester, 1962

Bate, G.R., *And So Make a City Here*, Thomasons Ltd, Hounslow, Middlesex, 1948

Bramson, Alan, *Bennett – Master Airman*, Airlife Publishing, 1985

Duffy, Paul *Russian Airliners*, Osprey Publishing, London, 1993

Gero, David, *Aviation Disasters (Since 1950)*, Patrick Stephens Ltd, Sparkford, 1993

Gilchrist, Peter, *Modern Civil Aircraft: 4 – Boeing 747*, Ian Allan, Shepperton, Surrey, 1985

Haddon, Richard, Harvey, Charles and Wolff, E.S., *The Modern World Book of Flying*, Sampson, Low, Marston & Co, London, 1957

Jackson, A.S., *Pathfinder Bennett – Airman Extraordinary*, Terence Dalton, Sudbury, 1991

Masefield, Sir Peter with Gunston, Bill, *Flight Path*, Airlife Books, 2002

Maxwell, Gordon S., *Highwayman's Heath*, Thomasons Ltd, Hounslow, Middlesex, 1935

Maynard, John, *Bennett and the Pathfinders*, Arms and Armour Press, London, 1996

McVeigh, S.A.J., *West Drayton Past and Present*, West Drayton Chamber of Trade, 1950

Robbins, Michael, *Middlesex*, Collins, 1953

Taylor, H. A., *Fairey Aircraft Since 1915*, Putnam & Co., London, 1974

Taylor, John, W.R., *Fairey Aviation*, Chalford, Stroud, 1997

Thetford, Owen G., *Ian Allen's ABC of Airports and Airliners*, Ian Allan, Shepperton, 1948 (reprinted 1998)

Thorne, James, *Handbook to the Environs of London*, Adams and Dart, Bath, 1876

Wright, Alan, *Classic Aircraft 2: Boeing 707*, Ian Allan Ltd, Shepperton, Surrey, 1990

Heathrow Airport Interim Master Plan (Draft for Consultation), BAA Heathrow, June 2005

Greater London Plan 1944, edited by Patrick Abercrombie, HMSO 1945

London Airport – Developments in the Central Terminal Area, Ministry of Transport and Civil Aviation, HMSO, 1954

London Airport Central Terminal Buildings for Ministry of Transport and Civil Aviation – Taylor Woodrow Construction Ltd publication, 1955

Many news items quoted in the book were sourced from Keesing's Contemporary Archives 1945–1966 and archives from the British Library Newspaper Library including: *Flight International, Air Pictorial, Aeroplane, Middlesex Chronicle, Evening Standard, Daily Express, Picture Post, Sunday Telegraph, The Times, Skyport, Sun, Daily Mail* and *Daily Herald.*

Thanks also to de Havilland Archives, George Cross Database and to various people in possession of material owned or produced by Brenard Press Ltd.

INDEX